W9-BEE-238

CIVILIZATION DYNAMICS I

Civilization Dynamics I

Fundamentals of a Model-Orientated Description

NORBERT MÜLLER
Professor of Empirical Social Research and Statistics
University of Osnabruck

Avebury

Aldershot · Brookfield USA · Hong Kong · Singapore · Sydney

Published by

Avebury

Gower Publishing Company Limited
Gower House
Croft Road
Aldershot
Hants GU11   3HR
England

Gower Publishing Company
Old Post Road
Brookfield
Vermont   05036
USA

H
61
M84
1989

British Library Cataloguing in Publication
Data
Muller, Norbert, *1945-*
   Civilization dynamics.
   Vol.1 : Fundamentals of a model oriented
   description.
   1. Civilization - Sociological perspectives
   306

ISBN   0 566 05516 3

Printed and Bound in Great Britain by
Athenaeum Press Ltd., Newcastle upon Tyne.

Contents

List of figures

List of tables

Glossary

$\mathcal{C}$	—	*head*; subsistence minimum unit
CATA	—	social catastrophe
DC	—	decision centre
$\mathcal{E}$	—	*energetic head*; subsistence minimum in energetic terms
HSDMEL	—	hierarchic-sequential decomposition of a regional system model of the Melle region, Lower Saxony, F.R.G.
LSU	—	large scale social unit
MABU	—	social catastrophes where concentrations or sensitive installations are involved
MISP	—	military-industrial-scientific-political complex
PC	—	power centre
PRIM	—	primary; face to face social context(s)
PT	—	power territory
PTR	—	power territory ruler
RM	—	rapid modelling
RS	—	real-structure ...
RSM	—	real-structure modelling
SEC	—	secondary; abstract social context(s)
V	—	virtual subsistence minima measured in $\mathcal{C}$; national product minus population

Glossary

ix

Preface

Nowadays in the industrialized states, productivity, technology and volume of production have brought about a morphogenetic potential which is capable of altering living structures with apparent matchless rapidity. Locally, at least, these production processes surmount the natural energetic transformations. Thus, civilizations are today capable of altering their natural and socio-economic life contexts with one prominent difference contrasted with earlier epochs, that being the speed that structural rearrangements of these life contexts now occur. Whereas, in former times, subsequent generations had to bear the consequences of structurally relevant activities - except situations of catastrophic structural ruptures - it can happen in present times that the initiators of structural change are still in charge when consequences become apparent.

It is obvious that rapid structural change diminishes the possibility of correcting misdevelopments by disposable operations. This calamity is aggravated by the large number of actors possessing a high potential to shape structures, because this can contribute to rapid structural change.

If the scale-order of the influence of human activities on life fonditions of the planet *TERRA* is insignificant compared with natural transformation processes, it may be justifiable to consider production or technology as a mere confrontation with (non-anthropogenic) nature. This approach is no longer appropriate. In the present situation, it will become indespensable to examine transformation processes in social systems also as self-directed. The (occidental) civilization process seems to have reached a threshold (or has already surpassed it) where conditions of existence and operation of living systems on *TERRA* depend to a significant degree upon transformation processes in social systems and as such become internal operating fields of social systems.

It appears that up to now the whole impact of this situation has become clear to only a few social and natural scientists. In exploring this situation we must try to find out how civilizations operate. In the long run we have to construct a unified *anthropo-ecological* theory so long as no qualitative new paths of civilizational development are taken e.g. orbital civilizations, genetic manipulation with human beings, or machine intelligence. This work is an attempt to approach the problem area of the operation principles of civilizations in a quasi-natural scientific manner and in this way we may perhaps come closer to the goal of an anthropo-ecological approach.

Osnabrück, autumn 1988

1 Introduction

In this book the operation of civilizations will be analyzed. *Operation* shall mean that persuant to a research project under consideration, properties selected as relevant by the researcher are regarded as influenced by other properties and that these influences are governed by rules determining their existence, structure, and dynamics. These rules shall be called *operational mechanisms*; the term "mechanism" not being meant to indicate a mechanistic approach.

Thus, analysis of the manner in which civilizations operate would mean to identify and describe their operational mechanisms. It must be pointed out that by taking this as a basic working hypothesis it has to be presumed that civilizations do function – until the contrary is proved. This is not obvious *a priori*. It would have to be an extremely difficult methodological and epistemological problem to indicate stop criteria, criteria after which the search for sufficiently durable operational mechanisms can be declared as having failed. We will proceed from the assumption that operational mechanisms do exist and their discovery is our aim.

On the basis of the writer's knowledge it cannot be taken for granted that the findings of this book hold for all civilizations. On the contrary, some present suppositions that are still speculative (see section 3.2.3) make the restriction to the occidental type of civilization. Instead of coping with concrete historic features, or development, of civilizations we prefer the general approach in choosing *large-scale social units* (LSUs) as our central research objects. This is based on the acceptably approved hypothesis that social

1

units cannot evolve to become civilizations until they have reached a certain scale-order. It has to be the subject of further research to answer the question as to whether LSUs can operate other than in a civilized framework. But for the purpose of this book the question is irrelevant and for sake of simplification LSUs will be regarded as civilized.

The state of knowledge shown in this book is not yet so developed that concrete historic features or developments of LSUs can be analyzed, let alone be forecasted. Instead we will cope with the question of whether and to what extent the operation of LSUs can be described by hard operational mechanisms in elementary fields of operation. It is difficult to define the concept "operation" of such a system. At this point there often exists a tendency to introduce non-explicit positions in functionalistic approaches. Just for the propositions of this book it is important to specify as far as possible a value-free concept of "operation". For this purpose, *operation* will mean the transformational relation between specified inputs and outputs. This can be compared to the meaning of the term "operation" if the question: "how does this machine operate?" is posed. Therefore, in order to understand the "operation" of a social unit, its inner 'real' transformation relations have to be analyzed.

An operational mechanism will be called *hard*,

- if its structure and effectivity are independent of influences that require the subjective evaluation of a large number of individuals (*objective-ness*) for their becoming effective,

  or,

- if it is defined through institutionalized durable standard routines.

Examples of operational mechanisms of the first category can be found in the generative reproduction e.g. the fact that children are borne by women is not dependent on a subjective evaluation. Examples of the second category can be found in the redistribution of economic surplus. In the F.R.G., the wage tax is collected according to clearly fixed routines and then forwarded to the treasury. These routines cannot subjectively be influenced by an executive administration clerk (e.g. an official for the wage tax administration of a firm, or a tax official in a revenue office) and even less by the tax payer.

Behind the emphasis on hard operational mechanisms there is the supposition that a considerable part of the operation of LSUs are governed by such mechanisms. It is the central issue of this book to find out whether this part would be large enough to specify soft operational mechanisms only in a simple manner. However, a final answer to this question cannot be given in this book. Its purpose shall be the development of the theoretical aspects of a LSU- specific approach, i.e. the *real-structure modelling* (RSM), by means of which this question can possibly be answered. However, the crucial point of the book is not a methodological one as this aspect has already been handled elsewhere, see [93].

In cases where the RS- approach is proved effective, substantial results of the analysis of LSUs will be outlined. While it would be presumptuous to suggest that a single researcher could work on the whole scope of an operating analysis of LSUs, this book is an attempt to make a virtue of necessity by outlining relevant research fields using RSM as an exploratory device.

We start with four elementary operation fields:

- population,
- production and technology,
- distribution and consumption,
- power and privilege.

It is hypothesized that the operation of LSUs could, in essence, be characterized by describing the relevant operational mechanisms of these four fields; in doing so – as is shown later – another important 'moderator'-operation field is added: *debt*. In a research-strategical sense it is postulated useful to consider only hard mechanisms as a first approximation in order, by that process, to find out the explanatory power of this approach.

It is perhaps the most serious simplification of this approximation to postulate that it would be sufficient merely to examine structures and not to recognize specific tasks in LSU areas. Behind this there is the working hypothesis that the operation of LSUs could be attributed to similar structures and operational mechanisms in all their areas. Regardless of whether it is public health, the educational system or religious rites, in all areas similar structures and operational mechanisms are assumed working. Again, it is not maintained that all these are real facts; what we want to find out is the extent to which such a simplification is appropriate. Of course, in that background it is assumed that this approximation works to a large degree. This assumption could be confirmed by systematic evidence, for example by the results of the research project HSDMEL ("Hierarchic-sequential decomposition of a regional systems model of the Melle region", sponsored by the Stiftung Volkswagenwerk), see [92,96,97].

A higher weight than that of the afore-mentioned substantial considerations is, however, carried by the research-logical argument for that method to proceed: only on a hard basis can the further differentiation within the areas, as well as the addition of further fields/areas, or the analysis of soft operational mechanisms seem to be meaningful. Paradoxically, to proceed by such a sequential method, i.e. *first hard, then soft*, is largely unusual within the social sciences; for a criticism of HABERMAS from a similar point of view see HEINSOHN [47], see also TAILOR [128] who, however, merely formulated a suggestion. One exception is the sociology of the PARETO tradition, see e.g. LOPREATO [73].

In particular, the specification of *hard basic models* and the attempt of thinking in *scale orders* on this ground is unusual within the social sciences. Often it is a surprise how large the explanatory power of a hard basic model can be simply by virtue of the right scale orders.

The insufficient orientation of many social science approaches to hard features and relations in object fields under consideration entails a neglect of social *selection*. Among other things this neglect is especially fatal from a methodological point of view. It is not infrequent that observational evidences can be traced back to a specific composition of the examined population, whereas this composition again can be the result of selection effects. If, in such a case, an attempt is made to explain the evidences by personality characteristics etc., then resultless data analysis or the production of research artifacts will be the consequences. OEVERMANN [102], as an example, found out that, frequently, girls from lower social classes attending a continuation school are especially successful pupils. He is right in attributing this to the selection effect according to which lower-class parents only send their daughters to continuation schools if they are convinced of their extraordinary intelligence. Neglecting this selection effect and searching instead for an early-child-determinant regarding this success in school would obviously be unreasonable as a first research step and would most probably be misleading. If a director dies in an accident and the vice president moves to his position, it is above all an advancement by chance and cannot be attributed to the vice president's dynamics. The political apathy of individuals in lower level political institutions is first of all not the result of personality structures, or manipulation, but a trivial product of the selection effect that the politically non-apathetic individuals usually hold positions at higher hierarchical levels. Since these individuals are not found at lower levels they cannot articulate any dynamics there. Further, such selection effects appear in longitudinal, e.g. biography, studies. For instance, in examining a representative sample of a country's population by means of a questionnaire, the answers to profession-oriented questions (for instance, position within the staff hierarchy) can plainly be explained by the fact that such questions do not appropriately relate to experiences of the test person's career. In general, each knot (life event) in a life tree, see [89], can be regarded as a selective device and individuals with the same edge sequences (biographies) can be regarded as clustering selectively in specific subpopulations.

However, the methodological problematic nature of subpopulation oriented research attempts is so manifold that it cannot be scrutinized in this book, for some aspects see [91], ARMINGER [3]; it would possibly require a new methodology, see [93].

The examples can be extended multiplicedly. They affirm once again the importance of a social science approach devoted to hard and concrete features and relations.

Some findings that, in the the writer's opinion, have not been given sufficient consideration lead to a central idea of this book, that is, to regard the 4th field, i.e. power and privilege (*Herrschaft*), as ranking equal to the others and not, as often done, as being derived from these. The power territory (*Erbhof*) (**PT**) is the central theoretic category here. It is maintained that *Herrschaft*, i.e. the durable capability to mobilize resources to exert influences, see [88], is organized in all LSU fields and is, with utmost priority, oriented to **PT** maintenance. In taking both together, we can make the conjecture that the equal-ranking relevance of the **PT** aspect and the universal organization principles of **PTs** ensure that the evolution of LSUs is, in essence, always characterized by the development, change, and breakdown of **PTs**. It is the writer's contention that the integration of this domination aspect in an approach comprising all 4 operational fields is the missing link for understanding the operation of LSUs. So the present book above all addresses itself to this integration task though focussing on the development of a *power territory approach*.

The approach of RSM developed in this realm is correctly called so because it refers to concrete units with their concrete hard operational parameters in elementary operation fields. It confines itself in the first research steps to stating explicitly what is in an obvious manner defined as *real* within LSUs. Notice, that it is not *systems* but social units that is being discussed; e.g. political communities or states. Starting from a RSM approach it cannot become clear, except in a relatively advanced research phase, whether parts of LSUs, e.g. several **PTs**, are organized as systems. Using the term *system* in a substantial way requires that in an LSU, energy transformation and information processes are related one to the other by certain systematics or rationality. This raises the interesting question of the designability of LSUs, a design capacity of a 'higher degree', *reflexivity*. The limits of the designability of LSUs will, among other things, be the subject of the propositions of this book.

A further basic aspect of this book is to define a uniform *real* standard for all economic activities. This standard will be specified as the *head* denoted by C . Following RICARDO and MARX a C will be operationalized as the *subsistence minimum* of an average individual. So, as an example, a certain number of C is produced in an LSU. The subsistence minimum will be fixed to 1 and in doing so all economic figures are standardized to the subsistence minimum. Behind this there is the supposition that the reference to the subsistence minimum is really effective in LSUs.

At this point the question arises whether such operationalizations and – even more basically – the focus on hard operational mechanisms are of universal adequacy. This question has to be answered with a clear *no*. This is just what RSM wants to be; a methodology that is adequate to "deep structures", BOULDING [11]. If *deep structures* change, the methodology has to change correspondingly. This methodologic relativism is a result of the fact that social 'reality' in LSUs is produced by *actors*. However, the existence of deep structures reflects that this production of reality is not an arbitrary one. Not until something has changed within the deep structures, which generally means a change within one or more operational fields, then according to the approach developed here the methodology would presumably have to change as well. A matriarchal civilization which does not exist anywhere on *TERRA* would probably have to be examined on the base of another methodology. A future 'society' wherein machine intelligence dominated exclusively would have to be analyzed in a 'sociological way' by machines. The methodology, therefore, has to be adapted to the developments within the elementary operational fields.

The *hard orientation* of RSM permits description of operational fields and mechanisms by means of formalized models. Because of the occurring non-linearities or because of the consideration of decision routines, to depict only two prominent difficulties, these models must be specified in the form of simulation models. The writer's present knowledge indicates that single models are taken under consideration for operational fields or relevant aspects, the other (external) operational fields being specified in a simple way. In a later research step, which presumably will be very complicated, it will be attempted to unify these part models to an overall LSU model.

If one should try to relate the approach developed in this book to a common research field there would be a relation in principal to ethnomethodologic considerations, though there are other focal points. In my opinion, the approach presented here is characterized best as a contribution to a materialistic anthropology of civilizations, see LENSKI, HARRIS, BOULDING and HOMANS [69,42,12,54]; as to sociobiology see as a survey BODGANY, FLOHR/TÖNNESMANN [9,29], and as an interesting entry into neighbouring research fields see GODFREY/COLE [35].

Perhaps the time will soon come when knowledge about the operation of civilizations will be important for survival.

2 Sectors of a societal operation model

Given the present state of social scientific research it may seem bold to design a societal operating model as is attempted in the following. An attempt such as this cannot be other than a kind of expedition into a research field that is little known up to now. However, considering the precarious situation of social scientific research, such a risktaking seems to be justified.

Following the principle of starting from obvious hard features and structures of social units to soft ones, the basic structures of the elementary fields of a societal operation model shall first be examined.

2.1 Population

The existence of human beings is the first obvious precondition for the analysis of social units. Although this may sound trivial, it certainly is not. Indeed, the fact that human beings are the actors of social units is in itself a social definition that is inflicted by profound epistemological and theoretical problems. Even the self-definition as *homo sapiens* is suspect of ideology. This aspect will not be pursued here, for reference see a.o. the paleo-anthropological literature, as an introduction see TUTTLE [130].

Without further preamble let the existence of human beings be taken as a starting point of the analysis. For the continued existence of the subject under examination it is also obvious that the species here has to reproduce itself, necessitating the participation of two sexes in the present reproduction organization. Thus, as a rule, social units have to be composed of couples of at least one male and one female. If descendents of this union are raised by at least one parent – and this is normally the case with all *primates* – it seems to be appropriate from a real-structural point of view to conceive social units at least as couples of male and female with their descendants. Such a social unit is called a *family*.

A hard basic model for population development would have to describe the process of birth as a dynamic tree of conditions with nodal points (events) as follows:

- age group

- in vocational training?

- partner?

- working?

- number of children

- frequency of intercourse

- contraception?

- abortion?

- miscarriage?

- live birth?

- one child/multiple birth?

- boy/girl? ,

similar to HOBCRAFT et al. [51] . Each path through this tree defines a subpopulation of women characterized by specific probabilities.

In such a modelling process it will successively turn out how far one has to resort to soft factors to determine single events. Possibly it is useful to divide the population of women into some subpopulations (e.g. after their religious confession and marital status). For each of these subpopulations such a model has to be specified, a research strategy that has not been followed until recently, e.g. HASSAN [44], for a general list of literature see UMBACH [131].

The resulting model complexity can be handled without effort by modern computers. The feature of this approach that dynamics have to be specified on a tree structure is more intricate, but we will not go into details here; however, for some reflections on this type of problem see Vol. 2.

Having defined the family as an elementary social unit in the field of population modelling, it has to be expected that factors explaining population reproduction have to be explored in the relation between the sexes, sexuality, pregnancy, and raising of children. It is noteworthy that in the social sciences these areas of explanation (which are obviously elementary) are used in connection with research fields classified as peripheral and are seldom handled concretely and fact-oriented, as e.g. in JANSSEN-JURREIT [57] or in CHAGNON/IRONS [16] .

After all what we presently have on hand of paleo-anthropological and anthropological evidence confirms that 'simple social units' indeed organize themselves in the form of families and the afore-stated fields of explanation factors really seem to be of great importance. It would be interesting to trace the question (which will not be treated here however) as to the extent that these elementary factors influenced the process of development towards 'complex social units' up to the formation of states and whether, despite civilizational covering, they possibly are effective even in very complex units. Curiously, such formulations of the question have scarcely arisen in the established social sciences.

Let us summarize that members of the species *homo sapiens* are organized in social units wherein a development from simple to complex units is presumed. This presumption has as a precondition that social units are comparable regarding the feature *complexity* and that they can be brought into a corresponding order relation. This, in turn, requires that complexity can only be related to one feature. [1] For instance, the degree of job differentiation indicated by the number of different job labels has been chosen as such an attribute. However, considering, for instance, the hunting of big game in hunter and gatherer societies makes it clear that this attribute seems to be of restricted appropriateness: Although these societies are unanimously classified as simple, hunting big game is an extremely job-differentiating work. Without further scrutinizing such attempts at definition, we postulate for the following:

Definition: A social unit is called the more simple,

- the more completely the course of action in this unit is performed by face-to-face contacts and,

- the larger is the number of members of this social unit who can observe such actions including their social consequences, face-to-face.

At least the second complexity feature is directly dependent upon the size of the social unit. Possibly there is an anthropogenic behavior disposition to sense anything that is beyond face-to-face control as strange and fear

---

[1]If it is related to several features, these features must have special ordering properties for providing an order relation (e.g. the suitability of a lexicographic ordering). However, these details will not be elaborated upon, here.

stimulating. If this "strangeness" component is a steady structure in a social unit it may be that, to provide fear control, subjection to leadership will become a structural feature of this social unit. Perhaps this is one of the anthropogenic causes for the ubiquity and longevity of structures of power, comp. [88], BOULDING [12], or religious rites.

The afore-mentioned shows how a population model has to be constituted. Hard influential factors for population development are: practices of infanticide [2], practices concerning nursing, contraception, abortion, kidnapping of women and violation, marriage laws (polyandry, polygamy, monogamy) as well as life expectancy of women.

However, population-theoretical approaches which are based on these obvious factors are an exception within the social sciences. [3]

2.2   Production and distribution

The will to survive is presumed a basic feature of every creature (be it in the form of individual survival or in the form of dispersion of its genes within the population). It is obvious that an individual survives until its 'natural death' if it

- doesn't die of illness before,

- is not killed by violence,

- cannot consume enough appropriate sustenance.

Illness shall not be discussed in detail here. We know that epidemics, caused through contacts with human beings from other parts of the world (e.g. Indians meeting with Europeans who carried germs unknown to the natives) have exterminated, or will exterminate, major parts of populations.

Killing by force can appear as

- non-human influence (for instance, accidents, natural disasters),

- or human actions (war, massacre, genocide, murder, suicide etc.).

---

[2]To a large extent, this was practiced up to the 19th century. Specific sexual killing rules (predominantly the killing of daughters) were made seemingly plausible to upper class parents by the custom that existed in India, as to CHAGNON/IRONS [16] . Whereas for parents of lower classes it seems to be more plausible to kill the sons, in that sons have to pay for a bride, comp. WHITE [134] .

[3]HEINSON/KNIEPER/STEIGER [45] at least took the course of such a 'hard' theory formation. Up to now, however, the proof is lacking that the deliberate birth control actions of individuals are directly determined by population control policy, see for instance BATES/LEES [6] . Concerning the relevance of reproduction behavior, see also BOULDING, HARRIS [12,43] .

Now in the social sciences and somewhat reluctantly it seems, natural disasters are examined as causes for evolutionary ruptures [4].

As regards the killing by force of human beings by human beings war seems to have the greatest importance. This is now evident on a level of development where overkill is possible – and will appear with probability 1 on *TERRA* by advancement of time. Wars, frequently accompanied by epidemics and famine have decimated populations, at all times temporarily (because mostly men have been killed and fertile women survived). Whether a war selectively accelerates social evolution, as long as it does not lead to a total genocide, is a question that an objective researcher might deal with thoroughly, comp. GROSSMANN [37] . We have to return to aspects of war elsewhere in this book.

The shortage of sustenance especially will be discussed here: Sustenance is above all a matter of food and particularly depending on climatic factors, shelter and clothing. 'Free commodities', air and water are part of the item food. Moreover, food has to be suitable for consumption, for example a certain concentration of pollution may not be exceeded in it, for a theoretical exposition of this problematic see METHE [84] .

2.2.1 Production and subsistence

It is important for an operational model of production and distribution to recall some *hard* economic aspects that possibly will appear banal to economists, see in particular SAMUELSON [112] . The population aspect is again the starting point. Sustenance can be regarded as products relevant for survival . An individual i survives if it in reference to this survival aspect, disposes of a minimum x_i of such products in a time interval that can be specified fairly precisely. As regards food, this time interval is such that a human being will die earlier from thirst than from hunger, and in determining the period of dying from thirst, it is lower for children than for adults. Generally, however, it will be adequate and sufficient to specify this minimum time period of death by thirst as some elementary interval of the life rythm, the day. Such a period may be indicated by 24 hours. Given a social units with N members, therefore, in a social unit a minimum day production of $X = \sum_{i=1}^{N} x_i$ has to be ensured. Assume the volume of production that i can produce per day to be P_i. E.g. $P_i = 0$ appears for children up to an age determined within the social unit, often also for individuals who have exceeded a certain age, sick people, invalids etc. It follows, in respect of the sustenance aspect, that all N members of the social unit will survive, if the

---

[4]Generally speaking it has to be contemplated whether the approaches of discontinuous processes predominantly developed in biology (e.g. of dissipative structures) can successfully be applied to social scientific research domains. Perhaps social scientific research deals too much with the 'normality' of social units and in this way loses the feeling for ruptures, transitions and structural change, being possibly the relevant phenomena in the social sciences, see LEMCKE [68].

following is fulfilled: $X = \sum_{i=1}^{N} P_i \geq X$. Those M individuals, $M \leq N$, for which $p > 0$ is fulfilled, shall be called *productive*. It is obvious that the P_i are not all equal. Reasons for this can be systematic (e.g. pregnancy of women) or accidental (e.g. productivity diminishing accidents). Moreover, it has to be taken into consideration that a part $Q = qY$ of the day production is unfit for use due to a variety of reasons, or is not at the consumers disposal (e.g. by robbery). Thus, P_i has to be specified as a random variable.

P_i shall be specified in terms of subsistence minima, i.e. in $\mathcal{C}$. So $P_i = 2$ means that i procures a product volume by which two persons of the social unit under consideration can be alimented at the subsistence minimum. If π denotes the average value $\pi = \frac{1}{M} \sum_{i=1}^{M} P_i$ the following formula can be defined:

$$P_i = \rho_i \pi \qquad , \qquad \rho_i \geq 0.$$

Because of the subsistence minimum it must hold that ρ_i should obey

$$\rho_i \pi \geq x_i .$$

On the average it must hold that $E(P) = \pi$ and $E(\rho) = 1$. In a first approximation it shall be presumed that the distribution of P_i is such that it is admissible to use the arithmetic mean π and the standard deviation σ_P .

Overproduction is unproblematic under survival aspects. Neglecting Q in a first consideration, it follows for a total social unit:

$$M(\pi - \alpha \sigma_P) \geq X, \tag{2.1}$$

where α denotes a risk parameter, which, as a result from experience, takes a certain value in a social unit. In a first approximation we can use the average minimum $E(x) =: \mathcal{C}$. Then it holds:

$$M(\pi - \alpha \sigma_P) \geq N \mathcal{C}. \tag{2.2}$$

Solved for π the result is

$$\pi \geq \frac{N}{M} \mathcal{C} + \alpha \sigma_P. \tag{2.3}$$

Taking into account Q, leads to:

$$\pi \geq \frac{N}{M} \frac{\mathcal{C}}{1-q} + \alpha \sigma_P. \tag{2.4}$$

In a first approximation, $\mathcal{C}$, σ_P and α can be specified as fixed terms, not capable of manipulation. M, N and Q remain as controllable terms to influence π. N is essentially dependent on population parameters. Obvious determinants of M first of all stem from demographic aspects such as age distribution (children and old people) or that section of individuals engaged in the raising of children (usually fertile women). Alone due to random influences, it must hold that $q > 0$. The value of q depends first on activities from other social units (robbery, destruction, poisoning) and further on the technology of conserving and refining sustenance. Enabling the latter to be effective, such technologies have to be known and applied. We will return to this in section 2.4 and Vol. 2.

As a rule, if no life stock is kept, there is no purpose in a robbery. Moreover, if social units do not dispose of appropriate technology in the sense afore-mentioned, q can be regarded as constant and not capable of manipulation. In this case the necessary π can only be reached by means of the parameters M and N.

However, the concrete π also depends on ecologic parameters and the available production technology. So these two parameters limit π from above. At a given point of time it can be specified: $\pi \leq \pi_{max}$. Thus, the interval of admissible values of π is given, and it holds:

$$\pi \in [\frac{N}{M}\frac{C}{1-q} + \alpha\sigma_P, \pi_{max}] =: \Pi \qquad (2.5)$$

An obvious condition for the survival of a social unit is, that Π is non-empty. If in a first approximation one chooses $q \in (0, 1)$ and when defining $r := M/N$, it can be comcluded:

$$r \geq C[(1-q)(\pi_{max} - \alpha\sigma_P)]^{-1}. \qquad (2.6)$$

Since the right hand side of 2.6 is fixed, it has to be achieved that r be enlarged. This implies, because r is a fraction, that M must be augmented, or N must be diminished. Naturally it must be provided that the right hand side of 2.6 remains admissible, i.e. it has to be inside the interval $[0, 1]$. In certain circumstances, the augmentation of M requires large organizational efforts (e.g. child labour). As the expected normal case it remains the reduction of N. By infanticide, the mothers can become labor-productive again quickly. Thus, the killing of new-born children can be expected as a practice to reduce N. In fact, this has been observed, see CHAGNON/IRONS and HARRIS [16, 43] in particular. Now and then one can also find the practice of eliminating aged people, as, for example, formerly in Eskimo societies.

Let us consider a *numerical example* for 2.6

$N = 100$, $\sigma_P = .5$, $\pi_{max} = 4$,
$C = 1.8$, $\alpha = 1$, $q = .1$,
then $r \geq .57$ results from 2.6
and from 2.5 $\pi_{min} = 2.5$ for $M = N$,
hence $\pi \in [2.5, 4]$.

For $r = .67$, the remaing terms being equal, results $\pi \in [3.49, 4]$.

However, since the children not killed are productive later provided they survive until the productive age, or are not excluded from production because of other reasons, a dynamic concerning the relation between r and the total production Y results which is by no means trivial. However, this shall not be gone into detail here.

Except in the case where all productive individuals produce the subsistence minimum, the problem of the distribution of surplus arises with each production. Let U_i denote the quantity of sustenance gained by $i(i = 1, 2, \ldots, N)$, again quantified in $\mathcal{C}$. i survives if $U_i \geq x_i$ is fulfilled. If production yields the subsistence minimum, then $U_i = X/N$ follows. Let us define the *surplus* as: $U' = Y(1 - q) - X$. Production on the level of subsistence minimum implies that U_i can only be increased by reduction of N. If there is a surplus, however, U_i is composed of the 'baseline' x_i of the subsistence minimum, and the appropriation of a part of the surplus; let this part be gained by i by virtue of the appropriation quota f_i. So the following can be stated:

$$U_i = \frac{X}{N} + f_i U' = \mathcal{C} + f_i U' \tag{2.7}$$

One form of surplus consumer is a non-productive individual who, although not belonging to the systematic non- productives, gains at least the subsistence minimum. M is lowered by this, so that this kind of appropriation has a tendency that $U' \to 0$. Another kind of surplus appropriation is that there are rules by virtue of which certain individuals receive more than an average productive individual does. Throughout this book, the subsistence minimum is standardized to 1 and production is regarded as multiples of 1. It is plausible to make the assumption that in case of surplus a productive individual receives more than 1. Let us denote that part of subsistence received by a productive individual by U_i^p (p for "productive").

Rules permitting a share that is larger than the arithmetic mean u^p shall be called *privileges*. If the plausible assumption is made that a privilege is identified when it clearly stands out from the mass, it follows that a privileged part has to be remarkably larger than u^p. Since in the case of $U' \to 0$, the U_i equalize, it results that privileges can only develop if there is a sufficiently large surplus. From these reflections it follows that the number of privileged is always very small in relation with N.

Let us regard an u^P as a reference value that results in the case of absence of privileges. For this reference it shall be supposed that all non-productives receive the subsistence minimum. From 2.3 it follows: M productives produce by virtue of $\pi = \frac{N}{M} \mathcal{C} + \alpha \sigma_P$ a volume of goods by which a number of $(1 - q)M\pi$ can be alimented, each receiving $\mathcal{C}$. According to the suppositions made, the following number of people have to be alimented:

$N \quad - \quad M$ persons at the level of 1 (subsistence minimum),

$$M \qquad \text{persons at the level of} \quad u^P.$$

Hence it must hold:

$$(N - M)\, C + M u^P = (1 - q) M \pi \qquad (2.8)$$

With the above π and solved for u^P, where $r = M/N$, it results;

$$u^P = 1 - \frac{q}{r} + (1 - q)\alpha\sigma_P, \qquad (2.9)$$

where, as already stated, $C = 1$.

Numerical example:

$$r = .6, \alpha = 1 \,, \sigma_P = 1 \,,$$
$$q = .1, \pi = 2.667 \,, u^P = 1.73 \,.$$

By lowering the subsistence minimum below 1 the 'working stress' of productives will be lowered and their alimentation allotment will increase. So e.g. at a C of .75, $\pi = 2.25$ and $u^P = 2.03$ result.

Conversely, for a given productivity, N and u^P, the necessary number of productives can be calculated. These and similar analyses are left to the reader.

Empirical distributions of assets can only be evaluated before the background of reference-distributions. The lower extreme results if, at a given productivity, exactly that volume is produced which provides the subsistence minimum to all N members of the social unit under consideration. Let this lower reference value be denoted by M_- . So, in 2.2 that M_- is examined for which it holds:

$$M_-(\pi - \alpha\sigma_P)(1 - q) = N$$

where again $C = 1$. Solved for M_- it results

$$M_- = N[(\pi - \alpha\sigma_P)(1 - q)]^{-1}. \qquad (2.10)$$

In the numerical example aforementioned, by inserting $\pi = 2.67$ and $N = 100$, it results: $M_- = 67$ and each receives $C = 1$.

At the opposite extreme one non-productive appropriates the total surplus and all other members of the social unit share the subsistence minimum. In the numerical example with $N = 100$, $M = 60$ and $\pi = 3.5$ it results:

- One receives $M(\pi - \alpha\sigma_P)(1 - q) - (N - 1) \cdot 1 = 36$

- 99 receive $C = 1$.

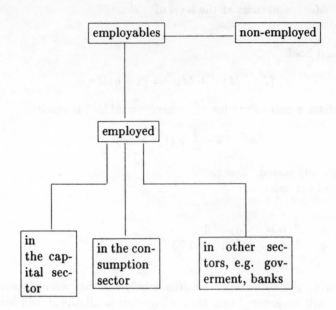

Figure 2.1: Subpopulation tree of employables

Only if such reference values are calculated can income distributions be evaluated. In particular, the justice of a distribution cannot be concluded from the equal distribution because it has to be taken into account how many productives have to work for how many non-productives.

With reference to the number of $\mathcal{C}$ produced it also becomes clear that the mere population number – so long as it does not increase to a number critical for production – plays a less important theoretical role with growing productivity. This can be demonstrated by the load put by a social unit on its territory, e.g. by pollution, demand for area. The normally used population density index N/F, where $F :=$ space of the territory, does not represent the real load. A more appropriate index would be

$$K/F : \quad = \quad \mathcal{C} \quad \text{per area}$$
$$= \quad (N - M + M\pi)/F = [N + M(\pi - 1)]/F.$$

In 1980, for the F.R.G. it held by scale-order (details in section 2.3.2): $K = (62 + 28 \cdot 7) \cdot 10^6 = 256 \cdot 10^6$ Thus, in 1980 the territory of the F.R.G. was loaded by some 256 millions of $\mathcal{C}$.

With a more complex differentiation of production and social structure the categories "productive" and "non-productive" are no longer adequate. Moreover, it has to be considered that the scope and character of production depends more and more on the use of machines.

For instance, considering the workers we must differentiate, resulting in a tree structure as displayed in fig. 2.1.

Among the productive employable persons the unemployed are of special importance. It would be very instructive to give a description of the time-varying behavior of this tree. Paradoxically, and not until recently, has the examination of this structural dynamics, e.g. the VASMA-Project, *Verglei-chende Analysen der Sozialstruktur mit Massendaten* (comparative analyses of social structure by means of mass data), been started at the University of Mannheim.

2.2.2 Production capacity determinants

As to production, the number of producible C is in the first instance obviously dependent on the *production capacity*:

$$P = \kappa K, \tag{2.11}$$

with $K :=$ capacity and $\kappa :=$ usage quota.
The *capacity* again is, in obvious manner, defined through

$$K = M f_0 \pi_M^s r, \tag{2.12}$$

where

$$
\begin{aligned}
M : \quad &= \quad \text{machines,} \\
f_0 : \quad &= \quad \text{maximal work hours per year,} \\
\pi_M^s : \quad &= \quad \text{machine productivity per hour and } C, \\
r : \quad &= \quad \text{external restrictions.}
\end{aligned}
$$

Thus, K denotes the *annual* capacity. Notice that only by r do the productives come into play. In a first approximation, however, we can set $r = 1$. The fact that machines are (still?) built and attended by human beings is expressed by κ, so to speak a disturbing variable to be controlled during the production process. If enough productive persons of the necessary qualification are available, then, in a first approximation P is not dependent on Q, the *laborforce*, at all. Of course, the degree of dependence of Q varies between the different sectors and the different branches. However, it diminishes by increasing rationalization. At any rate, for highly industrialized states it seems inappropriate to connect productivity with the productive persons and to speak of *labor productivity* as is normally the case. In section 2.4 we will return to these problems.

If K is inserted in 2.11 and the influence of the productive persons, e.g. in the case of a laborforce shortage, is specified by m_Q then it can be stated:

$$P = \kappa m_Q f M \pi_M r, \tag{2.13}$$

with

f : = operating hours per day   x   operating days per year/8760,

π_M : = machine output in the case of 8760 operating hours,

and $m_Q, f, r \in [0,1]$.

2.13 can be interpreted as the *main equation* of the machine-dependent production. Notice that all terms are time-dependent functions possibly requiring large models for the description of each of them. In addition, it is noteworthy that this is a sixfold non-linear dynamic. Dichotomizing each term results in 64 basic states. Conceptualizing dynamics in this case as the transitions between these 64 states results in 4096 possible transitions.

As an example, one could dichotomize in the following way:

κ –   high/low, e.g. lower half-interval/
        upper half-intervall of [.75,.92],

m_Q –   labor-intensive/ not labor-intensive,

f –   long/ short workday,

M –   many/few machines,

π_M –   high/low productivity,

r –   strong/weak influence of global restrictions.

Stemming from this, LSUs might be classified according to their position in the so spanned state-space.

P can also be interpreted as a projection of a six-dimensional state-space. Regarding the amount of non-linear complexity of this dynamic, the question rises immediately, how $P(t)$ avoid behaving chaotically at all. In the real processes this appears to be achieved by strategies to bring as many of the terms as possible under control in order to handle them as quasi-constants. Some examples may demonstrate this:

κ –   monopolization, trusts, commitments,
        legal regulations, market power

m_Q –   prevention of labor shortages,
        inside-firm education

f –   fixed working hours

M –   ?

π_Q –   ?

r –   ?

Thus a reduced complexity results:

$$P = cM\pi_M r \qquad . \qquad (2.14)$$

r depends among other things on international financial and trade relations as well as on natural resources. M is mainly dependent on investments. Assuming that the latter can strategically be controlled, all else depends on the technological progress and on external restrictions. Consequently, a situation must be regarded as extremely critical where these two areas come into conflict. It seems that this is presently happening in some civilizations.

2.2.3 Demand, cost and prices

So far *prices* have not been taken into account, i.e. we performed an analysis in real terms. As soon as we start to specify price aspects, very difficult problems arise. The reason for this is that demand, production, costs and financing behavior are coupled by prices. The situation is aggravated by the fact that all these relations can vary in different sectors, see for instance STEINDL [124]. Let us, therefore, roughly consider the following sectors [5]:

$$C \quad - \quad \text{final demand goods,}$$
$$M \quad - \quad \text{other goods (especially machines),}$$
$$POL \quad - \quad \text{political sector, more generally}$$
$$\text{the } \textbf{PT} \text{ sector,}$$
$$\$ \quad - \quad \text{banks and insurances.}$$

The export-import balance shall be zero so that this aspect is to be neglected.

There are two obvious factors for pricing:

1. the production is to be sold at least at cost,

2. if demand surmounts production capacity prices will generally rise.

ad 1.

From 1. it follows immediately:

$$\theta_w \overset{!}{\geq} L/P \quad , \quad (2.15)$$

or at least

$$\theta^* = L/P \quad ,$$

---

[5]An exact definition of a **PT** system will be given in section 2.3 and in chap. 4; in Vol. 2 this will be operationalized and modelled dynamically. In this section we often use the terms "state" or "government" for sake of conventional understanding. However, it must be underlined that the oligarchy of a far developed civilization comprises far more sectors than only the state.

where

$$\theta_w : \quad = \quad \text{price target,}$$
$$L : \quad = \quad \text{production cost in } C,$$
$$P : \quad = \quad \text{production in } C.$$

With θ as the price realized on the market, it holds

$$U_P = P\theta$$

which are the production dependent returns, and

$$G_P = U_P - L$$

which refers to the profits (resp. losses) from production.

Cost determinants are, therefore, of high importance in 1. They can be classified as follows neglecting, as aforementioned, imports and exports and balancing the aggregated inputs from other firms to zero. This macro balancing neglects sectoral differentiations and, as a consequence, can easily lead to aggregation artifacts. In a later stage of our considerations we have to overcome this simplification by an explicit sectoral modelling.

1. Costs of raw material, energy, and water,

2. Transport costs so long they are not included in the afore-mentioned zero-balance,

3. Wages (incl. the chief accountants),

4. Loan repayments and interest payments,

5. Cost of stock,

6. Depreciation,

7. Rents and lease payments,

8. Political costs (comprising more than governmental costs such as taxes, due to our **PT** approach),

9. Insurance payments,

10. Extraordinary costs.

Returns are composed of following intakes:

1. Income from sales,

2. Revenue from loan repayments and interests,

3. Revenue from rents and leases,

4. New debt,

5. Political revenue (such as government assistance),

6. Extraordinary revenue.

We shall go into some details of these variables in Vol. 2 and restrict our analysis at this time to some preliminary aspects.

Let E denote the sum of intakes 2 to 6. Then the whole returns are

$$U = U_p + E \quad ,$$

and the total profits resp. losses are given by

$$G = U - L \quad .$$

The amount of E depends on past decisions affecting profits and on the 'art of financing'. If, for instance, a firm is said to be capable of surviving as a bank this demonstrates a high share of E in U.

If E is regarded as extraordinary revenue not taken into account against the costs, full cost prices may be lowered in 2.15 leading to

$$\theta_- = (L - E)/P \tag{2.16}$$

and it holds

$$\theta_- \leq \theta^* \quad .$$

Therefore, in the case of an $E > 0$ and the pricing strategy θ^* an extra-profit results. It is well known that assistance from government sources like financial aids for research projects can result in such extra-profits. It is obvious that, following the pricing strategy θ^*, the demand oriented pricing strategy θ_c can have an influence on the price level only if $\theta_c > \theta^*$. It would be interesting to go into details of this point, but this must be left to other studies.

What we want to ask at this point is to what extent the cost variables mentioned above are, in principal, under management's control. If further, the share of each cost variable in the total cost is considered, then those cost variables can be regarded as critical which possess a high share and are only partially controllable. Three variables fall into this category: Wages, **PT** costs, and, in the case of a high dependence on external funds, repayments and interest payments.

With growing labor saving technological efficiency and, in the case of a low dependence on external funds, ultimately only the **PT** costs remain as critical ones. In the course of this book we shall pay specific attention to this structural conclusion.

Also of interest is the possible conflict between the intention in $ to maximize a high dependence on external funds in C and M and the target in C and M to realize a low dependence on external funds.

In any case, these considerations show the limitations of approaches which do not explicitly specify the sectors POL and $. Despite this conclusion, approaches which take $ into account are the exception in ordinary economics, whereas, at least since the thirties, government as a prominent part of the **PT** system has played an important part in economical analyses: for some recent publications see BACON/ELTIS or VOGT [5,133].

ad 2.

In case of machine dependent production, *demand* has at first to be differentiated into investment and consumer goods denoted by B_M and B_C resp. B_C in turn can be composed in a multiplicity of ways; however, we shall only distinguish between two types of demand: **PT**, in particular governmental, and private consumer demand and in the latter between mass and prestige demand. Moreover, the subsistence minimum, which depends on the standard of living, will be distinguished from the remaining demand. Finally, there are segments of consumer demand which can be subsidized by governmental regulations such as depreciations laws. A firm specialized in products whose buyers are capable to afford, the consumption of these products will by virtue of depreciation be less affected by economic cycles. In the long run such firms must gain a dominant market position even if there is only a slow positive growth rate trend so that they are in a position to make acquisitions of other firms and so on. Similar preferences exist for goods sold by the state, or state-like institutions, such as insurances; in the F.R.G., for example, this is the case in the medical sector.

Since the value of goods beyond the subsistence minimum is set by price, the demand for *prestige goods* can reach a considerable money value. This holds especially for situations where the total economic production is in manifold excess of the minimal subsistence production. Therefore, production P shall be decomposed into

$$P = V + N \quad , \qquad (2.17)$$

where

$$V : \quad = \quad virtual \text{ heads,}$$
$$N : \quad = \quad \text{population.}$$

Because of $N \cdot 1 = N$, V is the number of C beyond the subsistence minimum. In 1980, the V of the F.R.G. was (details in the following section)

$$V = 180 \cdot 10^6 \quad .$$

If V is very large compared with N , then it can happen that the prestige consumption has a money volume sufficient to influence economic growth considerably. In cases where this holds, the threshold

$$P^* = v^* N \quad ,$$

beyond which a self-sustainable prestige consumption on the macro-economic level starts would be of high theoretical importance. Beyond P^* an autocatalytic segregation process can begin which appears to be already observable nowadays in the U.S.A.

The demand for *final goods* can be defined as

$$B_C \quad = \quad B_N + B_{CPOL} \quad ,$$

and with

$$B_N \quad = \quad B_l + B_h$$

the result is

$$B_C \quad = \quad B_l + B_h + B_{CPOL} \quad , \quad (2.18)$$

where

$$B_l : \quad = \quad \text{mass consumption demand,}$$
$$B_h : \quad = \quad \text{prestige demand,}$$
$$B_{CPOL} : \quad = \quad \text{final demand of the \textbf{PT} system, in particular of the state.}$$

If B_M denotes the demand for investment goods, then P must be compared with the sum $B_C + B_M$. Therefore, it appears convenient to decompose P analoguously by

$$P = P_C + P_M \quad .$$

Moreover it seems reasonable to distinguish between political and economic demand in B_M, leading to

$$B_M = B_{MWi} + B_{MPOL} \quad . \quad (2.19)$$

Altogether, two ordering relations result:

$$P_M \overset{?}{\geq} B_{MWi} + B_{MPOL}$$
$$P_C \overset{?}{\geq} B_l + B_h + B_{CPOL} \quad . \quad (2.20)$$

As postulated before, returns must at least cover costs. Thus, pricing in M depends at first on L_M. From this it is interesting that investment costs in C are paid to the outside. In M, to the contrary, investment costs remain inside that sector, so that they balance to zero in an aggregation, leaving imports aside. If we assume that the volume of goods from C used in M is of considerably less volume than conversely, the interesting fact results that pricing in M can have a larger impact on the total economy than pricing in C. In addition the production in C is 'take it or leave it' dependent on machines, which in turn can give M the opportunity to realize a high pricing strategy successfully. Whether C can cope with such a pricing strategy depends heavily on its capability to pass on these costs to the final consumer. A necessary condition for this is that the final consumer possesses enough money.

A shortage of demand can be compensated by debt. Government is of special importance in this field. From this the question immediately arises whether there is, in principal, an upper limit to governmental debt. Assuming that repayments and interest payments are in turn financible by new debts and that the state is autonomous concerning its debt-strategy, there seems to be no argument in favor of such a limitation, provided there is an infinite time horizon which can be specified as included in the state's autonomy.

The total debt of an economy is composed by

$$D = D_N + D_C + D_M + D_{POL} + D_\$ \quad ,$$

where

$$
\begin{aligned}
D_N : &= \text{debts of private households,} \\
D_C : &= \text{debts in C,} \\
D_M : &= \text{debts in M,} \\
D_{POL} : &= \text{debts in POL,} \\
D_\$: &= \text{debts in the banking sector itself.}
\end{aligned}
$$

We can postulate that costs and earnings stemming from $D_\$$ balance to zero in \$. However, additional book-money is created due to this debt, but we shall not go into details of currency politics here. D_N can be regarded as limited by personal income. D_C and D_M strongly depend on the degree of dependence on external funds, i.e. on past profits and their usage. Repayments and interest payments can reach a considerable amount. Assuming, however, a restrictive strategy of external funding, the only critical debt remaining is D_{POL}. If the banking sector and especially the central bank are organized independently from the government, the latter's expenditure ultimately will be restricted by limits imposed on D_{POL}. Conversely, in the case of governmental autonomy it will be presumably only D_{POL} as that debt which tends to rise 'beyond all limits'. However, since debt is a smoothing device problematic consequences of high debt will occur only in long [6] cycles. We can resumé that in principal governmental debt is the only critical

---

[6]From this it is interesting to ask, whether there are limitations to the state's autonomy, for instance, in situations of extreme inflation which can be a consequence of a debt strategy as mentioned before. However, we have evidence that inflation rates of 100% p.a. do not affect a state's autonomy.

debt category. Thus, there is again a motivation to analyse the state or, in a broader realm, the **PT** system. We shall return to this later on, especially in combination with distributional politics.

A demand shortage in M can be extremely dramatic because it

- can lead in the long run to a lowering of K_M, thereby to a reduction of the production of investment goods and thereby from 2.13 to an overall reduction of the productive capacity of an economy which, by definition, results in a lowering of P;

- stimulates in the short run the augmentation of prices in M in order to keep the money value of P_M, from which a stagflation or a slow down can result.

An augmentation of B_{MPOL}, for example by military, energy, or space projects, therefore, can lead to a growth of P_M with a simultaneous price stability. Even a slight reduction of B_C, for example by a redistribution in favor of B_{MPOL}, can be acceptable if the reduction of consumer demand is compensated by a reduction of the costs of investment goods. The augmentation of P_M and *ceteris paribus* the resulting profit will generally be gained by those consumers who have a high demand for prestige goods. B_h will also rise as a result. In all, a possible cycle is discovered as displayed in fig. 2.2.

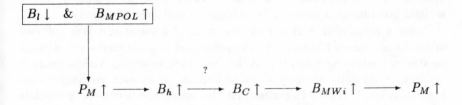

Figure 2.2: Distribution induced self–sustainable machine production growth

where $\uparrow$, $\downarrow$ denote augmentation and diminuation resp., and $\longrightarrow$ denotes a causal influence. The "?" refers to the question already posed above, whether an economic situation is possible in which this cycle will be self-sustainable.

The aforementioned cycle allows a strange conclusion. Workers already characterized in production as a disturbance factor controlled by labor saving and surveilling technologies may now be neutralized as a factor of consumer demand. Technological progress accompanied by certain redistribution politics can lead to a situation where B_l would be plafonded and by virtue of B_h, B_{CPOL}, and B_{MPOL} an *oligarchic economy* would appear. Could this be an aim of present conservative western politics?

In any case, the great importance of redistribution politics becomes clear. Economic models should contain production, distribution and debt in an explicit manner. In this book, naturally not all of these aspects can be analyzed completely. We must restrict our study to some aspects of apparent high relevance. According to the foregoing this is particularly the case in the political, or, in a broader sense, in the **PT** sector. However, because of the complex, non-linear structure of a model of this type it can only be performed in a simulation model. This will be the scope of Vol. 2.

2.3   Power territories

This book will examine civilizations exclusively, hence it will be of interest to study the existence of surplus. In the past 50,000 years LSUs without a surplus would have been an oddity: even a Shamanistic society requires a surplus, however modest. The question of distribution and allotment, to which we made some pertinent statements in the previous section, has a close connection with the existence of surplus. However, distribution and allotment are not only performed within but also between social units. Whereas within a social unit, the process of distribution and allotment can, beside exchange or robbery, be organized in the form of a central regulation (in simple social units e.g. by the chieftain or Shaman), between social units without supra-societal institutions, this can only proceed by exchange or robbery.

Since a social unit A that raids the stock of a social unit B is autocatalytically advantaged because A is in possession of additional stock with all its strategic advantages and B is at the same time weakened, violent quarrels between social units are very likely to happen; as to such mechanisms see [88]. However, it is easy to realise that this advantage is only permanent in the case of a small number of interacting social units (in a strict sense only in a dyadic relation). With an increasing number of interacting social units the violence principle tends collectively to harm all social units connected. So here for the first time we meet with a discrepancy that will attract our further attention in several aspects, i.e. the local-global problem.

If a social unit is successful in defending aquired surplus, this surplus, accrues to *property*. Since property, too, produces autocatalytic advantages as shown before, it will appear with high likelihood in all societies. In simple social units property especially refers to human beings (married) men, (married) women, children, slaves, animals (cattle), appliances (tools), weapons and territories (real estate).

Farming and cattle-breeding lead to a drastic rise in labor productivity and thus to higher surpluses. The appropriation of these surpluses become central problems of social units and some processes resulting from this are of special importance in understanding the operation of social units.

It is obvious that the distribution of surplus together with all activities related to it (storage, transport, business transaction, accounting etc.) cannot normally be effected by the immediately producing social units themselves. So, social units specialized in performing the distribution must exist. These have to be alimented from the surplus. Having subtracted this alimentation, only the remainder is at the disposal of distribution, exchange and appropriation. If the social units become more complex, and they get more complex by the existence of these social units specialised in distribution, or if productive social units are territorially separated from each other, a specific phenomenon of social development arises; social units emerge that can no more be controlled *face to face*.

Therefore, in essence, these social units are alimented by the surplus and are removed from primary control. Already these two features seem to be sufficient for the emergence of a social 'sphere' in which political power is sited. Some commonplace processes stem from these two features which have, nevertheless, strong power creating and power protecting effects. For instance, social units without socialization experiences in that 'sphere' neither have the time nor the energy – and as a rule don't get the idea at all – to become active in a power-critical sense. Further restrictions are productivity strain, fixation on family and immediate property.

The set of such simple, clear, concrete activities and social relations shall be called *primary context* (PRIM); individuals chacterized as mentioned before, are called *PRIM-centred*. Correspondingly, a social 'sphere', in which among other things political structures are sited, is designated as a *secondary context* (SEC).

If in rare cases PRIM-centred individuals break away from primary contexts, these activities are normally absorbed in SEC by acquisition of power positions. Now, as these few 'dynamic people' are dominant, they are missing from the dominated people so that political power entails over-proportional protection effects, for details about these mechanims see [88].

Thus, the central hypothesis is that SEC-structures do not require a specific, e.g. economic function in order to create their existence and durability, compare LENSKI and SERVICE [70,117]. In Vol. 2 models will show that these simple features alone are sufficient to create a social dynamic which, interestingly, is located in the political 'sphere'. This again proves SERVICE [117]. It cannot be ruled out, however, that for the purpose of legitimation, economic functions are maintained relevant by political institutions.

Dispositional power on the surplus and minor control on part of the producers, more generally on part of the PRIM-centred people, now leads to a new kind of redistribution.

Holders of social positions in SEC compete for shares in the surplus. As a rule, this appropriation does not happen in a direct way, e.g. by robbery or extortion. Rather, the access to the surplus is legitimized and guaranteed by privilege structures that are relatively durable, comp. LENSKI [70]. Presumably, this quickly entails competition no longer directly oriented to the share in surplus but to the participation in and enlargement of privilege structures. Then, surplus is only a necessary condition for the 'financing' of these structures, whereas, the form of these structures is no longer determined by economic conditions. Conversely, definition power in SEC leads to a high arbitrariness of privilege structures as long as they remain attractive.

A *privilege* can be characterized as the right to advantageous activities. Human beings strive or compete for such rights, and the mentioned activities are not regarded as inadmissible but, as a rule, even very legitimate.

Such rights establish themselves owing to the fact that individuals or social units succeed in decoupling 'society areas' from other 'society areas' and set up rules of domination within these areas, in particular by the definition of *competences*. Demarcation to the outside and internal rules of domination make it possible that external influences or influences of subordinated fields do not exist nor can be controlled internally: for more details about this see section 4.1. The demarcation is achieved e.g. by barriers (real bounds like walls, doors etc.), cultural symbols (e.g. profession-specific jargons), specific qualifications and ideologies. Often, rules of domination have the form of formal hierarchies.

Institutions and organizations, more seldom sub-institutions or sub-organizations, in such capsulated societal areas shall be called **PTs** and the holders of ruling positions within a **PT** their **PT**-*rulers* (**PTRs**). With high priority, the behaviour of those **PTRs** is oriented to the *securing* of their **PTs**, which means protecting it against external influences and not allowing themselves to be replaced by sub-ordinates or sub-**PTRs**. Such strategic behavior can be be summarized in the term **PT** *strategy*. Therefore, a **PT** strategy can be characterized as the *maximization of competences* under the side conditions of the stability of **PT** structures, resp. of the stability of the oligarchy structure on which there are more details below, and of the financability of the **PT** with all its structures and competences.

There is no need to mention the more or less trivial physical restrictions that naturally exist besides the social side conditions such as restriction of the time budget etc.

In other words, a **PT** could be characterized as a social unit wherein predominantly, possibly even entirely, the external unimpeachability of internal institutionalized structures is dealt with and to a lesser degree concrete contents of performances alleged to be the organizational aim. Casually formulated: **PTs** cope predominantly with power issues and not with substantial issues, comp. [88], see also the similar concept of "*Interesse an sich selbst*" (self-interest) by OFFE [103]. For further details see section 4.1.

Of far-reaching importance is the following conclusion that is a result of this **PT** approach and which will be presented in detail in chap. 4.

Proposition 1 *Explanations of the development and the operation of those LSUs producing a surplus must be explored, especially in areas associated with* **PT** *structures.*

It is not surprising that the form of *territorial* **PTs** was predominant from simple 'societies' to feudalism. One reason for this is surely, that here, surplus is above all achieved by agricultural production.

PTs emerge in the fields of religion, military, transport, architecture, art etc. at an early date. In complex 'societies' there are now all kinds of **PTs**, e.g. in the educational sector and public health.

If the proposition is correct that the development of LSUs is predominantly dependent upon developments and strategies inside **PTs**, then the hypothesis that the history of the human race would be the history of fights between the classes (MARX) becomes questionable. Instead, it has to be supposed that it is a history of quarrels between and within **PTs**: for evidence on this see LASSWELL/LERNER [64].

A key to the variability of cultural developments could possibly lie in the fact that **PTs** establish themselves by means of demarcations from other societal fields. This feature, if correct, would render the search for similarities of different cultures as not very promising and which could have some serious research-strategic consequences for comparative cultural analysis.

Under the condition of surplus, **PTs** will emerge in the course of time with probability 1 [7]. As is shown in detail in [88], they protect their internal structures without great friction. More problematic is the prevention against external influences, especially against competitive **PTs**. In section 4.2 there is a comprehensive explanation of the endemic violent **PT** strategies that can be expected, especially in 'societies' with a fixed or with a very slow growth of production. This is proved with the Yanomamö-Indians by CHAGNON [15] or for Madagaskar by BLOCH [8], where over centuries a war broke out approximately every 32th year. With some modifications, the same applies to Japan as for Madagaskar. It is interesting that in both cases cited this occured in island states. Perhaps in an insular or confined territory there is a greater need that one community must raid another for basic subsistence. In a broader generalization, territoriality could be one reason for the ubiquity of war, at least for partrilineal (agrarian) LSUs with surplus.

Finally, for the social-scientific analysis of LSUs, far-reaching methodological consequences result from **PT** importance, which are described in chap. 3,

---

[7] That oligarchies necessarily emerge from human interaction if two simple assumptions are made:

- the interaction is sufficiently complex,
- there exist interactions which are not orientated face-to-face (in the cited model "task-oriented groups"),

was shown in the stochastic process model of MAYHEW/LEVINGER [80].

for details see [93,97].

2.3.1   Existence and operation of power territories

A more detailed examination of **PT** structures now follows.

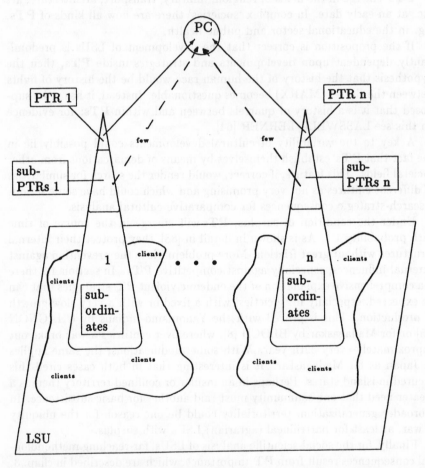

Figure 2.3: **PT** and *Herrschafts*structure in an LSU

At least three *existence* conditions and one *operation* condition can be stated:

Existence condition 1 (*competence*): At least one competence has to be defined for each **PT**. Below it is shown that oligarchic associations of

PTs possess definition power on these competences, i.e. they dispose of the competence on competence.

Existence condition 2 (*scope and effect*): Let individuals or social units in the competence field of a **PT** be called *clients* of the **PT**; the relation between the number of clients and the number of **PT** members may not fall under a certain minimum. It is obvious that this minimum is greater or equal to 1, i.e. that to each **PT** member there has to be allocated at least one client.

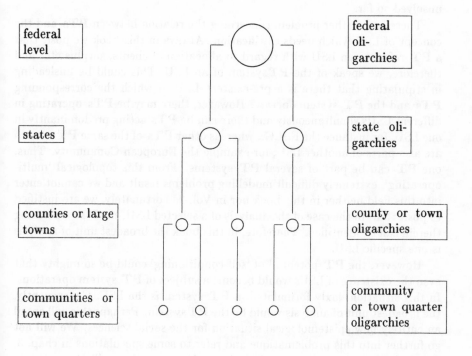

federal level

federal oli- garchies

states

state oli- garchies

counties or large towns

county or town oligarchies

communities or town quarters

community or town quarter oligarchies

Figure 2.4: Exemplary regional aggregates and *Herrschafts*hierarchy

This existence condition can also be defined as a *demarcation rule*; if the afore-stated relation should fall below 1, **PTs** within an LSU would no longer be in a position to delimit themselves. However, this holds only locally because **PT** members can be clients of other **PTs**. Regarding the members of an LSU there is an upper limit for the number of clients because of the limited time budget of an individual; there is a maximal number of client 'roles' per individual.

Existence condition 3 (*budget*): The **PT** has to dispose of sufficient financial assets.

Operation condition: If a **PT** exists, one central condition for its undisturbed operation is that **PT** strategies are effective.

The relation between **PT** structures and the operation of LSUs will be handled in chap. 4, but at this point it shall be underlined that **PTs** – if they operate – are in a position themselves to determine their existence conditions up to a certain degree. From this self-referentiality aspect intricate problems result which can affect great parts of civilizational operation and social science research. Only a minor part of these problems can be analyzed in this book due to the fact that the deep problems connected with self-referentiality are unsolved so far.

There is a further problem concerning the relation between **PTs** and the concept of LSU which needs clarification. Always in this book we posit that a **PT** refers to an LSU with regard to allocation of clients, surplus etc. and therefore, we speak of the **PT** system of an LSU. This could be misleading in stipulating that there is a pre-existent LSU in which the corresponding **PTs** and the **PT** system operate. However, there may be **PTs** operating in different LSUs simultaneously and there can be **PTs** acting predominantly in one LSU, for instance the F.R.G., whereas other **PTs** of the same **PT** system are also parts of another LSU, for example the European Community. Thus, one **PT** can be part of several **PT** systems. From this topological 'multi-operating', extremely difficult modelling problems result and we cannot enter into this field neither in this book nor in Vol. 2. Fortunately, we are justified to posit that, in the case of the analysis of a selected LSU, the **PTs** operating therein can be identified. Therefore, in this book the broadest unit of analysis is *one* specific LSU.

However, the **PT** potential of 'self-conditioning' could be so mighty that even the existence of LSUs would become a subject of **PT** system operations. In this situation, laxly formulated, a **PT** system *is* the LSU. Consequently, the broadest unit of analysis would be the **PT** system. Perhaps this will entail an entirely new epistemological situation for the social sciences. We will not go further into this problematique and refer to some speculations in chap. 3. All what we can do at present is to hope that some time will elapse before this situation is reached so that the contents of the two volumes of this work can be valid for for some years.

In this sense we shall speak of a **PT** system of an LSU in the following.

Propositions can be formulated concerning the relation between the number of LSU members and the number of **PTs** in a social unit. For this purpose the structure of a system of **PTs** shall at first be sketched as is shown in fig. 2.3.

As a rule, clients predominantly belong to one LSU only. This does not necessarily hold for **PT** members, because **PTRs** especially and sub-**PTRs** can hold power positions in different LSUs. The reason for this lies in the fact that position holders on higher hierarchy levels are mostly competent for regional aggregates. If the F.R.G. is taken as an example, a relation can be set up as sketched in fig. 2.4.

Thus, in this regional structure there are four types of LSUs together with the corresponding hierarchically arranged **PTs**.

Any unification of LSUs shall be called an *LSU system*. Let the number of LSUs at an aggregate level be denoted as the size m of this aggregate level. Especially, the simple fact that most times $m = 1$ holds for the highest aggregate level seems to be of great importance for the dynamic behavior of an LSU system that comprises all levels. These more complex problems, among other things the operating relevance of the sizes, will be examined in later chapters. First, some reflections on the operation of a single LSU shall be undertaken.

Notations:

$$
\begin{aligned}
E : &= \text{ set of } \textbf{PTRs} \text{ of the LSU,} \\
S : &= \text{ set of sub-}\textbf{PTRs} \text{ of the LSU,} \\
U : &= \text{ set of } \textbf{PT} \text{ subordinates of the LSU,} \\
N : &= \text{ number of the LSU members,} \\
H : &= \text{ set of members of the LSU } \textit{power centre } (\textbf{PC}), \\
OLI : &= \text{ set of the LSU oligarchs,} \\
SOLI : &= \text{ set of the LSU suboligarchs,} \\
A : &= \text{ set of all } \textbf{PT} \text{ members of the LSU,} \\
n : &= \text{ number of the } \textbf{PC} \text{ members,} \quad (2.21)
\end{aligned}
$$

The following set-theoretic relations are assumed:

$$
\begin{aligned}
A &= E \cup S \cup U \quad , \\
OLI &= E \cup (S \cap H) \quad , \\
SOLI &= S \setminus OLI \quad .
\end{aligned}
$$

$$(2.22)$$

From the set relations it follows:

$$|E| \leq |OLI| \leq |E \cup S| \quad ,$$

so that, by virtue of these set-theoretical postulates, some estimations concerning order relations can already be made.

2.3.2   Population size and the number of power territories

There seems to be a fixed relation between n and N:

Proposition 2 *(power concentration) Let N denote the number of members of an LSU and n the number of the members of its* **PC**. *Then it holds by virtue of scale-order:*

$$n = hN \qquad and \qquad h = 10^{-4} \qquad . \tag{2.23}$$

The scale-order of 10^{-4} has been proved for different LSUs, e.g. as to DYE [21] for the U.S.A, or [88] for a small town in Lower-Saxony ($N = 4.3 \cdot 10^4$). The chamber of magistrates of Venice elected 500 leading persons for each government period: the number of inhabitants of the republic of Venice including its colonies was $5 \cdot 10^6$, (see OTTEN [107], and personal communication). Since $|\ OLI\ |$ is small compared with N it can be approximated

$$n/(N - |\ OLI\ |) \approx n/N = h \qquad .$$

In the Venice example this relation was perfectly fulfilled.

The members of H (the **PC**) stem mostly from E, i.e. they are *top-oligarchs*. Only exceptionally do they stem from S. Let us posit:

$$|\ H\ |:|\ E\ | = 1 : 10 \qquad .$$

It can be supposed that the members of $E \backslash H$ will possess a significantly lower influence potential compared with that of the H-members if $|\ H\ |$ grows. Under this condition, therefore, the members of $E \backslash H$ must be considered as *suboligarchs*. Consequently, the members of $SOLI$ would be sub-suboligarchs. Conversely , in the case of small LSUs the members of E will be of higher importance. It can also be supposed that there exists upper thresholds for $|\ H\ |$ and $|\ E\ |$ beyond which **PC** and the oligarchy will become unsurveillably large. Let these thresholds be denoted by $|\ H\ |^*$ and $|\ E\ |^*$. From this the interesting question arises whether the size of LSUs is restricted by these thresholds; in other words, whether beyond those thresholds LSUs will collapse into new LSUs, or otherwise, whether LSUs can grow regardless of $|\ H\ |^*$ and $|\ E\ |^*$. It is plausible to presume that for

$$|\ H\ | \rightarrow |\ H\ |^* \text{ or } |\ E\ | \rightarrow |\ E\ |^*$$

new hierarchy levels or subsystems will emerge. By such differentiations, H-members will descend, resulting in $E \backslash H$ or S-members and the relations

$$\frac{|H|}{|OLI|} \qquad , \qquad \frac{|OLI|}{|SOLI|}$$

will diminish so that a reduction of ruling effort will result. We shall return to this in chap. 4 and in Vol. 2.

In 2.23 n was related proportionally to N, i.e. depending only on the number of LSU members. This may lead to some irritations at first sight since n is specified as independent from 'national', i.e. LSU, income. A possible explanation could be that the wealth of an LSU affects only $OLI \setminus H$ and $SOLI$ because instrumental aspects of ruling the (produced) C are located in these areas.

To derive the relation between population size and number of **PTs** from formal considerations, two approaches shall be portrayed. So far, it is still debatable which of the two approaches will be more appropriate in the end.

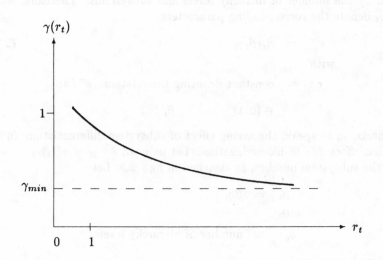

Figure 2.5: Saving effect due to subsystem differentiation

Notations: Let

$$n : = \text{ number of } \textbf{PC-PTRs},$$
$$s : = \text{ number of sub-}\textbf{PTRs},$$
$$e^- : = |E \setminus H|,$$
$$u : = \text{ number of subordinates of a } \textbf{PT},$$
$$\alpha : = |E| = n + e^-,$$

$$\sigma : \quad = \quad \text{sub-\textbf{PTRs} per \textbf{PT}},$$
$$\rho : \quad = \quad \text{subordinates per sub-\textbf{PTR}}.$$

$$(2.24)$$

Supposing that σ and ρ are fixed by organizational constraints, both can be specified as constants in a first approximation. Supposing further that there exists exactly one ruler per **PT**, it results that the number A of all **PT** members depends only on α:

$$A_t = \alpha_t(1 + \sigma + \sigma\rho)$$

and we have only to determine α to derive A. With 2.23 and e^- by definition it follows:

$$\alpha_t = hN_t + e_t^- \qquad . \qquad (2.25)$$

In our first approximation, as delivered here, we postulate that e^- is determined by the number of hierachy levels and subsystems. Therefore, let β_t and γ_t denote the corresponding parameters:

$$e_t^- \quad = \quad n_t \epsilon \beta_t \gamma_t \qquad\qquad (2.26)$$
with

$$\epsilon : \quad = \quad \text{constant denoting the relation} \quad e^-/n;$$

$$\gamma_t \in (0,1) \quad , \quad \beta_t \geq 1 \quad .$$

γ_t reflects, so to speak, the saving effect of subsystem differentiation, β_t the inflation effect due to hierarchization. Let us posit $\quad \gamma_t = \gamma(r_t)r_t \quad$ with r_t as the subsystem number, as sketched in fig. 2.5. Let

$$\beta_t \quad = \quad \beta g_t$$
with

$$g_t : \quad = \quad \text{number of hierarchy levels.}$$

In a first approximation:

$$\epsilon \quad = \quad 10 - 1 = 9$$
$$\beta_t \quad = \quad 1 \cdot 4 = 4$$
$$\gamma(r_t) \quad = \quad .1 \qquad\qquad \text{for} \quad t = 1980 .$$

Remark: -1 in the ϵ equation, because α can be regarded as being included; β is directly proportional to the number of regional levels.
Considering the F.R.G., it would hold by scale-order:

$$e_t^- \quad = \quad 6,000 \cdot 9 \cdot 4 \cdot .1 = 4,500$$
and

$$\alpha_t \quad = \quad 6,000 + 4,500 = 10,500 \qquad .$$

β_t and γ_t, especially, depend on the capability to finance them, thus, on the volume of produced $\mathcal{C}$, where σ and ρ must be noticed. Choosing

$$\sigma \;=\; \rho = 10 \quad \text{, it follows:}$$
$$A_t \;=\; 2.4 \cdot 10^6 \qquad \text{for the F.R.G. in} \quad t = 1980,$$

that is, around 10% of the productive population.

In the *second approach*, e^- is directly derived from the volume of produced $\mathcal{C}$. Let $P :=$ produced $\mathcal{C}$ per year, then let

$$V_t = P_t - N_t$$

denote the *virtual* $\mathcal{C}$. Now 2.23 shall be applied directly leading to

$$e_t^- = \hbar V_t \gamma_t \beta_t \qquad . \qquad (2.27)$$

As will be shown later, for 1980 the following is applicable for the F.R.G.:

$$P_t \;=\; 240 \cdot 10^6 \qquad ,$$

hence

$$V_t \;=\; 180 \cdot 10^6 \qquad ,$$

and

$$\alpha_t \;=\; 6,000 + 18,000 \cdot .1 \cdot 4 = 13,200 \quad .$$

Concerning these approaches some interesting questions can be posed which we shall analyse in more detail in chap. 4 and in Vol. 2, for instance:

- What is the relation between V and the number of clients?

- Can it be imagined that with the progress of artificial intelligence or biotechnology artificial $\mathcal{C}$ emerge?

- Where are the thresholds of hierarchization and subsystem differentiation?

If debt D_t is added to the terms considered (we will refer to this later), then we possibly have already specified the relevant terms for describing the dynamics of (occidental) civilizations in a first approximation. Hence, the following state space results:

$$\Phi_t = \{(\alpha_t, V_t, N_t, D_t)/t \in T\}$$

with $T :=$ set of time points. Notice, that the specification of the direct dependence on nature is lacking: in section 2.5 we shall cope with this area.

Let us assume that $e_t^-/n_t = .75$ is an equilibrium condition. Then it may be of interest to examine which processes lead back to the steady state in the case of departure from the equilibrium. If the fraction is less than .75, an increase in production or a decrease in population *ceteris paribus* leads back to the equilibrium state: if the fraction is greater than .75, **PT** partitions (S-members become E-members), new hierarchies or subsystems, the destruction of suboligarchies (war) or an increase in population *ceteris paribus* lead back to the equilibrium state. Presumably, the strategy of increase in population is the one with the least structural instability; LYON et al. and SIMON, J.E. [77,118] point out the existence of such mechanisms.

In the following, an attempt shall be made to derive n from a production-distribution-**PT** model. We call this a *derivation* and not a proof, because a model result cannot be a replacement for proof.

Derivation:

Definition 1 *Let N be divided in productives, systematically non-productives (children, aged, ill people...), and* **PT** *members.*

Remark: Notice, that, according to this definition, the **PT** subordinates, i.e. U, are non-productive, too.

Denoting the part of the productives of non-**PT** members with q, and

$$Q := \text{number of productives} \quad ,$$

we can state:

$$Q = (N - |A|)q \quad . \tag{2.28}$$

In 1980, for the F.R.G. it holds approximately that $q = .44$.

Definition 2 *All non-productives, i.e.* **PT** *members and systematically un-productives, are alimented from the surplus.*

It is not easy to state criteria which indicate who belongs to the productives. In the field of economy it may be useful to distinguish between small and large firms and to fix in a first approximation that **PTs** only appear in the latter class(comp. STEINDL, 0'CONNOR, OLSON [124,99,105], a survey on literature is given by GRUCHY [39], as to OLSON see also MÜLLER [86]).

Recall that economic production volumes in the form of C have been specified as a multiple of the subsistence minimum. The level of the subsistence minimum may vary depending on the standard of living, or on socio-structural conditions (e.g. number of the household members to be alimented as well), or whether the minimum is calculated in nominal terms. Since the present model is specified in a real-term and static way, the subsistence minimum is considered as a parameter which, of course, can be varied.

The model contains mean values averaged over all **PTs** and **PT** members of the LSU under consideration: a more differentiated model will be described in Vol. 2. The parameters of the model are drawn partly from empirical evidence, partly from obvious scale orders and partly from plausible guesses.

On the average, a **PT** member is assumed to inhabit K positions. If POS is the number of oligarchic **PT** positions, k results as

$$k := |POS| / |OLI|$$

In the study of DYE [21] the evidence was

$$K = 5,000/3,500 \approx 1.5$$

This evidence referred to the financial oligarchy of all states of the U.S. Presumably, K is greater at the lower levels, e.g. on the regional or municipal level. The relatively high value of 1.5 is assumed to be the result of the well-known interlocking between banks and company directorates in the U.S. On the highest level of the hierarchy of a state, k will be less than 1.5 (comp. also results of the model MUE & HIER in Vol. 2). In the F.R.G., we can distinguish four levels of regional institutions as was sketched in fig. 2.4. According to these assumptions the following should hold:

Conjecture 1 $k_{GEM} \geq k_{LK} \geq k_L \geq K_B$,
where

$$
\begin{aligned}
GEM: \quad &= \quad municipality\ or\ quarter, \\
LK: \quad &= \quad county\ or\ city\ without\ district, \\
L: \quad &= \quad state, \\
B: \quad &= \quad Federal\ Government.
\end{aligned}
$$

which, in a rough approximation, can be considered as levels of hierarchy.

As regards k_{GEM}, there is evidence from a communal élite study performed by the author ($N = 4.3 \cdot 10^4$) concerning the chiefs of decisions centres (parties, hospitals, important firms etc.) of this municipality: 23 of these 44 persons held at least one membership in a non-economic institution. If these 23 persons are selected, the corresponding findings are shown in table 2.1. A **PTR** is characterized by the feature that he holds at least one chair position. Hence, k must be calculated from the population of the 19 people (7+11+1) with at least one chair position, which yields the following average value:

$$k = (7 \cdot 1 + 11 \cdot 2 + 1 \cdot 3)/19 = 1.68$$

$k_{GEM} = 1.68$ is, according to conjecture 1, greater than $k = 1.5$ from DYE [21]. Owing to restrictions of the time budget, k_e must be supposed less than 2, where e denotes **PTRs**.

number of directorate positions

		0	1	2	3	sum
	1	2	1	2	0	5
number	2	5	2	2	0	9
of	3	0	0	2	1	3
memberships	4	4	1	3	0	8
in	5	1	2	1	0	4
organizations	6	2	1	0	0	3
	7	0	0	1	0	1
sum		14	7	11	1	23

Table 2.1: Multiple **PT** positions in a small German town

Because it is a matter of these 44 persons being already important deciders, that subpopulation with the following characteristic:

Number of organization memberships ≥ 1
and the number of chair positions $= 0$,

can be interpreted as the number of SOLIs waiting for achievement onto OLI-positions. Thus, $.44 = 14/32$ is the waiting/position relation. We can presume that this relation is a crucial parameter for the dynamics of a **PT** system. We shall return to that in the model MUE & HIER in Vol. 2.

Already at this point, it becomes clear that a more realistic model has to contain various regional as well as hierarchic-positional differentiations. In a first approximation we will omit that (more details in Vol. 2).

Let us return to the derivation of the proposition. We use the *first* approach, i.e. 2.25, in combination with 2.26. Let us recall:

$$\alpha = n + n\epsilon\beta\gamma = n(1 + \epsilon\beta\gamma) \qquad (2.29)$$

is the number of **PTRs**. Since one **PTR** holds k positions due to interlocking, the number of **PTs** ($=$ positions) is

$$\Omega = k\alpha \qquad .$$

Let the **PT** demand for produced $\mathcal{C}$ be composed of a local position demand and a global ruling (*Herrschafts*) demand, denoted by B_Ω and B_H, resp.:

$$B = B_\Omega + B_H \qquad , \qquad (2.30)$$

and

$$B_\Omega = (E + sS + uU)c_1 k\alpha \qquad ,$$
$$B_H = c_2 k\alpha^2 \qquad , \qquad (2.31)$$

where

$$E : \quad = \quad \text{alimentation of a mean } \textbf{PTR} \text{ in } \mathcal{C} \, ,$$

$$
\begin{aligned}
S : &= \text{ditto for sub-}\textbf{PTRs,} \\
U : &= \text{ditto for }\textbf{PT}\text{ subordinates,} \\
u : &= \text{number of subordinates per }\textbf{PT,} \\
s : &= \text{number of sub-}\textbf{PTRs}\text{ per }\textbf{PT.}
\end{aligned}
$$

c_1, c_2 are coefficients interpretable as interlocking saving effects.

That $B_H = f(k)$ and not $f(1/k)$ means that the ruling demand is larger the more concentrated the oligarchy. One can understand this by imagining the organizational efforts and energy input necessary to maintain an effective ruling of a highly concentrated oligarchy.

The specification of the quadratic term in B_H may be explained at this point by the fact that for maintaining power structures the interaction of **PTs** is necessary. Later on we shall see that this quadratic relation can be derived from hierarchy oriented considerations.

With reference to the whole LSU it must hold:

$$
P \geq A[N - \alpha(1 + s + u)] + B
$$

with

$$
\begin{aligned}
A : &= \text{alimentation of an average non-}\textbf{PT}\text{ member of the LSU,} \\
P : &= \text{total production of the LSU in } C , \\
N : &= \text{population of the LSU.}
\end{aligned}
$$

Notice, that the whole demand for machines and infrastructure is subsumed under B. This will be analyzed in a more differentiated manner in later chapters.

Let $\widetilde{E}$ denote the non-**PT** members of an LSU, that is,

$$
\widetilde{E} := N - \alpha(1 + s + u) \qquad .
$$

A part of $\widetilde{E}$ is productive, the remainder (elderly people, children,...) shall be considered systematic unproductive. The quota of productives shall be denoted by q , hence:

$$
Q = q\,\widetilde{E} \qquad .
$$

is the number of productives. Due to factors that are hard to change q is limited from above: a q of more than .6 is only imaginable in rare cases.

Let π_A denote labor productivity. For the sake of simplicity this productivity indicator is chosen here: in Vol. 2 we shall try to base the analysis on a machine productivity(see also the following section).

Provided Q and π_A are known, P is fixed, because trivially it holds

$$
P = Q\pi_A \qquad . \tag{2.32}
$$

Supposing that systematic unproductives are alimented lower than productives, the demand for alimentation of $\tilde{E}$ can be considered as being composed from

$$B_Q + B_N,$$

with

$$B_Q = QA_Q$$
$$B_N = (\tilde{E} - Q)A_N$$

Remarks:
B_Q denotes the alimentation demand of the productives, B_N denotes the alimentation demand of the systematic unproductives, and A_Q, A_N denote alimentations per individual. All terms are measured in C.

Notice that in this first approximation unemployed are omitted. In Vol. 2 they shall be introduced.
It must hold:

$$P \geq B_Q + B_N + B_\Omega + B_H.$$

Inserting the terms into the right side yields:

$$
\begin{aligned}
F &= q[N - \alpha(1 + s + u)]A_Q & &| B_Q \\
&+ \{N - q[N - \alpha(1 + s + u)]\}A_N & &| B_N \\
&+ (E + sS + uU)c_1 k\alpha & &| B_\Omega \\
&+ c_2 k\alpha^2 & &| B_H
\end{aligned}
\tag{2.33}
$$

Considering all terms except α as constants, it results that F depends only on α, and it must hold:

$$F(\alpha) \leq P.$$

Let α^* fulfil the equality, hence

$$F(\alpha^*) = P, \tag{2.34}$$

then it holds:

$$\alpha^* = \alpha_{max}.$$

Inserting $P = Q\pi_A$ into 2.34 results after sorting for exponentials and resolution for α^* in:

$$\alpha^*_{1,2} = -.5\frac{Y}{X} \pm \sqrt{.25(\frac{Y}{X})^2 - Z} \tag{2.35}$$

with

$$X = c_2 k$$
$$Y = dq(A_N - A_Q + \pi_A) + Dc_1 k$$
$$Z = N[q(A_Q - A_N - \pi_A) + A_N]$$
$$d = 1 + s + u$$
$$D = E + sS + uU$$

Since imaginary numbers of **PTRs** cannot exist, the term under the square root must be non-negative. Thus we have to control for

$$.25(\tfrac{Y}{X})^2 \overset{?}{\geq} Z \quad .$$

Let us first check *a fortiori* whether generally $Z \leq 0$ maintains because then the inequality is fulfilled in all cases. To perform this let us write the term in square brackets in another manner:

$$qA_Q + (1-q)A_N - q\pi_A \overset{?}{\leq} 0 \quad .$$

π_A must be greater than or equal to $A_Q + A_N$ in all cases, and under the condition of a positive **PT** demand it must even hold:

$$\pi_A > A_Q + A_N \quad .$$

In the minimum, i.e. for $\pi_A = A_Q + A_N$ and for $q = .5$, it follows:

$$A_Q + A_N - A_Q - A_N = 0 \quad .$$

Inserting plausible values of the parameters, hence, the argument of the root is positive.

Since there cannot be negative numbers of **PTRs**, only the postive solution α_1^* is meaningful. Let us calculate α_1^* as depending on X,Y and Z. The parameters shall be set as follows:

$$
\begin{aligned}
k &= 1.5 \quad \text{from DYE [21] and project HSDMEL} \\
d &= 1 + 10 + 60 = 71 \\
s &= 10 \quad \text{per scale-order} \\
u &= 60 \quad \text{from project HSDMEL} \\
A_N &= 1 \quad \text{as a plausible approximation} \\
D &= 10 + 10 \cdot 5 + 60 \cdot 1 = 120 \\
c_1, c_2 &= ? \in [0,1] \\
q &= ? \in [q_{min}, .6] \\
A_Q &= ?, \quad A_Q > A_N \\
\pi_A &= ?, \quad \pi_A \geq \pi_{min} \approx 1.7 \\
N &= ?
\end{aligned}
$$

The ? denote free parameters which must be inserted by the user. Taking together, we have:

$$X = X(c_2)$$
$$Y = Y(q, A_Q, c_1, \pi_A)$$
$$Z = Z(N, q, A_Q, \pi_A) \quad ,$$
and
$$\theta = \{c_1, c_2, q, A_Q, \pi_A, N\}$$

is the set of parameters to be inserted by the user.

From the statistical yearbook of the F.R.G. we take for 1980:

$$N = 61.658 \cdot 10^6$$
$$Q = 28.16 \cdot 10^6$$

From this it results using $\alpha = 10,500$ from above: $q = .46$, which appears plausible.

For the gross value added Y we find in the yearbook $Y = 1.429 \cdot 10^{12}$ DM.

Social care in 1980 per case was $l = 6,317$ DM/a.

Choosing in a first approximation l as the subsistence minimum, we can make the following approach:

$$Q\pi_A l = Y \quad ,$$
and from this
$$\pi_A = Y/(Ql) = 8.03 \approx 8 \quad .$$

Inserting

c_1	= .67	| plausible value
c_2	= .25	| 4 regional hierarchy levels
q	= .46	| F.R.G. 1980, see above
A_Q	= 3	| plausible
π_A	= 8	| F.R.G. 1980, see above

and the above N into the equation, it results:

$$\alpha^* = 10,004 \approx 10^4 \quad .$$

This result is near to the value of 10,500 derived above from the model. One could now insert 10^4, calculate a new α^*, and so on, but we do not think iteration is necessary due to the acceptable enough correspondence of our empirical calculations.

Notice that with an $\alpha = 10^4$ the number of **PTRs** in turn reach the scale-order of an LSU, which perhaps can have the impact to create additional hierarchy levels (perhaps the fifth level of the European Community). However, at this point we shall not pursue this topic further.

A closer inspection of 2.35 shows that Z is significantly dominant in the determination of α^*. For given N and q, therefore,

$$\pi_A - A_Q$$

is relevant. This is immediately plausible, because by this difference the distributable surplus is determined.

Let us now calculate α^* for some LSUs whose historical scale-orders are known or are of interest. This shall demonstrate whether the approach developed here delivers plausible scale-order results. The examples are listed in table 2.2.

type of society	N^+	c_1	c_2	q	A_Q	π_A	α^*
early agriculture	2E4	.9	.75	.6	1.5	2.2	3
late agriculture	1E6	.8	.67	.6	1.7	2.5	221
Venice	5E6	.8	.67	.6	1.7	2.5	566[a]
F.R.G.	61E6	.67	.25	.46	3	8	10,000
U.S.A.[b]	200E6	.67	.2	.45	3	9	20,616
future world system[b]	3.5E9	.6	.2	.1	5	17	32,073

Table 2.2: Societal types and their **PT** numbers
+) xEn means $x \cdot 10^n$
a) notice the good fit with the empirical value $\alpha - e^- = 500$
b) plausible values

If there are lower and upper limits for the parameters, then the root yields the effect that with growing N it becomes more and more difficult to create additional **PTs**. This can be interpreted by assuming an organizational limit to the growth of virtual C, see similar HIRSCH [50].

Finally, let us apply 2.23 to the case study of the HSDMEL project where data for an LSU of $4.3 \cdot 10^4$ inhabitants are available. Version 1 from above yields:

$$|H| = n = 10^{-4} \cdot N = 4.3 \approx 4 \quad,$$

and

$$|E \setminus H| = e^- = n\epsilon\beta\gamma \quad.$$

With $\quad \epsilon = 9, \gamma = .5 \quad$ it follows:

$$e^- = 4.3 \cdot 9 \cdot \beta \cdot .5 \approx 20\beta \quad .$$

In the élite study of HSDMEL the following evidence was produced (DC := decision centre) :

$\quad |E| = 44$, who adhere to 47 DCs,
and 97 important persons
were named in a snowball survey.

Let us suppose that the respondents gave their answers in a manner valid and reliable in accordance with the used questionnaire design. Then the evidence yields:

$$|OLI| = n + e^- = 92 \quad .$$

In 1972, the project region of HSDMEL was a newly established town formed from nine original former independent small towns of a county. Maybe this can explain the high number of 92 oligarchs. Anyway, this evidence requires further investigation which will not be made at this juncture. Let us apply our formulas directly. If in a first approximation, β is specified as directly proportional to the number of hierarchies then in the case of the project region, because of the county-town relation, this must be 2 . Thus it follows:

$$n + e^- = 4.3 + 4.3 \cdot 9 \cdot 2 \cdot .5 = 43 \quad .$$

This theoretical result corresponds significantly well to the observed number of the 44 **PTRs**, but is very much smaller than the named 92 important persons. In accordance with experiences from community power studies, the position oriented number should be considered as more trustworthy.

The *second* version yields after using the relation

$$P/N = 240 \cdot 10^6 / (61 \cdot 10^6) \approx 4$$

from the F.R.G. in the project region:

$$P = 4 \cdot 43 \cdot 10^3 = 172 \cdot 10^3 \quad ,$$
$$V = 172 \cdot 10^3 - 43 \cdot 10^3 = 129 \cdot 10^3,$$

and

$$n + e^- = 4 + 10^{-4} \cdot V \cdot 2 \cdot 5 = 17, \tag{2.36}$$

which is significantly smaller than 44 .

This discrepancy gives ground for some possible suggestions:

- On lower hierarchy levels the first version is more appropriate.

- The *second* version can possibly be an appropriate guess in the case of a large N, i.e. it could be supposed, that

$$\lim_{N \to \infty} \alpha_1 = \lim_{N \to \infty} \alpha_2 \quad ,$$

1,2 denote version 1, 2 resp.

- If this was correct, it must hold for large N,

$$N10^{-4} + (P - N)10^{-4}\gamma = N10^{-4} + \epsilon N10^{-4}\gamma,$$

and from this

$$V = \epsilon N \quad ,$$

and especially

$$\epsilon = V/N \quad , \tag{2.37}$$

where a rounding rule for ϵ is left to be specified. In the F.R.G. in 1980:

$$\epsilon = 180/60 = 3 \quad ,$$

which shows that if we take $\epsilon = 9$ (see above the remark after 2.26) as the exact value how far the F.R.G. is still distant from a real large V.

- It certainly is a rough simplification to specify an average **PT** over all hierarchy levels, which must be supposed to yield artificial results. In chap. 4 and Vol. 2 we shall undertake a hierarchy oriented differentiation of **PT**s.

Inserting $P = \tilde{q} N \pi_A$ into 2.37, where $\tilde{q} :=$ labor force quota of the population, leads because of $V = P - N$ to:

$$\epsilon = \tilde{q} \, \pi_A - 1 \quad ,$$

and it seems of interest to note that, for large N, ϵ no longer depends on N. Suppose there would in the future be the emergence of an LSU with a population large enough (maybe China or a world-wide LSU), then it would be interesting to analyse whether there could appear a situation $(\tilde{q}, \pi_A)$ to reach $\epsilon = 9$. In section 2.5 we shall see that due to saturation effects of technological progress $\pi_A = 9$ can be reached in the year 2035. It is immediately evident that $\epsilon = 9$ cannot be reached given this productivity. Therefore, let us consider a future society after 2035, supposing an exponential growth of π_A with the growth parameter r, provided labor productivity would also be a valid measure in this period, then the time points $t(\tilde{q}, r)$ can be calculated at which $\epsilon = 9$ is reached. The results for different $\tilde{q}$ and r are shown in tab. 2.3. r was chosen such that in the first case (.003) the next C will be reached in 30, in the second case in 25 years. The question, whether these threshold considerations and results can be interpreted substantially, however, must be answered by additional studies.

$\tilde{q}$	r	t	$\pi_A(t)$
.4	.003	2453	31.5
.3	.003	2525	39
.2	.003	2633	54
.4	.005	2286	31.5
.3	.005	2329	39
.2	.005	2394	54

Table 2.3: Reaching the hierachy level relation of 1:10 under the condition of a very large population depending on the labor force quota and the velocity of productivity growth

2.3.3   Power territory acquisition of surplus

In the derivation of proposition 2 we specified a surplus distributed over a number of average **PTs**. This 'monolithic' approach certainly is a great simplification. It would be more appropriate to differentiate **PTs** according to their distance from the power centre (**PC**) of the LSU and their distribution on hierachy levels, to mention only two aspects. If done, however, a distribution algorithm would need to be specified by which the surplus fraction for each **PT** could be calculated, a very difficult task. Considering the two aspects hierachy and **PC**-distance, a corresponding surplus distribution can be visualized as sketched in fig. 2.6 The numbers $1, 2, \cdots, r$ denote subsystems.

In the following a first rough sketch of a one-dimensional distribution algorithm shall be outlined. It shall serve only as a demonstration and not pretend to be an appropriate approach to solve the complicated problems in this research field.

Let the subsystems be numerated by $j = 1, 2, \cdots, r$. Suppose, there are m hierarchy levels, and **PTs** are present with a specific intensity on a hierarchy level $i = 1, \cdots, m$. Assuming, that the intensity of presence can be indicated by the proportion of **PT** personnel occupying positions on j, we may specify:

p_{ij} := proportion of **PTs** of a subsystem j
located on the hierarchy level i.

Let $w_i Z$ denote the surplus volume distributed to i with

$$Z : \quad = \quad \text{collective surplus of the LSU,}$$
$$w_i : \quad = \quad \text{quota of distribution to } i.$$

Let the subsystem j receive A_j with

$$A_j \quad = \quad q_j Z \quad ,$$
where
$$q_j : \quad = \quad \text{appropriation quota.}$$

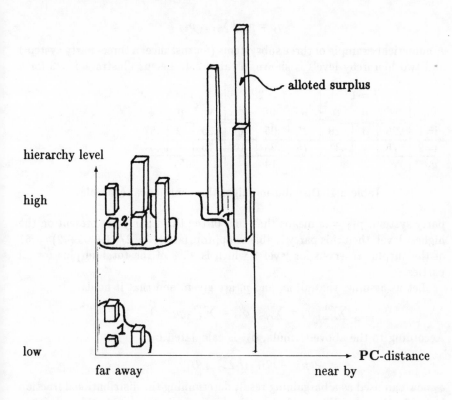

Figure 2.6: Hierarchy level, distance from the power centre and distributed surplus

We define

$$\phi_{ij} := \text{appropriation quota of } j \text{ on level } i$$

and postulate

$$q_j = \sum_{i=1}^{m} w_i p_{ij} \phi_{ij}$$

with

$$\phi_{ij} = w_i q_j p_{ij} / \sum_{j=1}^{r} q_j p_{ij} \quad,$$

that is, ϕ_{ij} is determined by q_j in combination with p_{ij}.

Assume, that q_j is determined by the presence on the highest hierarchy level, and let the levels be numbered by 1 for the highest and m for the lowest level. Supposing q_j to be determined directly proportional to the relative presence on the highest level leads to:

$$q_j = p_{1j} / \sum_{j=1}^{r} p_{1j}$$

A numerical example of three subsystems (for instance, a three- party system) and two hierarchy levels is shown in tab. 2.4. Let us illustrate $j = 3$ for a

	$j=1$			$j=2$			$j=3$		
	w	p	ϕ	w	p	ϕ	w	p	ϕ
i=1	.25	.1	.29	.25	.05	.14	.25	.2	.57
i=2	.75	.9	.31	.75	.95	.16	.75	.8	.54
q_j		.29			.14			.57	

Table 2.4: Distribution algorithm: numerical example

party system: $p_{13} = .2$ means that 20% of the third party are present on the highest level, then this party is able to appropriate $q_3 = .2/(.1+.05+.2) = .57$ of the surplus reserved for level 1 which is 25% of the total surplus for all parties.

Let us assume, that all w_i and p_i are given, and that it holds

$$\sum_{i=1}^{m} w_i = \sum_{j=1}^{r} \phi_{ij} = \sum_{i=1}^{m} p_i = 1 \quad .$$

According to the above formula, ϕ_{2j} is calculated by

$$\phi_{2j} = w_2 q_j p_{2j} / \sum_{j=1}^{r} q_j p_{2j} \quad .$$

q_2 now can used as a bargaining result determining the distributional fraction in $i = 3$ and so on. Notice, that a strict hierarchy is assumed in this approach.

If, finally, a recursive rule can be specified for the p_{1j}, the algorithm is complete. Let us define the following rule:

$$p_{1j,t} = p_{1j,t-1}(1 - E_{j,t-1}) \tag{2.38}$$

with

$$E_{jt} = (4G_{jt}L_{jt} - .5)(s - p_{1j,t-1})$$

where

$$\begin{aligned}
G_{jt} : \quad &= \quad \text{global \textbf{PT} effect,} \\
L_{jt} : \quad &= \quad \text{local \textbf{PT} effect,} \\
s : \quad &= \quad \text{saturation parameter} \\
&\quad\quad 0 < s_{min} \leq s \leq s_{max} \leq 1 \\
&\quad\quad s \text{ must be adjusted according} \\
&\quad\quad \text{to the other parameters} \\
4 \quad\quad &\quad\quad \text{standardizing factor,} \\
(s - p_{1j,t-1}) \quad\quad &\quad\quad \text{saturation factor,} \\
-.5 \quad\quad &\quad\quad \text{symmetry term.}
\end{aligned}$$

Naturally, the initial values of p have to be chosen accordingly.

The global **PT** effect yields an autocatalytic augmentation of **PT** presence on the highest hierarchy level. If the number of **PTs**, however, grows too much, the crowding effect L_{jt} yields a diminution of presence on the highest level.

Let us postulate:

$$G_{jt} = \{\min[1, n_{1j,t}/(\alpha_{jt} n_{1t}^*)]\}^{x_t} \qquad (2.39)$$

$$L_{jt} = (1 - n_{1j,t}/n_{1c})^{y_t} \qquad (2.40)$$

with

$n_{1j,t}:$ = number of **PTs** of the subsystem j on level 1,

$n_{1t}^*:$ = maximal number of **PTs** financable on level 1,

$\alpha_{jt}:$ = competition pressure from the other subsystems,

$\qquad \bar{\alpha}_{jt} \in [0,1]$,

$n_{1c}:$ = critical overcrowding number of **PTs** on level 1,

$x_t, y_t:$ = intensity parameter of the global resp. local **PT** effects.

Because

$$\sum_{j=1}^{r} n_{1j,t} \approx n_t^* = \sqrt{2 w_1 Z_t} \quad ,$$

where $w_1 Z$ denotes the surplus alloted to the **PC**, $n_{1j,t}^*$ must be calculated accordingly. Hence, we define the correction factor γ_t:

$$\gamma_t = 1/\sum_{j=1}^{r} \sqrt{q_{jt}}$$

and posit:

$$n_{1j,t}^* = \gamma_t \sqrt{2 w_1 q_{jt} Z_t} \quad .$$

n_{1t}^* may then result as:

$$n_{1t}^* = \sum_{j=1}^{r} n_{1j,t}^* \quad .$$

Let $n_{1j,t}$ be specified as the linear combination of the maximum $n_{1j,t}^*$ and the number of **PTs** resulting from the number of virtual $\mathcal{C}$ by formally applying 2.27:

$$n_{1j,t} = e_{jt} n_{1j,t}^* + (1 - e_{jt}) w_1 Z_t q_{jt} h,$$

where

$e_{jt}:$ = propensity to maximize the **PT** number,

$\qquad e_{jt} \in [0,1]$,

h is the already known **PT** constant 10^{-4}.

Depending on the choice of the parameter functions α_{jt}, x_t, y_t, e_{jt} and of the parameters w_1, n_c as well as of the input variable Z_t, complex behaviors of the equation system can result. The reader may verify that n_{1c} is of special importance.

As an example the simple case $x_t = y_1 = 1$ shall be analyzed. Choosing $s = 1$, in equilibrium it must hold:

$$G_{jt}L_{jt} = 1/8 \quad ,$$

and from this

the equilibrium solution results:

$$n^0_{1j,t} = .5n_{1c}(1 \pm \sqrt{1 - .5\alpha_{jt}n^*_{1t}/n_{1c}}) \quad .$$

Since the root argument must be non-negative, it follows:

$$n_{1c} \geq .5n^*_{1t} \quad ,$$

taking into account that $\alpha_{jt} = 1$ yields the maximal nominator. When choosing $n_{1c} = .5n^*_{1t}$, the equilibria values only depend on the surplus Z_t and the competition pressure α_{jt}.

Supposing a surplus not changeable short-term, then the competition behavior determines the presence on the highest hierarchy level and the equilibria **PT** numbers. This result is not surprising. Nevertheless, there are some competition rules leading to interestingly interpretable results. For instance, the rule that α_{jt} is directly proportional to the appropriation quota q_{jt}, that is, the competition pressure grows with an augmenting appropriation quota, leads to an equal distribution of quotas and hence, of **PT** numbers. One could call this the envy rule. On the other hand, if α_{jt} is inversely proportional to q_{jt}, i.e. a high receipt of surplus yielding a power bonus, then a two-party system is the consequence. The reader may analyse 2.38 further for himself and try in doing so the interesting functions

$$x_t = q_c(1 - q_{jt})^{-1} \quad , \quad y_t = p_c(1 - p_{1j,t})^{-1} \quad ,$$

where q_c and p_c are parameters.

Notice, that $G_j L_j$ describes a 'dialectical' formalization of the local/global relation, perhaps also a specification of considerable validity for other relations of this type, comp. SCHMEIKAL [113].

We have tried to derive that the number of **PTs** grows by increase of the population and production. We have considered that it could be plausible that **PT** structures divide into partialized structures after having reached a certain number of **PTs**. If this consideration is correct, then very large or rich states ought often to provide such a partitioning behavior. This process can be observed in the occidental civilization for some hundred years concerning territorial partitioning in its regional form. However, territorial partitioning of this kind does not seem to hold for large or rich states of the present.

On the contrary, here we observe tendencies of unification and agglomeration that are not accompanied by an immediate segregation process. What we observe here is that partioning takes the form of social differentiation, for instance, in creating new operational fields or institutions. Nevertheless, we also observe processes of concentrations in these fields. Thus, the mere number of **PTs** cannot be sufficient to describe these special findings. Presumably, the decisive role seem to play the parameters of hierarchization held constant in this section. In chapter 4 and Vol. 2 we shall make a dynamic analysis on this subject.

2.4   Technology

Let us recall the main equation of production:

$$P = \kappa m_Q f M \pi_M r \qquad . \qquad (2.41)$$

Thus, production equals

> *production capacity* (κ)
> - *restriction factor of working capacity* (m_Q)
> - *quota of operating hours* (f)
> - *mechanical equipment* (M)
> - *machine productivity for each machine installed* (π_M)
> - *global restrictive factor* (r) .
>
> $\uparrow$

Main Equation of Production

This equation holds for the individual firm as well as for the economy as a whole. We had realized that productivity π_M is a critical term because it is important and difficult to control. It appears astonishing that, in economic theory, this term has been specified as implicit or exogeneous for a long time. In economic theory, there was talk of a "neutral" technical progress which would leave the economic relations unaffected. Implicitly, technical progress was joined to the capital coefficient, but mostly this factor was also specified being constant. Although it has been entirely clear that economic models produce results of a striking difference due to the choice of the technical progress function; this maintains for Marxist- and for the neo-classic approaches as well.

Tackling the matter of how to deal with the problem of technology in model oriented economic approaches was first undertaken about two decades ago. In so doing it was realized that this was useful only in comprehensive considerations; see e.g. OGADIRI, PASINETTI [104,109], as a precursor STEINDL (1st issue 1952) [124].

By the term *technology* the following shall be understood: the quantity of possibilities known at a given time for the application of instruments of whatever kind by which a defined output can be realized. By the term *technique* the technology actually implemented is meant.

Particularly, a specific technology and technique belong to every production process. Therefore, 2.13 as a macro-relation is possibly an artificial aggregation with very different conditions in the individual sectors and with individual production processes. Because of the interdependencies between the single sectors and processes this aggregation can appropriately be described only on the basis of exchange matrices. That leads into the field of dynamic input-output tables with time-varying coefficients. However, we will not deal with these tables in this approach.

This differentiation can be continued inside the firm; e.g. in differentiating various kinds and fields of activities and then analyzing the relevant technologies and techniques for each combination. With reference to the place and kind of labor of productive people the *Statistisches Bundesamt* (federal office of statistics) elaborated upon a classification of 10 "where-kinds" and 11 "what-kinds" (Die Zeit, Nr. 35, 1984), leading to maximal 110 fields of technologies and techniques.

Technical progress means that the relation

$$target\ term/reference\ term$$

'ameliorates' in the course of time. In the production of goods technical progress relates to the amelioration of production and products. Thereby the amelioration may extend to a variety of aspects; e.g. a better quality, higher production output, savings in labor personnel, in capital, in energy or in raw material – just to state some aspects.

As each production can be understood as a process of energy transformation, special importance has to be given to the energy aspect, see GEORGESCU-ROEGEN, ODUM and HARRIS [32,100,42] as well as the considerations in the following section. In 2.3 this aspect enters into the term r.

As results from 2.13, a change of P can be determined by a change of the six variables. FROHN et al. [31] tried econometrically to determine technical progress in the F.R.G., differentiated according to 34 industrial fields. However, FROHN et al. did not proceed from 2.3, but from classical production functions in which the technical progress appears as residual term. With these simplified approaches it turned out to be very difficult to discriminate between the individual production factors. Finally they got the disillusioning result (93): [8]

"So müssen wir uns damit abfinden, daß es zur Zeit nicht möglich ist, die Rangordnung des technischen Fortschritts zu erklären".

---

[8]"So we have to face that at present it is not possible to explain the rank order of technical progress".

It would be fascinating to enter into a methodological discussion about how to tackle the empirical-statistical problems stemming from the complex non-linear dynamic of 2.13. However, we will continue without that: in the beginning of chap. 3 and Vol. 2 some details will be given on the matter.

The emergence of new technologies, as well as the manner and time of their implementation, depend strongly on the constellation of the other production factors such as a diminishing supply of cheap and sufficiently qualified workers which augments the pressure on the necessity of labor saving rationalization. Within certain limits, all terms can substitute each other in 2.13, and the reader easily realizes how such substitution strategies can work.

Since in 2.3, κ and m_Q are restricted to the interval $[0,1]$, P equals the theoretically maximum capacity for

$$\kappa = m_Q = f = r = 1 \quad .$$

The maximal capacity, therefore, depends only on M and π_M. Thus, ultimately, P is structurally determined by M and π_M. Hence, it can be concluded that first there is a labor saving rationalization, then capital saving rationalization (diminishment of cost for M and π_M).

Universally, we will design the relation

target term/reference term

as *productivity*, and in the following we will deal with the aspect of efficiency of a technology.

Still today, especially in the macro-economic approaches it is often common to choose the number of productives as the reference term. However, this choice seems inappropriate by virtue of increasing dependence of production upon machinery. So, it carries little conviction to say that productivity will increase simply by a higher rate of sick people or a higher unemployment rate – what really appears if the empirically frequent case arises that the production volume remains unchanged at least. If in strongly rationalized sectors the number of productives declines to zero, productivity would become infinitely large: this also does not seem very meaningful.

Since product and production innovation are accompanied by the purchase of new equipment, we will relate productivity to machines in a broad sense, denoted by π_M. Solving 2.13 for π_M,

$$\pi_M = P/(\kappa m_Q f M r)$$

results as the necessary *machine productivity*.

If *machines* are defined as a device for the execution of work that operates with *non-human energy*, then the above mentioned critique against labor productivity must also be objected to 2.13 immediately. This is because for simple societies which do not possess machines of the above defined kind, it would analogously hold that *ceteris paribus* $\pi_M \to \infty$ for $M \to 0$.

In order to get a universally valid approach, a definition of M is required that can be applied across all types of societies; e.g. the installed kwh could be such a definition. [9]. As HARRIS [42] shows, in the case of simple societies, human working power can throughout be calculated in kwh. Then, with reference to 2.13 the following dimensions can be stated:

$$P \;-\; \mathcal{C} \,,$$
$$M \;-\; \text{kwh},$$
$$f \;-\; \text{hours x days}/8760,$$
$$k, m_Q, r \qquad \text{dimensionless terms (quotas)}.$$

In addition, such a definition opens a direct way to the analysis of energy consumption and the problems connected with it.

Since labor-intensive sectors are also to be found in high-industrialized countries (e.g. crafts) empirical-statistical problems of discrimination would certainly not be unimportant. Again it has to be emphasized that, because of the complexity of 2.13 an increase in productivity does not have to be accompanied by an increase in production. It transpires that in the F.R.G. during the past twelve years considerable energy saving rationalizations took place which, according to the definition made before, led to an increase of π_M without a corresponding increase of P.

In the following we shall in a relatively simple manner take the average kwh-performance per machine in 2.13 so that, yet again M denotes the number of machines. Insertion of the energy term changes 2.13 to

$$P = \kappa m_Q f M l \pi_l r \qquad (2.42)$$

with

$$l : \;=\; \text{mean kwh-performance per machine,}$$
$$\pi_l : \;=\; \text{productivity measured in } \mathcal{C} \text{ per kwh,}$$
$$\text{multiplied with 8760.}$$

In distinguishing between a labor-intensive and a machine-intensive sector, we can differentiate the following:

$$P = \kappa m_Q f_M M l \pi_l r + (Q - Q_M) f_Q \pi_Q \qquad (2.43)$$

with

$$Q : \;=\; \text{employed people,}$$
$$Q_M : \;=\; \text{people employed}$$
$$\text{in the machine intensive sector,}$$

---

[9] I owe this idea to G. Klein, personal communication

q_M : = employed people per machine,

q : = quota of employed people

referring to population,

N : = population,

f_Q : = work hours x work days

per employed individual/8760,

f_M : = ditto per machine/8760,

π_Q : = labor productivity measured in C

per employed individual

multiplied with 8760.

In addition it must hold

$$Q - Q_M \geq 0 \quad .$$

2.4.1 Technical productivity of social units

Now, let us examine some typical societal production technologies. First an attempt shall be made to make a minimum calculation for the primordial society in order to find a reference. For the primordial society in can be stated:

$$P = Q f_Q \pi_Q \quad , \qquad Q = qN \quad . \tag{2.44}$$

Production and demand shall be calculated in energy units. As is well known, 1 kcal is equivalent to the amount of energy of 1.163 wh. Hence we define

$$e := 1.163 \cdot 10^{-3}$$

as the *scaling constant* in the transformation $kcal \rightarrow kwh$.

A healthy adult is able to do work on the scale of $.1\,kwh$. Per hour he needs an energy supply of $150kcal$ in the form of food. Thus, for this production capacity of an adult individual it holds:

$$p_{\mathcal{E}} = .1\,kwh$$

and for his food: [10]

$$
\begin{aligned}
b_{\mathcal{E}} : &= 150e && |\; kcal \cdot kwh/kcal \\
&= .175 && |\; kwh
\end{aligned}
$$

---

[10] According to ODUM [101, p. 556], energy balance models can be constructed analoguously. E.g. for the energy supply of the sun he states a value of 7,600 cal/sqm/day.

From this figure, 3,000 cal/sqm/day are allotted to Albedo, to Ozon 896 and to surface heating 1,400, so that 2,3000 cal/sqm/day are left for the photosynthesis. We will ignore such balance models, here.

Therefore, as minimum productivity for the subsistence minimum it results:

$$\pi^*_{\mathcal{E}} = p_{\mathcal{E}}/b_{\mathcal{E}} \quad . \tag{2.45}$$

Now we define the maximum annual capacity an adult is capable to furnish if he works $24 \cdot 365 = 8,760$ hours per annum:

$$\mathcal{E} := .1 \cdot 8,760 = 876\,kwh \quad ,$$

and denote $\mathcal{E}$ the energy "head", the analogue to $\mathcal{C}$, but now measured in energy terms.

Inserting $\mathcal{E}$ in 2.2 yields:

$$P_{\mathcal{E}} = Qf_Q\,\mathcal{E}\pi_{\mathcal{E}} \quad . \tag{2.46}$$

$\pi_{\mathcal{E}}$ denotes the *technology* in its proper sense, namely the production effect that goes beyond mere manual labor. Of course, $\pi_{\mathcal{E}}$ is also dependent upon the disposability of food and other provisions. On a low level of technical support P depends practically on f_Q alone and on the fertility of the territory considered. For that reason it is obvious that the first LSUs developed in fertile regions, e.g. by the Nile or in the Euphratus and Tigres region. As far as technological reasons are concerned the formation of states could have resulted from the necessity of coordinated irrigation, as WITTVOGEL [136] already worked out.

As to the collective demand, it is necassary to distinguish between productive and non-productive adults and the remainder of the population. Assume that food and other sustenance has to be provided every day of the year. Then the following equation can be formulated:

$$\begin{aligned} B_{\mathcal{E}} \;=\; & qWs365b_{\mathcal{E}} + qW(24-s)365b^-_{\mathcal{E}} \\ + \; & (1-q)W8760b^-_{\mathcal{E}} + (N-W)8760b^{--}_{\mathcal{E}} \end{aligned}$$

with

$$
\begin{aligned}
q : \;=\; & \text{quota of productives} \\
& \text{in reference to } W, \\
W : \;=\; & \text{number of adults,} \\
b^-_{\mathcal{E}} : \;=\; & \text{demand for food} \\
& \text{and other sustenance} \\
& \text{during recreation } (b^-_{\mathcal{E}} < b_{\mathcal{E}}), \\
b^{--}_{\mathcal{E}} : \;=\; & \text{demand for food} \\
& \text{and other sustenance} \\
& \text{of children and the elderly,} \\
s : \;=\; & \text{labor hours per day.}
\end{aligned}
$$

In a first approximation we equate $b^-_{\mathcal{E}} = b^{--}_{\mathcal{E}}$, and with

$$b^-_{\mathcal{E}} = (1 + b)\, \mathcal{E}/8760 \quad \text{and} \quad W = wN \quad ,$$

where w denotes the adult quota, the result after some rearrangements of terms is

$$
\begin{aligned}
B_{\mathcal{E}} = \ & \mathcal{E}N\{qW[f_s 1.75 + (1 - f_s)(1 + b)] \\
& + \ (1 - qw)(1 + b)\} \quad ,
\end{aligned}
\tag{2.47}
$$

where f_s denotes the labor hour quota per day. 2.47 is a collection of linear combinations which can be clearly interpreted.

Obviously $P_{\mathcal{E}} \geq B_{\mathcal{E}}$, and in the subsistence minimum $P_{\mathcal{E}} = B_{\mathcal{E}}$ must hold. The corresponding minimal $\pi_{\mathcal{E}}$, denoted by $\pi^0_{\mathcal{E}}$, then results as

$$\pi^0_{\mathcal{E}} = (qwf_s)^{-1}B \tag{2.48}$$

with $B = \{\cdot\}$ from 2.47. Regarding, in a first approximation, q, w, b as constant, $\pi^0_{\mathcal{E}}$ depends only on f_s in a non-linear manner. Since technology in the case of a simple society can be specified as exogenous or varying slowly, f_s as the necessary labor time quota per day is determined through $\pi^0_{\mathcal{E}}$. Let us choose as plausible figures

$$w = .67 \quad , \quad q = .95 \quad , \quad b = .25 \quad ;$$

then it follows:

$$f_s = \frac{1.96}{\pi^0_{\mathcal{E}} - .5} \tag{2.49}$$

For f_s to be admissible, i.e. stemming from $[0, 1]$,

$$\pi^0_{\mathcal{E}} \geq 2.46$$

must hold, and in the minimum $\pi^{0*}_{\mathcal{E}} = 2.46$. The relation

$$\omega := \pi^0_{\mathcal{E}}/\pi^{0*}_{\mathcal{E}}$$

represents the additional labor effort determined by ecological and socio-structural conditions.

These are boundary considerations. In reality, however, $f_s \ll 1$, so that $\pi^0_{\mathcal{E}} \gg \pi^{0*}_{\mathcal{E}}$. Let us choose the maximal f_s due to restrictions from darkness, tiredness etc. as $f_{s\,max} = .5$. From this the minimal productivity of 4.42 results, or $\omega \geq 2.53$ respectively. In this way plausible values of the necessary productivity can be deduced, which can serve as reference points for empirical investigations.

HARRIS [42] performed such studies. His results can be recalculated according to our approach, yielding the entries of tab. 2.5. Of considerable interest is the approximate identity of the energy based productivity per work hour, i.e. $\pi_{\mathcal{E}}/s$, and the labor productivity π_A.

HARRIS pp.	soc-iety	Q	$\pi_{\mathcal{E}}$	$\frac{\pi_{\mathcal{E}}}{s}$	ω	hours per day	P/a^a	labor product-ivity[b]
234f	!Kung bush-men	20	16.6	1.5	8.3	2.2	33	1.65
236	Hoe agri-cult.	334	19.5	1.8	11.2	2.3	640	1.92
245	Yunnan agri-cult.	418	93.4	12	53.3	3.1	3830	9.16

Table 2.5: Energy related technology and production for some selected societies
a)   production measured in $\mathcal{E}$ per year
b)   measured in C

We are now in the position to use the evidence of HARRIS to analyse the social structure of a simple society. Let us choose the !Kung because of the rich data base existing on this society. According to HARRIS, $Q = qwN = 20$ was observed. Equating $B_{\mathcal{E}} = P_{\mathcal{E}}$, it results from 2.47:

$$b = \frac{-N+24.8}{N-1.8} \quad ,$$

that is,

$$N \in [20, 24] \quad .$$

Dividing P/a by Q in tab. 2.5 results in an approximation of the labor productivity π_A documented in the last column, because

$$P = Q\pi_A \qquad . \tag{2.50}$$

It appears noteworthy that the labor productivity of the Yunnan agriculture is greater than the macro-economic labor productivity in the F.R.G. in 1980, which was calculated as $\pi_A = 8$ in the last section. HARRIS arrived at a similar result comparing that agriculture with the U.S. economy in the early seventies with respect to labor productivity.

Let us now choose the F.R.G. in 1980 as an example of an industrialized LSU to transform the C produced in that year into $\mathcal{E}$. Approximating

$$P \approx xb_{\mathcal{E}}P = P_{\mathcal{E}}$$

with x as a standard of living factor, from 2.43 with $\kappa = .85$, $m_Q = r = 1$ and $T = 8760$

$$xTb \,_{\mathcal{E}}P = .85 f_M M l \pi_l + (Q - Q_M) f_Q \,\mathcal{E}\pi\,_{\mathcal{E}}$$

results. We can identify the following correspondencies:

$$f_M \stackrel{\triangle}{=} f_Q \qquad ,$$
$$M \stackrel{\triangle}{=} Q - Q_M \quad ,$$
$$l \stackrel{\triangle}{=} \mathcal{E} \qquad ,$$
$$\pi_l \stackrel{\triangle}{=} \pi\,_{\mathcal{E}} \qquad .$$

The minimal productivity necessary to yield reproduction is:

$$\pi_l f_M = 1 \quad , \text{or,}$$
$$\pi\,_{\mathcal{E}} f_Q = 1 \quad \text{respectively.}$$

Productives in the service sector are included in this approach, whereas unproductives in this sector have to be subsumed under the **PT** system. A more realistic differentiation in which, among other things, the banking sector would be specified explicitly is confronted with great difficulties; and will not be persued in this jucture. In Vol. 2 an attempt is made on this aspect.

Let us choose a work day of 8 hours and 250 work days per year. By

$$f_M = f_Q = \varphi \frac{8 \cdot 250}{8760} = .23\varphi$$

then f_M and f_Q are parameterized. With $Q_M = q_M M$, where $q_M :=$ workers and staff people per machine, we then get:

$$\pi_l = \frac{Px - \varphi(Q - q_M M).113\pi\,_{\mathcal{E}}}{1.12\varphi l M} \qquad , \tag{2.51}$$

where x denotes the aforementioned standard of living factor. We choose the proportion $\pi\,_{\mathcal{E}} : \pi_A$ as holding analogously for the F.R.G and get from a comparison between the !Kung and the F.R.G.:

$$16.6 : 1.65 = \pi\,_{\mathcal{E}} : [8(Q - Q_M)/Q]$$

and from that

$$\pi\,_{\mathcal{E}} = 80(1 - \tfrac{q_M M}{Q}) \qquad .$$

Inserting this into 2.51 leads to:

$$\pi_l = \frac{Px - \varphi(Q - q_M M)^2 9/Q}{1.12\varphi l M}$$

With $x = \varphi = 1$, and because P and Q are known, the function

$$\pi_l = \pi_l(q_M, l, M)$$

results, where

l	$10^6 M$	π_l	$\pi_{\mathcal{E}}$
5	10	2.9	10.2
10	10	1.45	10.2
14.6	10	1	10.2
5	15	2.53	6.1
10	15	1.26	6.1
12.7	15	1	6.1
5	20	2.12	1.97^+
10	20	1.06	1.97
10.6	20	1	1.97

Table 2.6: Machine and body energetic productivity
+)   this line possibly plausible by scale order

$$q_M M \leq Q = 28 \cdot 10^6$$

must be fulfilled. For $q_M = 1.25$ some numerical results are displayed in tab. 2.6. In tab. 2.6 l ranges up to its maximal value l_{max}, resulting from $\pi_l \geq 1$. One easily recognizes that there are possible substitutions between the terms. The derivation of plausible values as displayed in tab. 2.6, of course, cannot replace empirical studies, but it can be a sound basis to scale order considerations.

In the case of a completely mechanized society, 2.43 went over to:

$$P = \kappa m_Q f_M M l \pi_l r \qquad . \qquad (2.52)$$

With $m_Q = r = 1$ some interesting recalculations in comparison with 2.50 can be made:

$$Q \pi_A = \kappa f_M M l \pi_l$$

and

$$\pi_A = \kappa f_M \frac{M}{Q} l \pi_l = \kappa f_M l \pi_l / q_M \qquad , \text{or,}$$

$$\pi_l = \frac{q_M \pi_A}{\kappa f_M l} \quad \text{respectively.}$$

Let us define:

$$i := \frac{q_M}{f_M l} \qquad .$$

With $q_M = 1.25$, $f_M = .23$, $l = 5$

$$i = 1.09 \approx 1$$

follows; hence, with $\kappa = .85$:

$$\pi_l \approx 1.18 \pi_A \qquad .$$

In postulating $i = 1$,

$$q_M = (f_M l)^{-1} \tag{2.53}$$

would result. This meant that rationalization, i.e. $q_M \downarrow$, be compensated always by $f_M \uparrow$ or $l \uparrow$. In the special case $q_M = 1$, $f_M = l^{-1}$ would result and the labor effort would be reversely proportional to the energy consumption of the machine.

q_M, however, cannot be specified as a single parameter, because it depends on *two variables*. Let us, therefore, regard Q/M again; then we get for i:

$$i = \frac{Q/M}{f_M l} \overset{!}{=} 1 \quad . \tag{2.54}$$

Fixing Q constant, it results that with a growing M the denominator must approach zero. Because, however, l is restricted from below (e.g. $l_{min} = 1$),

$$f_M \to 0 \quad for \quad M \to \infty$$

results. As plausible by scale order for the year 2000 in the case of the F.R.G. we can choose:

$$Q = 15 \cdot 10^6 \quad , \quad M = 30 \cdot 10^6 \quad , \quad l = 4 \quad .$$

Then it would result:

$$f_{M,2000} = .125 \quad ,$$

that is, in the case of 210 work days per year a daily work time of 5.2 hours, which appears plausible. The reader may perform additional calculations or analyse further societies. [11]

In particular, production and energy consumption are possibly related in a strict manner, at least near the boundary of an efficient energy saving technology. 2.52 can be used directly to perform energy oriented input/output calculations. Let us regard a technology as *energetically efficient* if in 2.52

$$\Omega^{-1} \Delta P \geq \Delta \pi_l \Delta l \tag{2.55}$$

with

$$\Omega := \kappa m_Q f_M M r \quad .$$

Let us analyse the case, where $\Delta \pi_l$ and Δl compensate each other. In this case it follows for yielding energetic efficiency that

$$(\Delta P)_{min} = \Omega \quad ;$$

---

[11] A *pure* slavery and working-cattle economy, for instance, cannot carry more than by scale order one million of total population. These internal restrictions possibly contributed to the break down of the Roman empire.

in the optimum approximately

$$\kappa = .92 \quad \text{and} \quad m_Q = r = 1 \quad ,$$

holds, so that

$$\Omega_{opt} = .92 f_M M \quad \text{, hence} \quad (\triangle P)_{min} = .92 f_M M \quad .$$

In particular in the case of a growing machine number, labor effort must be reduced to maintain energetic efficiency. For

$$\triangle \pi_l \triangle l = 1$$

it follows that

$$
\begin{aligned}
f_M &= .23 \quad \text{assuming an 8 hours work day,} \\
M &= 20 \cdot 10^6 \quad \text{and} \\
(\triangle P)_{min} &= 4.2 \cdot 10^6 \; C \quad .
\end{aligned}
$$

As to agricultural production, such input/output calculations concerning energetic efficiency are already carried out. Here it is defined: if more non-renewable energy input than the sun energy input is added, the corresponding agricultural production is *energetically inefficient*. Indeed, energy inefficient agricultural forms of produciton have been detected. For nuclear plants analogous calculations have been made; here there are cases where the energy input necessary for construction and running is larger than the plant supplies to the power system while operating. This, too, would have to be labelled energy inefficient.

2.4.2   Productivity and the production process

As worked out, the productivity π takes specific values according to the reference variable chosen. For each *production process j* a specific π_j is existent. Still more differentiated, for each *production factor i* in j there is a π_{ij}; e.g. a management technology in hard-coal-mining. By this means, thousands of technologies develop that can hardly be surveyed clearly. If in a rough approximation it is assumed that it is the production factors i that are decisive and have approximately a similar structure in all production processes, then only the π_i have to be considered, e.g. transportation-, information- and energy technology.

Only in situations of shortage do technology problems become very serious. In such case, the specific input/output quantities for every i must be specified, for instance, in the field of information technology, the

bit number/operating hour

per invested C.

Universally, let the *output* be denoted by y, the input by x. A shortage in technology arises if

$$\frac{\triangle y}{\triangle x} < 1$$

is realized. To perform such calculations about shortage, the contribution of the single techniques to the production output has to be considered. To this end, the components of the production process have to be considered and the technologies have to be analyzed correspondingly. A simple demonstration of the production process is displayed in fig. 2.7. Let us try to weigh the com-

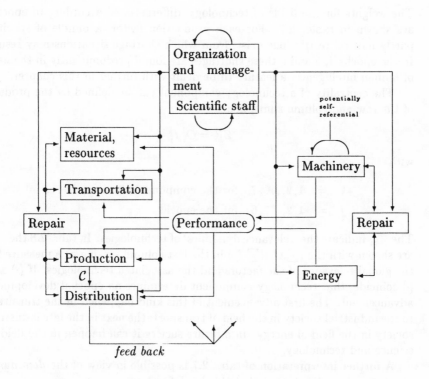

Figure 2.7: Production process and production factors

ponents with regard to their mutual importance for the epochal production lines. Of course, this is a rough-cast subjective weighing that cannot replace a detailed analysis of the production process. Nevertheless a rough analysis of this kind may deliver first insights into increases of technological niveau.

weighing: - unimportant

0 middle
+ important

"Important for →" := *row is important for column.*

1 :	=	neolithic epoch
2 :	=	developed agriculture
3 :	=	early industrialized society
4 :	=	industrialized society
5 :	=	forecast for the year 2000
6 :	=	speculations about the society thereafter

The weights for the fields of technology, differentiated according to epochs, are shown in table 2.7. For each production factor, a bundle of specific, partly natural restrictions exist, from which shortage situations may result. In the epochs 4, 5 and 6 these shortages are found predominantly in the field of human intelligence, a feature to be dealt with further in this chapter.

The centrality of a technology component can be defined by the product of the row and column sums, hence

$$Z_k^{ij} = O_i^k I_j^k$$

with

$$k = 1, 2, \ldots, 7 \quad \text{for the components "material"} \ldots,$$
$$i, j = 1, 2, \ldots, 6 \quad \text{for the epochs} \quad .$$

The Z_{kj} indicate the 'relevance dynamics' of technologies. In tab. 2.8 the Z_{kj} are shown with the $(\sum O_i)(\sum I_j)$ in the last column serving as a measure for the global relevance of the factors and the associated technologies. If $(\cdot)$ and $[\cdot]$ coincide, that technology component determines an epochal development advancement. The first advancement of this kind happened in the transition to the industrial society in the field of transport; the next in the late industrial society in the field of energy. In a future society it can happen in the field of science and technology.

A further interpretation of tab. 2.7 is possible in view of the *dominance* of a technology component. Let this be defined as:

$$d_k^{ij} := O_i^k / I_j^k \quad ,$$

that is, representing the relation

important for, but not dependent on ,

where $n/0 := n$ and $0/0 := 0$ are set by convention. This leads to the result shown in tab. 2.9. It is interesting that, after the dominance of science, machines will become dominant in future. Is the epoch of artificial intelligence reflected here? As to an optimistic valuation of such technologies see INOSE/PIERCE [56].

If tab. 2.8 and tab. 2.9 are regarded simultaneously, one realizes that the present is characterized by a gap between energy, which continues to be the most important field and organization and management that develop most dynamically. There will be a real advancement in the field of science in the epoch to come. Science and machines will be dominant in it. In regard to development during each epoch, energy and machines are the most important technological components.

A thorough invention and innovation model must describe all components explicitly. This will not be performed here, but for an attempt on Sweden, see JANSSON/ZUCETTO [58].

im-por-tant for →	re-quir-ed mat-erial	re-pair	mach-inery	trans-port	ener-gy	org-aniz. & man-ag.	scien-ce & tech-nol.	O_i $\sum$
requ. mater.		+0---0	--00++	-----0	000++0	--0++0	--0++0	100341 9
repair	----00		000000	-0++++	--0+++	-----0	----- -	001222 7
mach-inery	----0+	---0++	---0++	--0+++	--0+++	----0+	----0+	000247 13
trans-port	0+++++	-----0	----- -		--00+0	---00+	----00	011122 7
energy	--0+++	--+++0	-0+++0	00++++		--00+0	----00	003452 14
org.& man.	---000	00+++0	--00+0	-0+++0	--00++	--00++	---00+	002253 12
sci.& tech.	--0+++	---0+0	--0++0	---0++	--0+++	---0++	---00+	000365 14
I_j	123456 011334	123456 102241	123456 001252	123456 003344	123456 000464	123456 000144	123456 000113	
$\sum$	12	10	10	14	14	9	5	

Table 2.7: Relations between production factors in different epochs

Legend: O_i := Sum of all "+" per row and epoch
I_j := Sum of all "+" per column and epoch
- := unimportant 0 := neutral + := important
main diagonal non-empty means:
production factor is (potentially) self-referential

Epoch	1	2	3	4	5	6	$(\sum O_i)(\sum I_j)$
Material	0	0	0	9	12	4	108
Repair	0	0	2	4	8	2	70
Machinery	0	0	0	4	20	14	130
Transport	0	0	[(3)]	3	8	8	98
Energy	0	0	0	[(16)]	(30)	8	196
Org.&Man.	0	0	0	2	[20]	12	108
Sci.&Tec.	0	0	0	3	2	[(15)]	60

Table 2.8: Relevance of production factor technologies

Legend: (·) := maximum per epoch
        [·] := strong augmentation compared with previous epoch

Epoch	1	2	3	4	5	6
Material	[(1)]	0	0	1	1.33	.25
Repair	0	0	.5	1	.5	2
Machinery	0	0	0	1	.8	[(3.5)]
Transport	0	[(1)]	.33	.33	.5	.5
Energy	0	0	[(3)]	1	.83	.5
Org.&Man.	0	0	2	2	1.25	.75
Sci.&Tec.	0	0	0	[(3)]	[(6)]	1.67

Table 2.9: Dominance of production factor technologies
The (·) and [·] denote the same as in tab. 2.8.

2.4.3   Invention and innovation

Seven production determinants have been worked out. By this, P is bound from above by the availibility of these determinants, or by restrictions affecting them. In an obvious manner, m_Q is restricted by the population N:

$$m_Q = m_Q(qN, \ldots) \qquad ,$$

where $q :=$ quota of employable people. Roughly guessed, $q \leq .6$ must hold. In the best case, $m_Q = 1$. Analogously, $r = 1$ is the maximal value of r. Also obvious f_M is restricted through T, that is, $f_M \in [0,1]$. In a first approximation, $f_M \leq .5$ is plausible. κ can empirically be restricted to $\kappa \leq .92$. After this, the determinants $Ml\pi_l$ remain, and we can collect the other terms into one constant, $C^* = .475$. From this

$$P^* \quad = \quad C^* Ml\pi_l \quad \text{results, or,}$$
$$2.1053 P^* \quad = \quad Ml\pi_l \quad \text{,rounded :}$$
$$P^* \quad \approx \quad .5Ml\pi_l \quad .$$

Production-neutral technical progress means, therefore, that

$$\Delta l \Delta \pi_l = 1 \qquad ,$$

so that

$$\Delta P^* = \Delta M \qquad ,$$

that is, a pure economic relation. This 'economistic' position, however, does not take into account the influence stemming from the **PT** dynamics worked out in the last section. A growth in **PT** demand can under certain circumstances be supplied at cost of investment and, therefore, of M, similarly suggested by OLSON [105].

With a technological progress that is not production neutral and which we must presume as a rule, the development of π is of central importance. Hence, its structural and dynamic analysis is a relevant task to which we will devote ourselves in the following.

In the first instance, invention and innovation shall be differentiated. *Invention* means the discovery, *innovation* the implementation of inventions in transformation processes (here, in particular, in production processes). Again, global and local inventions are to be distinguished. Local inventions refer to 'little' inventions within a technological line, e.g., regarding a flint, the knock-off angles becoming steeper for providing stone blades, or the transition from the single to the double ploughshare. In contrast to that, global inventions refer to the discovery of new technological lines; e.g. the discovery of fire, the wheel, the steam-engine or the electric motor.

Until now, local inventions and their innovations have been examined more thoroughly. MENSCH [83], however, maintains that the long-term dynamic of P depends on global inventions. This corresponds to the above reflections. MARCETTI [79] found out that local inventions and their innovations can be described by logistic curves.

Logistic productivity function: an agricultural example

A common technological logistic function is defined as follows:

$$\pi(t) = \frac{\pi_\nu^*}{1 + e^{a - bt - c\pi_{0\nu} e^{gt}}}$$

with

π_ν^* : $=$ productivity maximum in the technology line ν,

g : $=$ 'technicity' (rapidity of approaching saturation),

a, b, c : $=$ parameters,

$\pi_{0\nu}$: $=$ initial value of π in the technology line ν.

As is denoted by ν, a single logistic function would be inappropriate to describe technological progress. Rather, there seems to be a hierarchy of technological levels. For instance, there is an 'epochal' structural change which overlays the global innovations, e.g. the transition from the agricultural society to the industrial society. Let us assume that these epochal changes occur when the global inventions belonging to an epoch have approached their saturation limit. Assume, moreover, that the envelope of global inventions are also shaped in the form of the logistic function, then it may be the case throughout that the line segment corresponding to the period from 1775 to 1975 is an approximate linear part of the logistic function. As a result, an explanation for the equidistancy of the innovation advancements (according to MARCETTI [79]) could be given.

The transition of the invention envelope into the saturation region is of special interest. As to that, LEM [67] contributed interesting considerations in expecting this transition by the time of 1990. From this he concluded the possible beginning of a new epoch, namely, that predominated by artificial intelligence. According to LEM the shortages of technical civilizations arising in the saturation phase can only be overcome in time if about in 1991 the first prototype of an adequate computer generation could be innovated. Following LEM, this computer must be capable of auto-programming. A group of Japanese firms and scientists has announced the first prototype of the 5th generation's computer for the year 1991; its new feature is said to be its capability of auto-programming.

It would be necessary to examine whether epochal structural change is decisively determined by global inventions. In this book, conclusions are drawn in favor of the hypothesis that the dynamics of an LSU's operation can be traced to the interdependent relations between the factors of production and distribution. Only a system model that contains all these factors can explain which factors are more important than others, thus determining the relevant driving forces of the system. Only on the basis of such a general model can a clarification be made, in particular about the controversy between 'business cycle' and 'innovation' theorists on the question whether the dynamic of the economic process can be attributed predominantly to machines or to productivity.

Taking the example of agricultural productivity of the F.R.G., we want to demonstrate a simple logistic technology function in which the aforementioned "technicity" is neglected.

Let the number of persons alimented per farmer in the F.R.G. be denoted by π_L. According to figures published by the federal office for nutrition, agriculture and forestry, republished in the Neue Osnabrücker Zeitung of 15th February 1986, this relation develops from 1950 to 1985 as displayed in tab. 2.10.

We formulate the logistic function as follows:

π_L	$\Delta\pi_L$ decade average	year
10	0	1950
18	$\grave{}$.8	1960
32	1.4	1970
57	2.5	1980
77^b	2^b	1990^a
92^c	1.5^c	2000
102^c	1^c	2010
107^c	$.5^c$	2020
107^c	$\approx 0^c$	2030
$\downarrow$		
≈ 110		

Table 2.10: Agricultural productivity in the F.R.G.
a) data up to 1985 are available, from that a $\Delta\pi_L = 2$ results in 1985
b) continuation (see a) up to 1990
c) plausible assumption: $\Delta\pi_L$ decreases by 0.5 per annum

$$\pi_{Lt} = \frac{K}{1+ae^{-bt}}$$

From tab. 2.10, $K = 110$ results as the saturation limit. a, b are estimated from the linearized function

$$ln(K/\pi_{Lt} - 1) = a - bt \qquad ,$$

and it results from least square estimation

$$\pi_{Lt}^{lin} = 156.66 - .079\,t$$

In tab. 2.11, π_L and the estimated $\hat{\pi}_L$ are displayed. The tables show that

year	1950	1960	1970	1980	1983	1984	1985	1990	2020
π_L	10	18	32	57	62	65	67	77^c	107^c
$\hat{\pi}_L$	9.4	18.8	34.4	55.1	61.6	63.7	65.8	75.8	105.6

Table 2.11: Agricultural productivity in the F.R.G.: data and estimations
c) as in tab. 2.10 $\qquad r^2 = .99$

the simple logistic approximation is quite sustainable here. It is of interest that the present agricultural technology line will have reached its saturation around the year 2030. We shall see that other saturation phenomena also are expected at that time.

Innovation and population growth on TERRA

What can be said about productivity? It is obvious that implementation depends on previous invention. Thus, inventions are the decisive point. It is further obvious that the quantity and quality of the inventions depend on the creative potential within an LSU. As long as there is no creative artificial intelligence, inventions are made by human beings. Even if it is alleged that all members of an LSU are equally creative (with regard to intelligence tests, creativity is only to a moderate degree correlated with intelligence), a natural restriction results from the population. LIETH [71] examined these facts with

Population size	Innovation speed	Epoch (in years before today)	Societal type
10^9	5	today	industrial society
10^8	500	500	agricultural society
10^7	50,000	50,000	neolithic society
10^6	5 mio	5 mio	early hominids

Table 2.12: Types of society and innovation speed

regard to the observed reduction of the periods between the beginning and the success of an innovation (innovation period) and found out:

$$t = (K/M)^2$$

where

t : = innovation period in years,

K : = proportionality constant,

M : = population in the innovation-oriented states.

For M, he chose the population of the industrial states. He got t from empirical examinations. As a first approximation he found that:

$$K = 2.25 \cdot 10^9 \qquad .$$

For 1950

$$t = [K/(.751 \cdot 10^9)]^2 = 9$$

results, and as a forecast to the year 2000:

$$t = [K/(1.4 \cdot 10^9)]^2 = 2.58 \qquad .$$

If types of societies are taken, in accordance with LIETH, the survey in tab. 2.12 results. It is interesting that the dating of society type emergence is, by scale order, fairly in accordance with historical, archeological and paleo-ontological findings.

In a first approximation we can assume that the minimal innovation period lasts for two years so that industrial societies will have reached this saturation limit in the year 2000 approximately. This is in fair accordance with the statements of LEM [67] cited in the previous section.

2.4.4 Technological progress, human intelligence distribution, and large scale projects

It is obvious that not all members of an LSU are equally creative. Let the maximal creative potential be defined as:

$$K^0 = \theta N \qquad ,$$

where θ denotes the maximal creativity quota. It depends on manifold organization factors to what extent K^0 is really used. Let this be posited as

$$K = q_K K^0 \qquad ,$$

where q_K denotes the usage quota. It is obvious that invention and innovation depend on people applying themselves to it. In a first approximation, consideration is given to those who professionally deal with inventions and innovations. As to the field of invention, the people concerned are scientists occupied in basic research and, as to innovation, the experts working in the production field. This is stated in the following equation:

$$W = W_g + W_p ,$$

where

$W :\ =$ actors concerned with invention and innovation,

$W_g :\ =$ in basic research,

$W_p :\ =$ in production.

In principle, two kinds of invention and and innovation can be distinguished; those directed to the creation of (virtual and in the future possibly also natural or artificial) "heads" in their own LSU and those intent upon the destruction of "heads" in other LSUs, or even in their own LSU. Let the former be denoted by the index 1, the latter by 0. Then, the following equations result:

$$W = W_{g1} + W_{g0} + W_{p1} + W_{p0}$$
$$W_g = W_{g1} + W_{g0}$$
$$W_p = W_{p1} + W_{p0}$$
$$W \leq K^0 .$$

W/K^0, in approaching 1, definitely has as one result that the technological progress cannot increase exponentially any longer, at least in the form of π. Even a devolution can happen if

$$\frac{d\pi}{dt} = f(W/K^0) < 0 .$$

In all, a complicated distribution problem arises since the mobilized creative potential within an LSU must be distributed among four sectors. Moreover, as a result of this, a distribution problem of the surplus arises because, in addition to the demand sectors stated in the sections 2.2.3 and 2.3(and its subsections), military and science have now to be considered.

Assuming that there are also military and scientific **PTs**, their numbers are in turn limited by financial restrictions. Thus, altogether a manifold restricted, non-linear, dynamic distribution problem arises. Notice, that a growing relevance of **PT** strategies in science areas can be at the cost of creativity so that, in addition, intricate feed-back relations have to be considered; briefly: the distribution problem that results can only be examined in a large scale and comprehensive model. Phenomenologically, only rough indications can be given here, see e.g. deSOLLA PRICE [120].

One possibility to postpone the problems expected here, would be to establish a military-industrial-scientific-political complex(MISP). Perhaps this is one motivation for SDI. So, a renunciation of SDI would raise a twofold problem. First, growth problems caused by **PT** dynamics would appear earlier; second, the military power in this earlier crisis would diminish. Recall the previously mentioned relevance of sequential problems in LSU-rivalries.

However, if the results from the last section are right, it has to be expected that programs like SDI where several scale orders more than 10^4 virtual C , i.e. V in our notation, are fed in, give rise to new **PTs** in the project field. Hence, we will examine whether a program like SDI is able to reach a crucial scale order in which predominantly no substantial project output except **PT** structures are financed.

Let us use the second approach from section 2.3.2 and choose 2.27 in its simplified form yielding the minimal number of project **PTs** denoted by n_p^- ,

$$n_p^- = h V_p$$

with

$$V_p : = \text{project volume in } C ,$$
$$h = 10^{-4} .$$

The maximal number of financable **PTs** can be derived from the **PT** demand

$$B_{Ep} = n_p A_p + c_p n_p^2$$

by equating $B_{Ep} = V_p$, where

$$A_p : = \text{alimentation per } \mathbf{PT},$$
$$c_p : = \text{project specific constant.}$$

The result is:

$$n_p^* = -.5 A_p / c_p + \sqrt{.25 A_p^2 / c_p^2 + V_p / c_p} .$$

Since large scale projects are considered here, V_p dominates so strongly (e.g. in case of a project volume of 10^9 the term V_p/c_p determines 97% of the result) that it appears admissible to approximate as follows:

$$n_p^* = \sqrt{c_p^{-1} V_p} . \tag{2.56}$$

The realized number of project **PTs**, thus, will fall into the interval between n_p^- and n_p^*. Let us, therefore, define a parameter called **PT** *affinity* denoted by ϵ_p and posit:

$$n_p = (1 - \epsilon_p) n_p^- + \epsilon_p n_p^* \tag{2.57}$$

with

$$\epsilon_p \in [0, 1]$$

Let us propose for ϵ_p:

$$\epsilon_p \;=\; (n_p^-/n_p^*)^{1-e_p} \tag{2.58}$$

with

$$e_p : \;=\; \text{intensity parameter of } \mathbf{PT} \text{ affinity.}$$

Example: Let the project volume be 10^9 \$ in a certain year. The corresponding virtual "heads" V_p are calculated as in section 2.3.2 from the subsistence minimum which shall be set as 4500 \$/a in the U.S.A. in 1986. Hence ($c_p = .5,\ A_p = 120$):

$$V_p \;=\; \frac{10^9}{4,500} = 222,222 \qquad | \; C$$

$$n_p^- \;=\; 22 \quad , \qquad n_p^* = 667, \quad ,$$

and for $e_p = .6$ an $\epsilon_p = .26$ results, that is, $n_p = 187$, around 28% of n_p^*.

If, in respect of the project, a predominant substantial orientation is requested then the relation

$$B_{Ep} \ll V_p$$

must be fulfilled, or, in a parameterized way:

$$B_{Ep} \leq qV_p \qquad and \qquad 0 < q \ll 1.$$

With n_p from 2.57 and q^* as a free parameter to be inserted deliberately,

$$V_p^* = B_{Ep}/q^*$$

results as the critical project volume. q can be interpreted as the *overhead* **PT** quota, and $1 - q$ would indicate the ouput *efficiency* of the project. Denoting the subsistence minimum by L, the critical project volume can be calculated back to currency units. In the case of the U.S.A., for instance,

$$V_\$^* = V_p^* L \qquad .$$

V_p^* depends on A_p, c_p, e_p, q^*. Some values are displayed in tab. 2.13, where L was chosen as in the above example and $A_p = 120$.

For the year 1986, in the federal budget of the U.S., \$ 3 billion was officially allocated for SDI. Since, at the outset of the project, the **PT** formation was not yet fully developed, but rather enlarges in the course of the project, the **PT** formation achieved would not only depend finally on the original budget, but also from a year's maximum project budget. Later, however, we shall see that an original budget can be of decisive importance. Within an unfavourable parameter situation even the original budget of \$ 3 billion could represent a critical scale order. The investigation results of the Shuttle

c_p	e_p	q^*	ϵ_p	n_p^-	n_p^*	$n_p^{+)}$	V_p^* $(10^9\$/a)$
.25	0	.05	.125	313	2500	586	14.06
.5	0	.05	.086	148	1718	283	6.64
.75	0	.05	.07	96	1386	185	4.32
.25	0	.1	.224	1000	4472	1776	45.0
.5	0	.1	.15	455	3017	841	20.48
.75	0	.1	.12	295	2429	554	13.28
.25	.25	.1	.26	550	3317	1296	24.75
.5	.25	.1	.18	205	2025	532	9.23
.75	.25	.1	.145	117	1530	323	5.27
.25	.33	.1	.267	390	2793	1033	17.55
.5	.33	.1	.184	128	1600	399	5.76
.75	.33	.1	.15	68	1162	231	3.04

Table 2.13: Project **PT** formation and critical project volume
+) It is neglected that there can be a **PT** crowding, more to this problem in the last section of this chap.

catastrophe show how justified the consideration of **PT** formation is in an analysis of the project efficiency.

The reflections made before on the timing of a project handling also illustrate the restricted explanative power of a static analysis, as it is expressed in 2.14.... At this point, however, we will omit a dynamic model of a **PT** formation in a large scale project.

In a problem statement reverse to tab. 2.13 it can be calculated which project overhead **PT** quota q results if V_p $(e_p = 0, c_p = .5)$ is given. The results are displayed in tab. 2.14. Notice, that the entries in tab. 2.14 hold

V_p^* $(10^9\$/a)$	ϵ_p	n_p^-	n_p^*	$n_p^{+)}$	q
10	.033	222	2108	420	.028
20	.15	444	2981	825	.098
30	.183	667	3651	1213	.130
50	.24	1111	4714	1976	.194

Table 2.14: Project budget and overhead **PT** quota
+) as in the foregoing table

a fortiori because $e_p = 0$, and $c_p = .5$ are figures conservatively chosen.

Finally, we will calculate how sensitively q reacts on a 10% change of c_p, e_p.

$$\frac{\Delta q}{\Delta c_p} = 1.18 \quad \text{for} \quad e_p = 0$$

$$\frac{\Delta q}{\Delta e_p} = 1.176 \quad \text{for} \quad c_p = 0 \quad .$$

In the previous calculations, the **PT**s have not been specified hierarchically; in the form of α only the **PT**s on the highest hierarchical level (more precisely in the **PC**) have been given regard. Of course, the blocking effect of the **PT** formation [12] increases dramatically if we assume that **PT**s also establish on lower hierarchical levels. However, we shall not return to this aspect until the model MUE & HIER in Vol. 2 and we will merely note at this time that there are quite realistic project budgets where a considerable **PT** blocking effect must be expected. SDI is likely to be arranged in this scale order. Thus, with such a scale order the success of the project depends above all on success in reducing the propensity towards **PT** formation. With reference to the parameters of q this means that e_p and c_p have to be shaped as small as possible. Is that possibly one of the reasons for 'Japanese efficiency'?

If n_p could be restricted to n_p^-, an overhead **PT** q would result as stated in tab. 2.15. Hence, the question of how to reduce the degree of **PT** formation

V_p^* $(10^9\$/a)$	c_p	n_p^-	q
10	.5	22	.013
25	.5	556	.04
50	.5	1111	.068

Table 2.15: Project **PT** overhead in case of minimal **PT** formation

is indeed a relevant research question.

2.4.5 CARNEIRO's theory of societal organization re-examined

In a carefully selected sample of 46 simple societies CARNEIRO [14] found, by regression methods, the empirical relation

$$N = P^{.594} \quad ,$$

---

[12] Notice the results of the MX missile mismanagement investigation showing analogous characteristics just as in the case of the Shuttle catastrophe. Conversely, if there is a large enough budget, typical **PT** behavior can reduce temporarily, as was observed in the reduced competition between the US forces following the tremendous augmentation in the military budget during the Reagan era.

that is, approximately

$$N = \sqrt{P} \quad ,$$

where

$P :$ = size of population, and

$N :$ = "number of organizational traits".

Inserting $c_p = 1$ in 2.56 and choosing in our notation N, i.e. the population size, for V_p which is a plausible specification for simple societies near the subsistence minimum, CARNEIRO's formula results, and n_p^* is the number of traits in CARNEIRO's terminology.

CARNEIRO could only state the deviation of his exponent .594 from .5. Based on our **PT** approach, however, we are in the position to formulate the following hypothesis. Recall, that c_p represents, so to speak, the saving effect of hierarchical coordination. Assuming a small surplus also for simple societies, we have not to insert N but the production volume P measured in C which must be slightly greater than N. Thus, taking for granted the .594 from CARNEIRO, we can formulate the following equation:

$$N^{.594} = P^{.5}/\sqrt{c_p} \quad ,$$

and after solving for P ,

$$P = c_p N^{1.188} \quad .$$

Assuming two hierarchy levels without interlocking for simple societies, we can choose $c_p = .5$, [13] and hence get for a population of $N = 100$ a $P = 159$. Choosing the structurally maximal labor force quota of .6 which seems plausible for simple societies, $P/60$ yields the labor productivity of 1.98 which is, at least, plausible by scale order.

Notice, that an exponent of .5 implies the case of the subsistence minimum, where obviously $c_p = 1$ must hold, because there is no surplus to finance any hierarchy level beyond the trivial level one. Thus, CARNEIRO's approximation in reality is the lower boundary to the exponent.

We can interpret the results of this section in stating that the operation of simple societies is one big project bringing the expected number of project-**PTs** into being. If this held also for LSUs, far-reaching conclusions could possibly be drawn concerning the understanding of societal evolution. It is too early, however, at this moment to substantiate these still speculative considerations.

2.4.6   Dynamics of invention and innovation

Since innovations are realizations of previous inventions we can formulate:

$$\pi_{t+1}^* = (1 + \beta_t)\pi_t^*$$

---

[13]Interstingly, $c_p = .5$ is repeatedly confirmed in this book, so that we may presume, that hierarchy and interlocking effects approximately compensate, for details see chap. 4.

$$\pi_{t+1} = \pi_t + \alpha_t I_t$$
$$I_t = \pi_t^* - \pi_t \qquad (2.59)$$

with

π_t^* : $=$ level of inventions in year t,

π_t : $=$ level of innovations in year t,

I_t : $=$ invention lead over innovation,

α_t, β_t := parameters determining the speed of invention and innovation. One could call π_t^* the possible and π_t the realized productivity in year t.

$$R_t = I_t/\pi_t \qquad (2.60)$$

shall be called the relative invention lead.

In the case of constant parameters, recursive inserting yields the following analytical solution:

$$\begin{aligned}
\pi_t &= \alpha(1+\beta)^{t-1}\pi_0^* + \alpha(1-\alpha)(1+\beta)^{t-2}\pi_0^* \\
&+ [\alpha(1-\alpha)^{t-2}(1+\beta) + \alpha(1-\alpha)^{t-1}]\pi_0^* \\
&+ (1-\alpha)^t\pi_0
\end{aligned}$$

Putting $\alpha\pi_0^*$ outside parantheses leads to:

$$\pi_t = (1-\alpha)^t\pi_0 + \alpha\chi(\alpha,\beta,t)\pi_0^*$$

with

$$\begin{aligned}
\chi(.) &= (1+\beta)^{t-1} + (1-\alpha)(1+\beta)^{t-2} \\
&+ (1-\alpha)^{t-2}(1+\beta) + (1-\alpha)^{t-1}
\end{aligned}$$

and for π_t^* it holds:

$$\pi_t^* = (1+\beta)^t\pi_0^* \qquad .$$

Following MARCETTI [79] it holds since around 1700:

$$\pi_{t+50} = \pi_t^* \qquad .$$

Inserting this we are in the position to search for $\pi_0, \pi_0^*, \alpha, \beta$ so that

$$\frac{(1+\alpha)^{t+50}}{(1+\alpha)^t - \alpha\chi(\alpha,\beta,t+50)} = \pi_0^*/\pi_0 =: C$$

holds. Choosing $\beta = .01$ and $C = 1.5$, hence, for each t that $\alpha(t)$ is searched for which fulfils the equation. Some results are displayed in tab. 2.16.

The dynamics of the processes described by 2.59 must depend on the factors determining α_t and β_t. For α_t the following guess is possible: when relating the maximal innovation speed to the doubling period of π_t, the minimum of the latter must be identifiable. Let this be denoted by d_0. Since in course of one year not more than I_t can be innovated it follows:

t	α_t	doubling time of $\pi_A^{+)}$ in years	π_{At}
0	.01115	114^{++}	8.0
1	.0107	187	8.0045
$\vdots$	$\vdots$	$\vdots$	$\vdots$
50	.0001		

Table 2.16: Productivity growth and doubling periods based on the MAR-CETTI approach

+) for $\pi_{At}^* = 12 = 1.5 \cdot \pi_{A,1980}$

++) compare tab. 2.17, reference footnote d

$$\alpha_t \in [0,1] \quad .$$

Defining the innovation speed as

$$d_t = \delta_t/d_0 \quad ,$$

with $\delta_t :=$ realization quota of the maximal speed (hence $\delta_t = 1$ means the maximal innovation speed), we get:

$$\pi_{t+1} = \pi_t + d_t\pi_t \quad .$$

By the way, this formula was used to calculate the doubling periods in tab. 2.16, i.e. they are linearly approximated.

By comparison with 2.59 we get:

$$\alpha_t I_t = d_t\pi_t \quad .$$

With 2.60 $\alpha_t = d_t R_t^{-1}$ results, and since

$$d_t \leq d_0^{-1} \quad ,$$

$$\alpha_{tmax} = \min[1, (d_0 R_t)^{-1}] \tag{2.61}$$

results. If I_t is small compared with π_t, then

$$R_t^{-1} \geq d_0^{-1} \quad ,$$

and $\alpha_{tmax} = 1$. With this information, it can now be concluded that the innovation (not to be confused with invention) process must speed up in approaching its development line threshold. Setting α_t direct proportional to $(d_0 R_t)^{-1}$, it follows:

$$\alpha_t I_t = d_0^{-1}\pi_t \quad ,$$
$$\text{and}$$
$$\pi_{t+1} = \pi_t + d_0^{-1}\pi_t \quad ,$$

that is, π_t grows at its greatest speed exponentially, as described by

$$\pi_t = (1 + d_0^{-1})^t \pi_0 \quad .$$

As is easily recognized, the innovation is more rapid from invention to invention in this model. Even these simple assumptions yield an innovation process corresponding to that proposed by MARCETTI [79]. Let us, in particular, capture that the inverse of the relative invention lead is relevant for α_t.

A Hierarchy of Invention and Innovation

Recall the above-mentioned four levels of the technological development:

- local innovations referring to a local invention,

- local invention,

- global invention,

- epochal invention.

Let us now reflect that each level be the innovation of the next higher level. Then there would be only one essential invention, namely, the epochal one. Using 2.59 ... one gets the following equation system:

$$
\begin{aligned}
\pi_{t+1} &= \pi_t + \alpha_{\pi t} I_{\pi t} \\
I_{\pi t} &= L_t - \pi_t \\
\alpha_{\pi t max} &= \min[1, (d_\pi R_{\pi t})^{-1}] \\
R_{\pi t} &= I_{\pi t}/\pi_t
\end{aligned}
\tag{2.62}
$$

for *local* innovation

$$
\begin{aligned}
L_{t+1} &= L_t + \alpha_{Lt} I_{Lt} \\
I_{Lt} &= G_t - L_t \\
\alpha_{Lt max} &= \min[1, (d_L R_{Lt})^{-1}] \\
R_{Lt} &= I_{Lt}/L_t
\end{aligned}
\tag{2.63}
$$

for *local* invention

$$
\begin{aligned}
G_{t+1} &= G_t + \alpha_{Gt} I_{Gt} \\
I_{Gt} &= E_t - G_t \\
\alpha_{Gt max} &= \min[1, (d_G R_{Gt})^{-1}] \\
R_{Gt} &= I_{Gt}/G_t
\end{aligned}
\tag{2.64}
$$

for *global* invention

$$E_{t+1} = E_t + \alpha_{Et} I_{Et}$$
$$I_{Et} = \Pi^0 - E_t$$
$$\alpha_{Etmax} = \min[1, (d_E R_{Et})^{-1}]$$
$$R_{Et} = I_{Et}/E_t \qquad (2.65)$$
$$\text{for } epochal \text{ invention}$$

Π^0 denotes the physically maximal productivity. If the four initial values π_0, L_0, G_0, E_0 and that absolute maximum is known, the equation system can be solved, and the universal process of technological development would be describable.

Let us make an attempt to reach plausible results based on as simple as possible assumptions and oriented only to scale orders.

Assumption 1: $\Pi^0 = 50$ be the value of the maximal labor labor productivity; recall that for the F.R.G. in 1980 this took the value 8: the present epoch has its saturation at 17 approximately.

Assumption 2: The only free parameter shall be α_π and the remaining innovation speeds be dependent on α_π as follows:

$$d_L = \alpha_\pi/2 \quad , \quad d_G = d_L/2 \quad , \quad d_E = d_G/2 \quad .$$

Assumption 3: That the 'demand for invention' of the next lower level be the driving force of the inventions on the level under consideration; it depends further on the capability of invention on the next higher level, formulated exemplary for level 3 by

$$(L_t/G_t)^{E_t/G_t} \qquad .$$

Assumption 4: A retardation factor that supports the premise that an invention is more difficult the narrower the remaining invention scope at a given point of time, formulated exemplary for level 3 by

$$1 - G_t/E_t \qquad .$$

Assumption 5: That only on the first level is there a real innnovation. Therefore, the retardation factor of assumption 4 is not specified here.

On the whole one gets:

$$\alpha_{\pi t} = d_\pi^{-1} c_t \quad , \qquad c_t \in [0,1]$$
$$\alpha_{Lt} = d_L^{-1}(\pi_t/L_t)^{G_t/L_t}(1 - L_t/G_t)$$
$$\alpha_{Gt} = d_G^{-1}(L_t/G_t)^{E_t/G_t}(1 - G_t/E_t)$$
$$\alpha_{Et} = d_E^{-1}(G_t/E_t)^{\Pi^0/E_t}(1 - E_t/\Pi^0) \qquad (2.66)$$

Inserting plausible values for epochal societal types results in the figures displayed in the three tab. 2.17..., wherein α_t is set directly, that is, not by virtue of d_π and c_t. The doubling periods $V_{\{\cdot\}}$ are linearly approximated by

$$V_{\{\cdot\}t} = (\frac{X_{t+1}}{X_t} - 1)^{-1} \quad , \qquad (2.67)$$

where X_t serves as a symbol for the diverse variables on the different levels. For the transition from a technology line under consideration to a new one the following approach shall be made:

Approach: Let

$$V_t^i \geq rV_t^{i+1}$$

with $i :=$ level index for some t. Let in t^* the identity

$$V_{t^*}^i = rV_{t^*}^{i+1}$$

hold. Then, at the time point t^*, $X_t^i = X_{t^*}^{i+1}$ is set where X_t is again a dummy symbol as in 2.67. That is, after t^* a new technological line starts, and the old line is characterized by a residual small developmental potential. r must be chosen appropriately. Notice, that the entries for

year	π	L	G	E	societal type
t	1.7	1.76	2.2	3	early
t+1	1.7006	1.7604	2.2004	3.0003	horticulture
t	3	3.1	4.1	6.2	early
t+1	3.002	3.1023	4.1023	6.203	agriculture
t	3	3.125	4.1	6.3	early
t+1	3.0025	3.1272	4.1025	6.3032	agriculture^c
t	6.3	6.5	9	13.5	early
t+1	6.308	6.5133	9.0092	13.53	indust. soc.
t	8	8.2	13.5	15	F.R.G. 1980

Table 2.17: Invention and innovation dynamics for some societal types: productivity
c) see references in tab. 2.19

the F.R.G. 1980 show a particular shortage of global inventions which can imply the advent of a new epoch. Tab. 2.17 and the following two tabels show some plausibility. If 2.62 ... and 2.66 represent a correct description, then technological development can be regarded as following a specific 'eigendynamics', because the equation system contains, except d_i, no terms which are not determined recursively. If this approach is a correct framework to analyse whole civilization development lines like the occidental it certainly is not concrete enough for single LSUs. In the latter case, technological

year	$\alpha_\pi 10^{-2}$	$\alpha_L 10^{-3}$	$\alpha_G 10^{-4}$	$\alpha_E 10^{-5}$	
t	1	.96	4.92	.67	early
t+1	1	.96	4.92	.67	horticulture
t	2	2.3	11.096	7.8	early
t+1	2	2.33	11.098	7.82	agriculture
t	2	2.25	11.504	7.225	early
t+1	2	2.254	11.503	7.224	agriculture^c
t	4	5.32	20.46	81.3	early
t+1	4	5.3	20.53	81.15	indust. soc.
t	4	7.54	5.75	246	F.R.G. 1980

Table 2.18: Invention and innovation dynamics for some societal types: invention and innovation speed
c) see reference in tab. 2.19

development must be explained by concrete mechanisms. We can suppose from the results of this book so far that these mechanisms are found in the complex relations between

- destruction of material or energetic C ,

- distribution of material or energetic C on the different demand sectors,

- non-war and war technologies.

It is not proposed to elaborate further on the foregoing conclusions.

The consistency of the entries of tab. 2.17 ⋯ can be checked by comparison of the starting time points of epochs with those derived from the table. For instance, let us regard the epoch ahead:

Choosing the beginning of the industrialized society
approximately at 1700 it holds on behalf of
V_E(early industrialized society) = 455

$$1700 + 455 = 2155 \quad .$$

Comparing this with an analysis of the F.R.G.
one can confirm:

$$1980 + 174 = 2154 \quad .$$

year	V_π	V_L	V_G	V_E	
t	2833	4177	5592	9549	early
t+1	2844^a	4178^a	5594^a	9533	horticulture
t	1500	1327^b	1759	1815	early
t+1	1497	1329^a	1760^a	1812	agriculture
t	1200	1422	1620	1995	early
t+1	1203^a	1423^a	1621^a	1991	agriculture^c
t	788	489^b	978	455^b	early
t+1	768^a	492^a	971	457^a	indust. soc.
t	1000	205	15661	174^d	F.R.G. 1980

Table 2.19: Invention and innovation dynamics for some societal types: productivity doubling times
a) Since $V_{t+1} > V_t$, the saturation threshold is reached
b) Since $V^i > V^{i+1}$, already in the beginning of line i a strong invention pressure is existent
c) Variant without an invention pressure of type b)
d) compare with tab. 2.16, there reference ++)

The results of tab. 2.17 $\cdots$ enable calculations backwards to earlier epochs:

	1980	
$-$	281	$(= 455 - 174)$
$=$	1699	(start of industr. soc.)
$-$	1995	(V_E agricult. soc.)
$=$	296 bC	(start of agricult. soc.)
$-$	9549	(V_E horticult. soc.)
$=$	9845 bC	(start of horticult. soc.)

As one recognizes, this backward calculation yields plausible historical dates. Notice, that the assumptions used are quite simple. More is not intended in this book.

Creative potential, PT formation, and innovation speed

Without extensive foundation, an approach to determine α_t and β_t shall be given.
Let $\alpha_t^0 = \alpha_{tmax}$;

$$\alpha_t = \min\{\alpha_t^0, (W_{pt}/cN_t)^{a_1}[1 - (\alpha_t/\alpha_t^*)^{b_1}]^{c_1} \min[F_t, (V_{wt}/E_t)^{d_1}]\}$$
$$\beta_t = (1 - \pi_t/\Pi^0)^r \rho_t$$
$$\rho_t = (W_{gt}/cN_t)^{a_2}\{1 - [\alpha_{wt}/(\alpha_{wt}^* D_t)]^{b_2}\}^{d_2}(H_t/H_t^0)^{d_2} \qquad (2.68)$$

with

W_{gt} : = number of scientists employed in basic research,

$N_t :$ = population size of the LSU under consideration,

$c :$ = quota of creatives,

$\alpha_{wt} :$ = numer of scientific **PTRs**,

$\alpha_{wt}^* :$ = maximal number of scientific **PTRs** due to financial restrictions,

$D_t :$ = number of scientific disciplines,

$W_{pt} :$ = number of scientists employed in production,

$\alpha_t :$ = number of **PTRs** in the **PC** of the LSU,

$\alpha_t^* :$ = maximal number of **PTRs** in the **PC** of the LSU due to financial restrictions,

$F_t :$ = fraction of mean personal income related to E_t,

$E_t :$ = mean income of a **PTR** in the **PC**,

$V_{wt} :$ = mean income of a scientist,

$H_t :$ = $\displaystyle\sum_{i=1}^{D_t} p_{it}\ln(1/p_{it})$, $p_{it} := W_{it}/W_t$,

$W_{it} :$ = number of scientists in discipline i, $i = 1,...,D_t$,

$W_t :$ = number of all scientists,

$H_t^0 :$ = $\ln(D_t)$

$a_1,...,d_1,r,a_2,...,d_2 :=$ parameters,

$t :$ = time points.

In the most simple case, $a_1 = ... = d_2 = 1$ holds, and $F_t = V_{wt}/E_t = 1$. The results of this version are displayed in tab. 2.20.

The table can be summarized as follows:

Summarizing for the F.R.G. 1980

$W_{pt} = 5\cdot 10^5$	$N_t = 61\cdot 10^6$	$c = .05$	$\alpha_t/\alpha_t^* = .75$
$\pi_t/\Pi^0 = 8/50 = .16$	$W_{gt} = 35,000$	$\alpha_{wt}/\alpha_{wt}^* = .75$	
$D_t = 25$	$H_t/H_t^0 = .8$		

Summarizing for an agricultural society

$W_p = 2,500$	$N_t = 10^6$	$c = .05$	$\alpha/\alpha^* = .75$	
$\pi = 3.5$	$W_{gt} = 500$	$\alpha_w/\alpha_w^* = .8$	$D = 4$	$H/H^0 = .25$

Summarizing for an horticultural society

$W_p = 10$	$N = 10^4$	$c = .05$	$\alpha/\alpha^* = .75$	
$\pi = 2$	$W_g = 1$	$\alpha_w/\alpha_w^* = 1$	$D = 2$	$H/H^0 = .1$

With these considerations and the results from tab. 2.20 we can identify the distribution of the societal creative potential to the different areas of invention and innovation as the crucial problem, the solution to which is perhaps a central issue maintaining stability of high civilized LSUs.

societal type	F.R.G. 1980	agricult. soc.	horticult. soc.
W_{pt}/cN_t	.1639	.05	.02
α_t/α_t^*	.75	.75	.75
π_t/Π^0	.16	.07	.04
W_{gt}/cN_t	.0015	.01	.002
$\alpha_{wt}/(\alpha_{wt}^* D_t)$	.03	.2	.45
H_t/H_t^0	.8	.25	.1
β	.0075	.00186	.00002
α	.041	.0125	.005
doubling period of π^*	133^b	538	9470
doubling period of π	35^a	1400^c	2667

Table 2.20: Developmental speed of technological progress depending on socio-structural factors
a) From tab. 2.18, there entry 13.5, in combination with $I_t = 13.5 - 8$ and $V_t = [(\pi_{t+1} - \pi_t)/\pi_t - 1]^{-1}$
b) In tab. 2.19, 174 years were necessary to reach a $\pi = 15$, here 133 years are necessary to arrive at $\pi^* = 16$.
c) $I_t = .2$

In the previous sections the relevance of an MISP has been worked out repeatedly. LEM [67] points out that inventions occur almost without exception in the area of basic research. One possible conclusion, in particular with **PTRs**, would be to join basic and politically sponsored (especially military) large scale research projects. Two pitfalls, however, would result from such a strategy; it would no longer be pure basic research and large scale projects have a tendency towards **PT** formation. Thus, the creative potential would be twice reduced. The strategy to search for the applicable results of an autonomous basic research appears to be more sophisticated. This would reduce costs due to the low **PT** demand and strengthen the creative power. An imaginable result could be a conspirative organizational structure devoted to the hidden appropriation of basic research results to use this for the aims of the MISP. The reader may speculate how far such structures are already established.

From 2.67 it holds for the doubling period of π_t:

$$V = (\pi_{t+1}/\pi_t - 1)^{-1} \qquad .$$

Let Γ_{wt} denote the doubling period of the stock of scientific "know how" W_t (regardless of how operationalized). Let us make the approach:

$$W \;=\; W(qcN, V_w)$$

with

$q:$ $=$ usage quota of the creative potential cN,

$V_w:$ $=$ surplus transfer to W.

Let W depend synergetically from cN with σ as the parameter representing the synergetic effect:

$$W = (qcN)^\sigma \quad .$$

Let σ be reversely proportional to the amount of **PT** formation in W, hence

$$\sigma = s\alpha_c/\alpha_w$$

with

$\alpha_c:$ $=$ critical **PT** number,

$\alpha_w:$ $=$ actual **PT** number in W,

$s:$ $=$ parameter,

$$\alpha_w \leq \alpha_c \quad , \quad \alpha_w \leq \alpha_w^* \quad , \quad \alpha_w \leq qcN \quad ,$$

and hence

$$\alpha_w \leq \min(\alpha_c, \alpha_w^*, qcN) \tag{2.69}$$

Let α_w^* be calculated in a simple manner as done in 2.56:

$$\alpha_w^* = \sqrt{2V_w} \quad ,$$

where, again, a "saving parameter" of .5 is supposed. Analogous to 2.57 we write:

$$\alpha_w = (1 - \epsilon_w)hV_w + \epsilon_w\alpha_w^* \quad , \quad \epsilon_w \in [0,1] \tag{2.70}$$

It is obvious that the scientific-technological progress must slow down for $\Gamma_w > \Gamma_\pi$.

Let B_w denote the alimentation demand in W. It shall be posited

$$V_w \leq B_w < P$$

with

$P:$ $=$ production per year in C

in the LSU under consideration.

Let us now consider $V_w = vB_w$, $v \geq 0$, generally v stems from a surrounding of 1. B_w is composed of the **PT** and the remaining (pertinence oriented) demand, that is,

$$B_w = E_w + S_w$$

with

$$E_w = \alpha_w A_w + p_w\alpha_w^2 \quad ,$$

wherin

$$A_w : = \text{personnel costs in the } \mathbf{PT} \text{ system,}$$
$$p_w : = w\text{-specific } Herrschfts \text{ parameter,}$$

and

$$S_w = qcNw(1 + d^{\gamma/\Gamma_\pi})$$

with

$$w : = \text{alimentation per scientist,}$$
$$d, \gamma : = \text{parameters.}$$

Let us assume that the shorter the doubling period of π, the faster it is that S_w grows exponentially. Altogether we get:

$$W = (qcN)^\sigma$$
$$\sigma = s_0 \frac{\alpha_w}{\alpha_c} + s_1(1 - \frac{\alpha_w}{\alpha_c})$$
$$\alpha_w \leq \min(\alpha_c, \alpha_w^*, qcN)$$
$$\alpha_w^* = \sqrt{2vB_w}$$
$$B_w = E_w + S_w$$
$$E_w = \alpha_w A_w + p_w \alpha_w^2$$
$$S_w = qcNw(1 + d^{\gamma/\Gamma_\pi}) \qquad (2.71)$$

It shall hold now

$$\Gamma_w \overset{!}{\leq} \Gamma_\pi \quad .$$

From this results, in considering

$$\Gamma_{wt} = (\frac{W_{t+1}}{W_t} - 1)^{-1} \quad ,$$

the following equation that is not easy to solve:

$$\Gamma_w(\Gamma_\pi) \leq \Gamma_\pi .$$

However, we are not forced to investigate this equation because with a growing V_w and N we can posit that α_c is that restriction factor which is the first to be relevant. Note, that this simplification does not hold for diminishing population. Thus, it is sufficient to examine the limit value $\alpha_w/\alpha_c = 1$, i.e.

$$W = (qcN)^{s_0} \quad .$$

Supposing for approximation a $q = 1$, a maximal $c_{max} =: c^*$, and $s_0 = 1$, then it results:

$$W_{t+1} = c^* N_{t+1} \quad ,$$

hence

$$\Gamma_{wt}^* = (\frac{c^* N_{t+1}}{c^* N_t} - 1)^{-1} = (\frac{N_{t+1}}{N_t} - 1)^{-1} \quad .$$

Near the limit, the question for achievable scientific progress reduces itself to the question whether to this end population grows rapidly enough. Since with increasing N, the number of **PTs** generally grows, $q = 1$ thus means that LSUs having reached that saturation, that is, entering a situation of serious stress, switch over to admit only scientific **PTs**.

The foregoing reflections present a formalization of the argumentation of LEM [67]. SIMON [118] also points out that for the development of civilization the "ultimate resource" lies in population because of civilizational dependence on the inventory power of human beings. We have to elucidate from this the explosive effect of a diminishing population. On the other hand it becomes clear how outstanding is the fact that the Peoples's Republic of China is capable of maintaining an LSU of 10^9 members.

Denoting the growth rate of population with ρ, in the above-mentioned limit it holds immediately:

$$\Gamma_{wt}^* = \rho^{-1} \qquad ,$$

hence, for instance, in case of a population growth rate of 1%, a doubling period of 100 years results. LEM [67] argues consistently in proposing that only artificial intelligence could overcome the inescapable saturation problems in the scientific- technological progress. However, it can be presumed that the necessity to transit to this new epoch becomes acute only when reaching the limit described above. Since, in that situation a population shortage already exists, the transition to the new epoch can, if at all, be attained only by attracting creative potential from other LSUs. Thus, an LSU with a reducing population faces 'double' problems.

In our terminology this would mean that artificial "heads" N_a emerge in this new epoch which can be added to N, so that now, in the above equation system the sum $N + N_a$ can be considered instead of N. However, at present we can only speculate on N_a.

However, the above considerations only hold for a 'monolithic' V_w. If it happens that scientific fields are differentiated from each other permanently with a minimum of mutual interdependencies and in the form of $i = 1 \ldots D_t$ disciplines, then the term W_i can be considered instead of W. Hence, interdisciplinary cooperation would have to be tranformed into new disciplines. By steady splitting, α_w can be kept smaller than α_c. However, it must be taken into account that from the population, only qcN is available as scientific personnel. Thus, the strategy of the scientific-disciplinary differentiation can only help temporarily, since from combinatorial calculations

$$D_t \quad = \quad \delta_t(2^{D_{t-1}} - 1)$$

with

$$\delta_t : \quad = \quad \text{growth quota}$$

must be considered. Even with a very small δ,

$$D_t \quad * \quad \text{(scientist per each} \quad D_t)$$

rapidly exceeds the limit qcN. Here, there is the danger that c will be manipulated, i.e. non-creatives being defined as creatives, and this in turn can lead to disadvantages in those aspects of LSU competition where the quality niveau is of high importance. Moreover, because of the necessary basic stock financing for each new discipline, the demand

$$B_{wt} = \sum_i^{D_t} B_{wi_t}$$

rapidly reaches the limit P_t.

It would appear at first glance that only one conclusion seems plausible; the **PT** formation within the scientific field has to be kept as small as possible. However, if taken by itself, this is a false conclusion: how can the state of scientific know-how be arrived at, if not authoritatively by means of **PT**-decision? If we accept this, the problem results that an agreement on know-how is either not achieved due to lack of **PT** influence or is the result of oligarchic-strategical competition due to **PT** formation in this field.

Thus, an α_c^- must exist that, at least, is necessary for allowing an agreement on know-how. Emanating from this the difficult control problem arises as follows: Γ_{wt} has to be minimized under the side condition

$$\alpha_w \in [\alpha_c^-, \min(\alpha_c, \alpha_w^*, qcN)] =: \Omega_c \quad .$$

This means that there exists a limit resulting from α_c^- for the number of disciplines and, thus, indirectly for scientific discovery (unless artificial intelligence is ignored). However, these strange-sounding conclusions are valid only if established disciplines have a very long life time. If enough 'old' disciplines are surrendered, α_w can be maintained in Ω_c. But how can it be decided which 'old' disciplines have to be abandoned in favour of which 'new' disciplines and how can it be guaranteed that no creative potential is lost accidentally in this way? On this level at the latest, one can no longer avoid specifying an 'objective' success criterion for the progress of scientific-technological know-how. Since ultimately the definition concerning scientific truth cannot be more convincingly asserted than by killing the scientific 'opponent' and as **PTs** have chosen militant force as ultima ratio at all times, it is convenient to base the aforementioned criterion on superiority of the killing technology. Ultimately, as MAHR [78] has also stated, this must result in a technological world war which, however, needs 'territories' where the superiority can be verified by a confrontation of the opposing technologies. Moreover, it has to be considered that in the atmosphere of a technological world war the appropriation of foreign know-how could possibly be effected more readily. Perhaps these are further reasons for SDI and the STAR WARS intention could be to establish the territory in which this confrontation can take place far away from *TERRA*.

We will now analyse the field of militarily relevant HI TEC, briefly denoted by θ, under the problem stated in 2.71. In θ we are proceeding from the fact that the allocation of the potential

$$q_\theta c_\theta N_\theta$$

available on *TERRA* is the matter in question, where N_θ shall mean that only certain people (for instance those in highly civilized states) on *TERRA* are competent in this field. Let us suppose that this potential is mobile in principle, and hence is not linked to one LSU. Then, in a first approximation, for N_θ the number of people on *TERRA* that can be regarded is that which is allocable by one LSU. Let q_θ denote the quota of the allocation success.

However, the regrouping of disciplines in favour of θ is affected by the problem that the intelligence stored in the old disciplines can as a rule, not be regrouped either. Hence, in the regrouping strategy only the rising generation can fill the field θ with scientific personnel. As we may presume that θ-talent is not ubiquitous, it results in addition that

$$c_\theta \ll c$$

with

$$c_\theta : \quad = \quad \text{quota of the } \theta\text{-talents.}$$

The doubling period Γ_θ has to be short enough to win the technology world war. From this, we can posit:

$$
\begin{aligned}
W_\theta &= (q_\theta c_\theta N_\theta)^{\sigma_\theta} \\
\sigma_\theta &= s_0 \frac{\alpha_\theta}{\alpha_c} + s_1 (1 - \frac{\alpha_\theta}{\alpha_c}) \\
\alpha_\theta &\in \Omega_\theta \\
\alpha_\theta^* &= \sqrt{2V_\theta} ,
\end{aligned}
\qquad (2.72)
$$

provided θ is monolithic.

Let Γ_θ^* be the doubling period necessary for the victory, and W_θ^* the corresponding know-how. Let $W_{0\theta}$ be the presently available know-how. Then

$$\lambda_\theta = \frac{W_{0\theta}}{W_\theta^*}$$

is the actual know-how quota. Let us assume that λ_θ could be indicated by experts' judgements. Finally, let T_θ be the time in years scheduled by the LSU for the achievement of the technological world domination. Then

$$\Gamma_\theta^* = T_\theta \ln(2)(\ln \frac{1}{\lambda_\theta})^{-1} \qquad (2.73)$$

is the required shortest doubling period of the θ-knowledge. As there are only fixed terms on the right side of 2.73, Γ_θ^* can be regarded as given.

However, the linear appproximation

$$\hat{\Gamma}_\theta = \left(\frac{W_{\theta\,t+1}}{W_{\theta t}} - 1\right)^{-1} = p^{-1}$$

with

$$p \qquad \text{from } W_{\theta\,t+1} = (1+p)W_{\theta t}$$

is larger than the real Γ_θ. Hence, $\hat{\Gamma}_\theta$ must be multiplied by the correction factor

$$KF(\lambda_\theta, T_\theta) \qquad .$$

It is calculated:

$$KF(\lambda_\theta, T_\theta) = \frac{T_\theta \ln(2)(\ln\frac{1}{\lambda_\theta})^{-1}}{[\exp(\frac{1}{T_\theta}\ln\frac{1}{\lambda_\theta})-1]^{-1}}$$

Hence, $KF(.)$ is fixed provided Γ_θ^* is given, and we can make use of $\hat{\Gamma}_\theta$.

Now we can formulate the following problem:

$$\hat{\Gamma}_{\theta t} = \left[\frac{(W_{\theta\,t+1})^{\sigma_{\theta\,t+1}}}{(W_{\theta t})^{\sigma_{\theta t}}} - 1\right]^{-1}$$

and

$$\hat{\Gamma}_{\theta t}\, KF(\lambda_\theta, T_\theta) \overset{!}{\leq} \Gamma_\theta^*(\lambda_\theta, T_\theta) \qquad . \tag{2.74}$$

Let us first display $KF(\lambda_\theta, T_\theta)$ and $\Gamma_\theta^*(\lambda_\theta, T_\theta)$ as be shown in tab. 2.21. There is no reason to fear that $\alpha_\theta < \alpha_c^-$, i.e. we can neglect this case in our

λ_θ	T_θ	$KF(\cdot)$	Γ_θ^*
.05	50	.7143	11.57
.05	100	.7036	23.14
.05	150	.7	34.71
.05	200	.6984	46.28
.05	216	.698	50
.1	50	.7094	15.05
.1	100	.701	30.1
.1	150	.6985	45.15
.1	166	.698	50
.25	50	.7028	25
.25	100	.698	50
.5	50	.698	50

Table 2.21: Selected parameters in the optimized technological innovation speed

analysis. Again, we chose \$ 4,500 as the subsistence minimum in the U.S. in 1986, the C , and get from this:

$$\alpha_\theta^* = \sqrt{2V_{\theta\,1986}}$$

In the following we will skip the index 1986. Notice, that α_θ^* is a guess *a fortiori*, because the budget of 1986 was chosen. Presumably, the budget will not become smaller in the future.

Let us assume a maximal quadratic synergetic effect, hence $s_0 = 1$, $s_1 = 2$. With α_θ analogous to 2.70 in combination with 2.58 on p. 77

$$\sigma_\theta = \sigma_\theta(V_{\theta t}, \epsilon_\theta)$$

is given, too. What remains is the problem in stating something about α_c. Recall that the critical scale order for an LSU, at which **PTs** emerge, is $h^{-1} = 10,000$. We can assume that the critical crowding-size within an already highly organized field is considerably smaller than h^{-1}. Let us assume that θ be monolithic in its starting phase. Effects resulting from hierarchization and subsystem formation may mutually compensate. Let α_c be posited as

$$\alpha_c = i_c h^{-1}/S$$

with

$$i_c : = \text{critical interaction density,}$$
$$S : = \text{number of subsystems.}$$

Numerical example: $\alpha_c = 5 \cdot 10,000/50 = 1,000$.

Let us, therefore, posit $\alpha_c = 10^3$ by order of magnitude. Then the important parameters necessary for an analysis of the θ-development process can be calculated. Some results are displayed in table 2.22. Since we undertake

V_θ $10^9\$$ in 1980	e_θ	ϵ_θ	α_θ^-	α_θ^*	α_θ	σ_θ
10	0	.033	22	667	44	1.96
20	0	.15	444	2981	823	1.18
30	0	.183	667	3651	1212	.79
40	0	.21	889	4216	1590	.41
50	0	.236	1111	4714	1960	.04
10	.25	.078	22	667	72	1.93
20	.25	.24	444	2981	1053	.947
30	.25	.28	667	3651	1500	.5
40	.25	.31	889	4216	1924	.076

Table 2.22: HI TEC financial volume, **PTs** and creativity

a guess *a fortiori*, as mentioned above, in 2.74 we can posit

$$\sigma_{\theta\,t+1} = \sigma_{\theta t} =: \sigma_\theta$$

and get

$$\hat{\Gamma}_{\theta t} = [(\frac{W_{\theta t+1}}{W_{\theta t}})^{\sigma_\theta} - 1]^{-1}$$

and

$$\triangle W_\theta = q_\theta c_\theta \triangle N$$

Recall our assumption, that $c_\theta \ll c$. If we take, as before, $c = .05$ and presume that every thousand of the corresponding creative potential be θ-qualifiable, then $c_\theta = .5 \cdot 10^{-4}$ results. Let us postulate that the population of the whole developed industrialized world can be taken into consideration for the support of θ. Let this be posited as 10^9. The population p_N shall be taken as .005. Then the following results:

$$W_{\theta t+1} = W_{\theta t} + .25 q_\theta N 10^{-9}$$

Under the assumptions made, the necessary technological development in θ cannot be achieved within 50 years. The resulting question is whether the target on the velocity of that development can be achieved at all with a somewhat realistic parameter constellation q_θ, c_θ, p_N. In addition, we have to take into account that, because of the time delay in education, $p_{N,t-25}$ must be considered, and by this we can choose a greater p_N due to the high birth rates 25 years before 1986. The results of this examination are displayed in tab. 2.23. In the first line there is, in my opinion, a realistic parameter

W_θ	$c_\theta \cdot 10^{-2}$	q_θ	σ_θ	$\hat{\Gamma}(\lambda_\theta, 50)$	
50,000	.005	.25	1.18	242	
$20,000^+$	.0237	.544	1.18	11.5	
$20,000^+$	$.0275^+$	.38	1.18	11.5	←
$20,000^+$	.0275	.575	.79	11.5	

Table 2.23: Parameter constellation within the HI TEC sector and reaching the target of rapid sectoral development
+) mids of interval

constellation. In all lines $\lambda_\theta = .05$ was chosen (what already appears quite a large value). p_N was chosen .01. The stated variables resp. parameters have been varied in the restrictions

$$W_\theta \geq 10^4 \quad , \quad c_\theta \leq .05 \cdot 10^{-2} \quad , \quad q_\theta \leq .75 \quad .$$

Moreover, the following assumption was made: If c_θ or q_θ approach their limits, then σ_θ approaches .79.
Example: In the row marked by ← the following interpretations seem appropriate:

1.) every 182nd $(c_\theta q_\theta / c)$ scientist must be mobilized for θ;
2.) this means, expressed in faculties, that 5.5 times
as many θ-special fields have to be procured as existed in 1986.
Assuming 50 non-θ-faculties, it follows
that approximately every 10th these 'old' faculties
has to be regrouped;
3.) Referring to q_θ the marked line tells us, that 38%
of the whole growth of θ can factually be mobilized for θ.

Naturally, the question remains whether an intelligence potential of .0275 % for θ is available at all in the occidental industrialized world. This means for the F.R.G. a number of θ-scientists amounting to 16,500. As this is already remarkably above 10^4 for one LSU, a growth in the financing volume and hence a drop of σ_θ must be expected because of the **PT** costs. This has been examined in the last row of tab. 2.23. Here, 57.5 % of the whole θ-growth in intelligence potential would have to be mobilized. With reference to the F.R.G., that would be 9,500 scientists within one year. Assuming that 2/3 of these scientists have to be newly educated in the starting phase of the θ program, it would result in a demand for 153 study faculties. Presuming a studying period of 12 semester and 500 students per study faculty, some 14 study faculties per federal state, i.e. approximately 1 faculty per university would be required. In fact, this could be the reason for the fact that nowadays each university in the F.R.G. receives a θ-faculty. Altogether it becomes clear that the realization of the above described θ-target plan of 50 years is only achievable by enormous efforts on the part of the occidental countries: however, there are no entirely unrealistic prospects for success under **PT** aspects which are under consideration here. Because we derived some strong saturation tendencies to be expected by the year 2030 in some of the most important technology fields the choice of a time period of 50 years seems plausible.

Finally it seems interesting to examine how large is the quota of substantial output orientation $1 - q$ (recall tab. 2.14) in the field θ. In tab. 2.24 the dependence of $1 - q$ on e_p is displayed, where a financing volume of $30 \cdot 10^9$ \$ is presumed. By scale order we can assume that with $1 - q < .75$ the propen-

e_p	0	.1	.2	.3	.4	.5
$1 - q$	.87	.85	.82	.79	.74	.68

Table 2.24: Propensity towards **PT** formation and quota of substantial output orientation

sity becomes very strong to consider results in θ oligarchic-strategically as success, regardless of the actual performance (recall the definition power of **PTs**). An inclination towards **PT** formation of .38 (i.e. 38 % more **PTs** in

θ are established than with the minimum of $10^{-4}V_\theta$) is already sufficient for such a pretention strategy. The reader may decide whether she/he thinks this to be realistic. If it can be regarded as realistic then θ would not be able to fail merely because of oligarchic-strategical reasons. Taking STAR WARS as an example a possible rude awakening could happen only in the case of an emergency.

By this, we see again how much is dependent on slowing down **PT** dynamics. How can this be achieved? It raises basic questions of civilization development which, however, will not be discussed here.

2.5 Natural environment

We characterized the civilization process by the fact that to a growing extent natural determinants are replaced by those that are socially controlled. We have seen that **PT** dynamics require a growing surplus, and therefore, that more and more virtual "heads" V have to be produced. Hence, two questions arise:

A) To what extent can civilizations decouple from nature?
Are there zones in the state space of Ω wherein
the civilization process collides with natural features?
B) Where are the limits of production, productivity and growth?

To **A**:
As will be shown in the model MUE & SYN in Vol. 2, such *critical zones* are quite realistic since they are in a certain respect a destabilization of social areas which instantaneously collapse when confronted with specific natural features. The reverse case, the collapse of natural fields by influence of social activities is possible as well. Then, the extent to which the operation of LSUs is disturbed by such collapses shows how far the decoupling from nature has actually succeeded.

Social activities like search for or production of food, wars, infrastructural constructions etc. have at all times affected local parts of nature and have even destroyed them. The history of occidental civilization development is full of examples for these facts, e.g. the cutting down of the Spanish forests, farming of the North-American prairie, or the excessive extension of large areas used as meadows by sheep and goats with the consequent destruction of many forests in middle Europe.

However, the systematic wide-range damage of the natural system by industrial production, having application also to agriculture, has been observed in the developed occidental civilizations only in the last 30 years. An outstandingly important question for the understanding of the relation between civilization and natural environment is whether this kind of production has always existed in the occidental civilization ("Be fruitful and multiply, and replenish the earth, and subdue it") or whether it was a matter of the last (machine-oriented) developing phase that production and technology created these problems. In the first case, the occidental civilization field could be regarded as a general ecological system displacer.

Already the comparing of the basic components of natural ecosystems and civilizations shows that civilizations are competitors to ecological systems. Namely, both possess population, production and consumption as elementary operation fields. However, a decisive difference exists in the facts that within LSUs, population, production and consumption can, at least on a local level, be more or less systematically controlled *and* of a scale order of energy flow etc. comparable to that of large natural systems. Thus, civilizations could also be regarded as "artificial ecological systems". Technical civilizations succeeded especially in producing large quantities of stuff that cannot or rarely be found in pure nature. By this, to a growing extent natural products are replaced by artificial ones. By the creation of *artificial* "heads" (genetic manipulation of human beings, artificial intelligence) LSUs would switch over to adopting this displacement principle to themselves.

Thus, the decisive question is whether civilizations (at least the occidental) are principally on a collision course with nature or whether the affections of natural systems can be corrected without revision of civilizational basic structures. According to the approach of this book, the causes for a systematic collision course must be investigated in Ω, and here, in particular, in the fields of surplus and **PT** dynamics. Both can, under certain circumstances, lead to serious local concentrations of surplus production and consumption.

Systematic collision course means that elementary operation principles of LSUs are incompatible with a 'wise' way of dealing with nature. This question cannot be discussed here: SCHNEIDER/MORTON [115] refer to that in a normative respect.

However, by growing production of C, LSUs would not only have to get on a collision course with nature but also with themselves, because, as supposed in section 3.2.2, the production of V entails a growing complexity of the system structures and this in turn increases the likelihood of getting into critical zones. This must aggravate tremendously when a civilization is affected by a large scale damaging feedback from nature.

Presumably, there is, in addition, a relation between productivity and rapidity of structural change of LSUs. In the last sections we denoted labor productivity measured in C with π_A. Perhaps structural change, the transition from one to the next *generation* of an LSU (in analogy to cultural or technological generations) is directly dependent on the transition

$$\pi_A^* \to \pi_A^* + 1 \quad , \quad \text{where} \quad \pi_A^* \in \{\pi_A \mid \pi_A \in \mathbf{N}\},$$

i.e. are positive full numbers.

By scale order, a new LSU generation could result at each full number increase of π_A. This new generation would be indicated by the appearance of new subsystems or hierarchies. Denoting the generation number of an LSU by λ, *structural change* could be defined as follows:

$$\lambda_t := \pi^*_{At} - 1 \qquad .$$

Since π_A must systematically be greater than 1, $\lambda = 0$ is inserted for $\pi_A < 2$. Thus, the following correspondence results:

π_A	< 2	2	3	...
λ	0	1	2	...

Let us postulate a logistic envelope covering the two industrial epochs, the first of which started approximately in 1600, whereas the second started in 1980. We assume,therefore, in a first approximation, a logistic growth function for π_A,

$$\pi_{At} = \frac{K}{1+ae^{-bt}} \qquad .$$

We choose for $t = 1600$ the value $\pi_A = 2.5$. For $t = 1980$ we take the empirical value $\pi_A = 8$, as was made out above for the F.R.G. We presume that maximal rapidity of structural change will be reached in the year 2000. Because of the central symmetry of the logistic function,

$$\pi_{A,2000} = .5K$$

results, and by iteration

$$K = 17.6$$

is calculated. [14] From these informations, a and b can be estimated as

$$\hat{a} = 5,448 \qquad , \qquad \hat{b} = .00425 \qquad ,$$

where $\wedge$ denotes estimation. Tab. 2.25 shows the behavior of λ and π_A in dependence of t. The entries of tab. 2.25 could be interpreted as follows:

t	1600	1652	1736	1806	1870	1927	1980	2035
π_A	2.5	3	4	5	6	7	8	9
λ	1	2	3	4	5	6	7	8

Table 2.25: Productivity and epochal change

1652 - approximately Westphalian peace treaty,
    Fr. Wilhelm der Große, Grand Duke.
1736 - peace treaty of Vienna, birth of James Watt,
    approximate beginning of capitalism.

---

[14]Recall that the saturation threshold of approximately 17 for the present epoch is repeatedly found in this book, for instance in tab. 2.2 and section 2.4.6.

1806 - dissolution of the German Reich with its old borders.
1870 - German/French war, German Reich with its new borders.
1927 - approximate beginning of world economy crisis and fascism.
1980 - approximate beginning of electronic and industrial revolution.
2035 - ? (beginning of orbital societies).

Surely, the reproduction of some historically relevant dates can happen by chance. In this regard only the plausible scale order of periods of structural change is important. Because of the simple assumptions this cannot be more than an outlining of the systems behavior.

In the approach of both volumes of Civilizational Dynamics, synenergetic coupling effects between civilizational and 'natural' operational mechanisms are not considered – except the model MUE & SYN in Vol. 2. That model, however, is specified for simple societies. To disregard natural restrictions implicitly means that LSUs would be successful in their strategy of decoupling from nature. If they are not, then the endogeneous consideration of nature in Ω is absolutely necessary. This would require an approach that could be labelled ecologically comprehensive, namely, in describing nature and human beings in a unified approach.

At first there may appear to be an objection that the approach of this book is misleading from the beginning, since nature is more 'powerful' at the rate of 10th powers than are human societies. For instance, in the decade 1970–1980, despite all production growth the predominant share in atmospherical dust was still to be traced back to natural causes (volcanic eruption, Savanna fires etc.). This objection may be globally valid (i.e. on a world-wide standard or world average), it overlooks, however, the capability of civilizations to concentrate activities locally and, in doing so, to local-selectively follow evolutionary paths that are globally impossible (e.g. the take off into the orbit).

From this the decisive question arises whether local energy flow maximation (generally: the maximum-power-principle) can by many small local successes become dominant at the global scale in the end. We will reserve this problem for other researches.

To B)

As regards modelling, B is easier to handle, because restrictions of production are dealt with here. For instance, in world models this has repeatedly been considered, see e.g. MEADOWS, ODUM [82,100]. Produced goods are the result of human, animal or mechanical labor. Every labor is connected with energy transformation processes. With each energy transformation a part of the energy is definitively lost. The extent of this loss, however, depends on the kind of technology used. In the long run, unless no energy resources independent from sun energy inflow are explored, we only dispose of sun energy as energy-input. From this, the possible size of the world society can be calculated which is, according to LIETH [71], approximately $3.5 \cdot 10^9$ human beings. If the activities of LSUs consume more energy than the sun energy input this has inevitably to be to the expense of non-renewable, e. g. fossil energy reserves. The consequences of this wasteful exploitation are shifted over temporarily to subsequent generations, regionally to the energy suppliers and in a sectoral sense possibly finally to the quality of the 'natural' environment.

Let us posit that most of natural restriction impacts can be indicated by using energy consumption figures. Hence, in Ω the additional term E_t has to be integrated leading to

$$\Omega_t = \{(\alpha_t, V_t, N_t, D_t, E_t) \mid t \in T\} \quad ,$$

where $\cdot$

$E_t : =$ energy consumption in the LSU

measured in $\mathcal{E}$ (see section 2.4.1),

and

$T : =$ set of time points.

In the approach of this book, the natural restrictions of the production and other activities of LSUs are exogenuously fixed, hence, no explicit energy balance models are specified. The decisive question is that of the sequence of internal and external restriction impacts. Thus, the design to specify natural restrictions as exogenous implies to examine the question whether LSUs reach internal restrictions earlier than external ones, or expressed technically that the state space of the old Ω is a subspace of the state space enlarged by E. Should it become evident that LSUs are able to evolve within the exogenously given natural restrictions without collapsing and hence only enter problematic zones at the margins of the 'natural niche' it would be inevitable to specify these restrictions as endogeneous. If not, LSUs would collapse before reaching these margins because of internal problems, and the specification of natural restrictions would be unnecessary. However, the possible integration of natural and human sciences has to be reserved to other researches.

3 Epistemological and methodological reflections

In section 2.2 we distinguished between population N and virtual "heads" V, i.e.

$$P = V + N \quad .$$

Between this decomposition and a real-structural decomposition, there is an interesting relation. Following MÜLLER [93], variables Y can be decomposed into

$$Y = Y_{DC} + Y_{MASS} \quad ,$$

that is, data produced by DC behavior and data produced by mass behavior. Example: Concerning a region of 43,000 inhabitants it was found approximately for 1979 that 2% of 1,200 business tax payers of a region pay 60% of that business tax within one year. In absolute figures:

$$
\begin{aligned}
Y &= 6 \cdot 10^6 \quad \text{DM/a} \\
&= 3.6 \cdot 10^6 \quad \text{DM/a} + 2.4 \cdot 10^6 \quad \text{DM/a},
\end{aligned}
$$

and the number of DCs was 24 and that of the remaining MASS 1176.

We can assume that institutions, particularly DCs, establish in the domain of virtual "heads", hence, in the distribution mass V. DYE and MÜLLER [21,88,93] found out that it appears appropriate to posit the following 75% rule:

Proposition 3 *DCs refer to those minimal ensembles of positions upon which 75% of Y is generated.*

This fraction, interestingly, corresponds to the quota

$$V/P = 180/240 = 3/4 \quad ,$$

as was observed for the F.R.G. in 1980. This evidence shall be generalized yielding the following, although this perhaps is a little speculative:

Conjecture 2 *In each time point t there exists a fraction p_t according to which the operation of organizationable fields of LSUs are determined by DC decisions, and it holds:*

$$p_t = V_t/P_t \quad . \tag{3.1}$$

With P from 2.53 $i = q_M/(f_M l)$ from 2.55 and

$$Q = q_M M = qN$$

it results :

$$P = \kappa m_Q i^{-1} N \pi_l r \quad ,$$

omitting t for the sake of simplicity. Let us posit $i = 1$; hence, supposing $m_Q = r = 1$,

$$P = \kappa N \pi_l \quad ,$$

and :

$$p_t = 1 - (\kappa_t \pi_{lt})^{-1} \quad . \tag{3.2}$$

Recall, that π_l is measured in (produced C /kwh) x 8760.

To compare different epochs let us choose the labor productivity π_A and utilizing $P = Q\pi_A$ and $Q = qN$

$$p_t = 1 - (q_t \pi_{At})^{-1} \tag{3.3}$$

results. The figures corresponding to the epochs are shown in Tab. 3.1. Interestingly, at the end of the agricultural society $p = .5$ holds and this approximately coincides with $\pi_A = 4$. It would be interesting to speculate whether epochal upheavals coincide with the powers of two of π_A, i.e. they happen when

$$\pi_A = 2, 4, 8, 16, \dots$$

is fulfilled (recall section 2.5).

Furthermore it must be noted that p increases by a declining population number. However, in this case the problem can arise that there are not enough members in an LSU to fill the **PT** positions.

3.2 is an interesting formalization of the statement that living conditions determine the consciousness of people (MARX). For with $p \to 1$, Y

epoch	π_A	q	p
premordial society	1.7	.6	.02
developed agriculture	3	.55	.4
F.R.G. 1980	8	.44	.72
F.R.G. $\approx$ 2035	9	.4	.72

Table 3.1: Social structure, productivity, and DC-Relevance in different epochs

approaches $Y = Y_{DC}$. From this, the situation would be that reality, at least in its social dimension, would largely be shaped by oligarchic structures. If we assume that DCs have definition power over social reality, would then cognition processes also be structured by oligarchic influences? Is social science perhaps an ideology serving as a veil to MASS perceptions? However, doesn't just such an artificial (or in our terminology 'virtual') social science correspond to the dominance of V_t? We can conclude: in many respects a growing p_t leads to problems of self-referentiality whose epistemoligical explosiveness does not seem to be sounded, so far. We shall not go further into this aspect here.

If by a high DC-share in Y the macro- and micro level are 'short-circuited', unexpected phase transitions in the behavior of $Y(t)$ appear, as WUNDER-LIN/HAKEN [138] have shown in some examples. We will come back to this in section 3.2. If it is assumed that local phase transitions are located in DC areas and global phase transitions in MASS areas, then social structural change would finally, i.e. in case of nearly total oligarchization of LSUs, be the result of local structural change of DCs only. Thus, by a growing p a situation could arise in which relatively long-lasting development phases (due to the slow structural change in MASS) change abruptly into a chaotic situation.

In particular from a methodological point of view, a growing p is relevant because this entails that traditional research instruments which are quite appropriate for mass phenomena, can become inappropriate. This, therefore, requires a new methodology. Some of its possible components are described in [93]. Special methodological problems can arise by the facts that DCs tend to keep function-relevant informations secret, see TEFFT [129] who, however, does not deal with methodological problems: some aspects are considered in [88] and in MÜLLER/SCHÖN/THOBER [97]. We will not deal further with these problems here.

At this point we will focus on one aspect, namely the methodological consequences of rapid structural change in LSUs. We have seen that, with a growing productivity, Y is more and more completely determined by Y_{DC}. Thus, great methodological impacts must stem from the fact that structural change is frequent in DCs. In the project HSDMEL it could be proven that in at least one DC of the project region a structural rupture happened every year. Let a *structural rupture* be defined as a change by which a relevant variable disappears, or emerges, or if a parameter function changes its basic structure, e.g. its degree n in $Y = f(X^n)$. In an extreme case, DCs emerge or disappear completely within one time period, for instance, if there happens to be a bankruptcy of an economic DC. If structural ruptures of DCs have heavy impacts on Y and if no meta-theories on structural ruptures of DCs exist then the corresponding model must be revalidated. To perform this needs some time. As a consequence, a real-time-problem of a special type appears in the social sciences. Real-time-problems usually refer to the speed of calculating certain terms (for instance, the position of a rocket or a pollutant cloud). This is called real-time-computing. In the case of LSU modelling, however, the problem of *real-time-modelling* arises: model results should not refer to a system outmoded due to structural ruptures. Thus, a technology of *Rapid Modelling* (RM) is desirable. We will now analyse whether there can be scale-orders of DC numbers in an LSU under consideration where even the most rapid RM-technology has to fail systematically.

For this purpose, let the number of DCs involved in the generation of Y be denoted by n. Let p_i be the probability that a structural rupture in DC_i happens at least one time per year and let us posit that the arithmetic mean $p = \frac{1}{n}\sum_{i=1}^{n} p_i$ is a valid description. Furthermore, structural ruptures in different DCs shall be stochastically independent, though this implies a considerable simplification. Then the binomial model can be adopted and it holds for 1 year:

$$W(1) = 1 - (1-p)^n \quad .$$

If Y is not artificially aggregated, but decomposed in a sub-system-specific, hierarchical and regional way, refer to [97], then, generally, n is not very large. If we posit (recall section 2.3)

$$n \quad = \quad 11hN_H sr$$
$$\text{with}$$
$$N_H : \quad = \quad \text{population size on hierarchy level} \quad H,$$
$$s, r \quad \in [0,1] \quad \text{are subsystem resp. regional parameters,}$$

then it holds:

$$W(1) = 1 - (1-p)^{11hN_H sr} \quad .$$

If we choose $p = .05$, which is too small, as we will prove subsequently, the following would result for the F.R.G., see tab. 3.2. Resulting from this it would appear to be fruitful to develop an RM-technology first for a community. If this should fail it would fail on higher levels of hierarchy *a fortiori*.

	F.R.G.	federal state[a]	county	community[b]
N_H	$60 \cdot 10^6$	$15 \cdot 10^6$	$1 \cdot 10^6$	$40 \cdot 10^3$
s	.01	.015	.05	.10
r	.10	.200	.33	1
n	66	50	18	5
$W(1 \mid p = .05)$	.97	.92	.60	.23

Table 3.2: Territorial regions and probability of structural rupture
a) scale order of NorthRhine Westfalia
b) scale order of the project region of HSDMEL

Let us assume that a future RM-technology is so effective that it permits a revalidating within 1 month of an invalidated model (possibly model system). Let us posit further that model results must remain valid at least 50% of the period considered. For a period of one year, therefore, it results that 6 structural ruptures is the maximum allowed. Then, the critical probability, at which the disturbing event appears, is

$$\alpha = 1 - W(6)$$

with

$$W(6) = \sum_{i=0}^{6} \binom{n}{i} p^i (1-p)^{n-i} \quad .$$

For $p = .05$ the result on the top (federal) hierarchical level $H = 1$ in the example of tab. 3.2 is:

$$\alpha = .047 \approx .05 \quad .$$

Since for lower hierarchical levels α turns out to be smaller the result is valid *a fortiori*. Thus, under the assumption made, with prob $=.05$ the RM-technology is not rapid enough.

$p = .05$ means that a structural rupture happens on average every 20 years. This, however, is very optimistic taking today's conditions into account. If we take 8 years as the average rupture free period (we shall return to this duration of 8 years in chap. 4.3.8) , $p = .125$ results. For this, it holds on level $H = 1$:

$$W(1) = .99985$$

and

$$\alpha = .73 \quad .$$

The dependence between the necessary validation speed and α is shown in tab. 3.3. So in a realistic scale order of structural change we have to develop an RM-technology which, under extreme circumstances, must be capable to

necessary validation speed in months per structural rupture	α
1.70	.590
1.50	.440
1.33	.310
1.20	.195
1.09	.114
1.00	.057

Table 3.3: Validation speed of RM-technology und probability of its failure

validate whole model systems within one month, if we wish to restrict the failure probability to approximately 5%.

Surely, this aim could only be achieved if DCs were coupled online with the RM-technology software systems. Disregarding aspects of privacy protection and oligarchic strategies of keeping data secret, which argue against such a solution, it would demand a financing that would presumably lead to at least one new **PT** in the operation field of the RM-technology. By this, the structural rupture problems would become self-referential. If that would entail the oligarchization of science, which seems to be highly plausible, this would arrive finally at models validated **PT**-strategically. Such facts can be observed throughout, for instance, in politically predetermined experts' behavior. The reflexions made here, however, go beyond such a pragmatic dimension in suggesting that 'objective' social science, (in the meaning of absence of power-strategical research manipulation) is impossible at least on the top (of the macro-) level. Thus, an impossibility theorem perhaps is hidden behind this problematique. I think there is no alternative other than to formulate theories on the level of structural ruptures, refer to GROSSMANN [38].

3.1   Gender relations and scientific bias

As shown in the section about population, the family is the elementary social unit at the micro level. Herein, the relation between the sexes is fundamental. Findings from primate research permit the following generalization: Primates are predominantly polygyneously organized, males compete for females, and a hierarchy of sexual privileges exists; females prefer dominant males. Though interesting deviations of this model are observable, this can be regarded as the average case.

It is undecided, however, whether these findings can be transferred to *homo sapiens.* In particular no simple connection between the organization of sex relations and social sex dominance (matri and patrilineality resp.) seems to exist. It is true that societies examined up to now, across all levels of 'development' (from tribes to civilized states), are predominantly organized polygyn and patrilineal, but there is a series of interesting exceptions, as described for instance by JANNSEN-JURREIT [57]. Evidently, and this requires further research, the organizational forms of the relations between the sexes are of great variability in different 'cultures' and in the course of time, see e.g. GREELEY [36].

However, as high as the variability may be, some features and structures of the organization of gender relations are evidently invariant for long time periods:

(1) Males are more aggressive than females,
(2) in patrilineal societies females prefer dominant males;
    in societies with a class structure this means
    hat females prefer males from higher classes
    ("Cinderella effect").

As to the Cinderella effect under the aspect of class-specific mobility see LENSKI [70]. If this effect is operationalized as follows:

Cinderella effect := women marry men with a higher school graduation
                     than her own,

interestingly this effect has decreased remarkably for West-German women born later than 1945, compared with women born before that date (crosstab analysis of the corresponding variables of the West-German NATIONAL SURVEY 1980). This could be an indicator of change in gender relations that requires careful further investigation. By means of the NATIONAL SURVEY 1980 the author could not make out a significant association coefficient between sex of children and class of their mothers and fathers (however, these properties are only indirectly indicated by the variables of the survey). For primates, however, a significant association coefficient has been proved between birth sex ratio and social rank, SIMPSON, SIMPSON [119].

From (2), DICKEMANN [19] derives a model for the preferential infanticide of daughters within upper classes in some societies. In general, the following should hold: If, because of sex-specific lineage children of a certain sex are preferred (e.g. sons in patrilineal and daughters in matrilineal social units), then children of the non-preferred sex are undesired. If, in addition, the short life expectancy of women, and the contraception effect from the combined influence of nursing practices and food quality, are considered it is plausible that especially the first-born children of undesired sex are discriminated or even killed. Hence, it has to be expected that in matrilineal social units first-born sons are killed and in partilineal social units first-born daughters. These killing practices [1] are indeed observed for many "societies".

---

[1] The suggestion may be interesting here, that the exclusive right to kill puppies of a wolf pack in ecological stress situations is by a dominant female.

(3) Essential features of civilizations are
the suppression of female sexual initiative
or orgiastic potency, SHERFEY [116],
as well as the predominance of formally
monogamous inter-sexual organizational forms.

male dominance	female dominance
female infanticide	male infanticide
monogamy	polygamy of woman
shyness of woman	erotic development of woman
sexual initiative of man	sexual initiative of woman

Table 3.4: Gender relations organizational types

The types in tab.   3.4 are extreme types that really only appear in mixed forms.

Relevant scientific explorations could be undertaken in 'matrilineal experiments' that seem to be performable in some 'developed' western civilizations. Evidence from such 'social experiments' is produced by the observation of subpopulations created in these experiments. The case discussed here is a matrilineal subpopulation which could have the following features:

- it consists predominantly of women,

- older women care for the children of women in the fertile age,

- the alimentation of children, pregnant women and old people is realized by property (see the next item) and by redistribution of revenues of the employed women,

- preferentially, property is left to the daughters,

- sexual initiative and erotic development of the women are positively sanctioned.

Special attention in the observation of such subpopulation must be directed to the exploration of new social and political organization forms.

In methodological respect the question has to be asked whether a research pertinent to this would, in the established disciplines, not be subject to a patrialistic bias, comp. BENARD/SCHLAFFER, FISHER, GILLIGAN, JANSSEN-JURREIT, [7,27,33,57]. At any rate, a combination of ethnology, anthropology and sexual research could be a research field of highest relevance. Presently, however, it is of only marginal importance in the established disciplines. Perhaps the 'women studies' will more intensively deal with this field of research.

The broad occupation with the problems discussed before is made here because, as already stated above, it cannot be excluded that operation principles of LSUs can remarkably vary dependent on gender relations. The case of KIK (civil movement "child in hospital") in Wiesbaden (F.R.G.) can be regarded as an evidence in favor of this. According to DILLMANN [20] the civil movement was unusually organized, hardly corruptible, did not develop internal **PTs** and was able to dissolve after relatively successful termination. The movement consisted predominantly of women.

3.2 The civilization process and social evolution

In the following sections some model-theoretical reflections and suggestions shall be pointed out. The model-theoretical reflections are preliminary; they will be extended in Vol. 2. The suggestions are to a certain extent speculative. However, speculations can also be fruitful, particularly in a field like social evolution where scientific knowledge is in its infancy.

3.2.1 Model-theoretical preliminary notes

In the following, the development of civilizations shall be regarded as an evolutionary process. In general, *evolution* shall denote the directional change in structures of a system of populations. *Directional* shall mean that principles can be found, for example energy flow maximization, by which the evolutionary process is driven. Emergence and decline of subpopulations are of special interest; 'sleeping' subpopulations can become dominant. Often such creative processes are synergetic effects of the combination of population system features, as is shown in the example of the decline of a population in the model MUE & SYN in Vol. 2. New structures can develop by contacts between members of different subpopulations. Historically, for example, this has repeatedly been the case with contacts between different cultures.

Today it is common to subsume the change of structures under the term *morphogenesis*. Morphogenetic processes can be precisely analyzed e.g. by methods of *cellular automata*. If the analysis of these morphogenetic processes shows that structures establish borders towards other structures by obeying certain rules in doing so, this is called a system generation process which, recently, under the term of *autopoiesis* was the subject of system-theoretical considerations, see ZELENY, LUHMANN [139,140,75]. We will not discuss the question of the autopoeitic character of social units ('systems') but will confine ourselves to examine the structural changes of population features. Should a change of relevant structures happen this may be called *evolutive branching* (in the case of two emerging properties *bifurcation*). The identification and analysis of such branchings is of central importance for

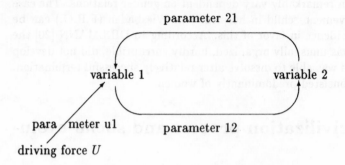

Figure 3.1: Signal flow diagram of a system

the understanding of civilization processes, because often in such instances,
'developmental advancements' take place.

Topologically, a branching can be described as follows. Let the state
space S contain all possible combinations of the realizations of the features
of interest to the researcher. Generally, in the case of complex populations,
as for example civilizations, S is high-dimensional. Let the number of these
features be denoted by n. Thus, at each moment considered, these n features
realize a certain combination. If, for example, we consider both features size
P and the total monthly income Y in the subpopulation of catholics, the
following combinations can appear:

$$
\begin{aligned}
(P,Y)_{t=1} &= (30 \cdot 10^6, 60 \cdot 10^6) \\
(P,Y)_{t=25} &= (25 \cdot 10^6, 68 \cdot 10^6) \\
(P,Y)_{t=6327} &= (3 \cdot 10^3, 3 \cdot 10^4)
\end{aligned}
$$

Notice, that catholics have been regarded as subpopulation and not as a variable as is often done, misleadingly, in empirical social science. In principle, if
the interdependencies between the features and the driving forces are known,
the realization combinations during time can be stated. This motion in the n-
dimensional state space is called the *trajectory* of the process. *Driving forces*
are those terms which, theoretically, enable the features to move. As a rule
they are outside influences, i.e. no interrelations with the features considered
are specified such as energy input from the sun.

The manner in which these driving forces are effective and how the interdependencies between the features are characterized, is stated by causal
parameters, see fig. 3.1. If features and parameters are fixed, a certain trajectory results for each driving force influence. Since the driving forces are

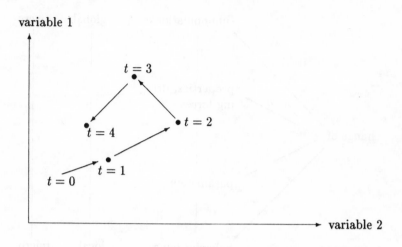

Figure 3.2: Trajectory of a system

subject to certain restrictions not every point of the n-dimensional space can be reached by the trajectories. The remaining partial space is called the *state space*. A trajectory of two features is shown in fig. 3.2 exemplary. Let us assume that civilizational processes can be characterized by trajectories that are at least over a certain time period [2] governed by certain rules, producing motion figures like that of fig. 3.2 showing an inward directed spiral. Let these be called *behavior figures*. If in certain state space areas such behavior figures can be identified, then the object examined is said to behave *locally ordered*, if not, it is said to behave *locally chaotic*. Behaviors that are locally ordered can be *globally chaotic*. Although these local- global-phenomena are not as yet completely understood they seem to be one of the keys for a deeper insight into the operation of civilizations. Order and stability ought not to be confused. An outward directed spiral describes an instable operation, although it is an identifiable behavior figure.

3.2.2   Levels of civilizational structural change

Now, we will consider four levels of structural change, ordered hierarchically, due to the extent that the object under consideration is affected by this

---

[2]The physical time itself is an operational construct, hence a theoretic feature. However, we will not probe further into the problems connected therewith.

change, see fig.   3.3.   A special monograph would be necessary to enable

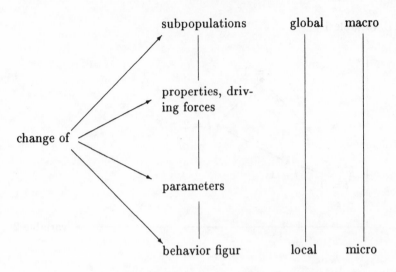

Figure 3.3: Hierarchy of structural change

elaboration of this hierarchy precisely. The differentiation between variables and subpopulations, especially, would be laborious having regard to the broad conceptual imprecision in the social sciences.

Here, we will confine ourselves to the rough definition of a *subpopulation* as being an accumulation of social units or individuals whose activities differ systematically and basically from those of other subpopulations in at least one of the relevant operational fields (e.g. generative reproduction, production, consumption, power and privilege). Features which in this manner stipulate subpopulation formation, are called *subpopulative features*. For example, gender is presumably, without exception, such a subpopulative feature.

Structural change on the top level means that subpopulations emerge or disappear. The associated elements on the lower hierarchical levels emerge or disappear accordingly. From a topological view, entire (possibly high-dimensional) parts of state spaces emerge or disappear in these cases. New social classes, or confessions, can be examples of this type of structural change. We have to take into consideration that serious sequential problems will arise by such branchings that open or close partial spaces. Future developments (trajectory courses) become possible or are ruled out by these changed behavior spaces.

The qualitative change of the non-subpopulative features being considered and driving forces is located on the second level from above. In extreme events, features or driving forces also disappear or emerge in such cases. Thus, this case is not considerably different from that of the subpopulative structural change. Examples are new technologies, changing forms of settlement etc.. Such changes can initiate subpopulative structural changes. We have to note, however, that fig. 3.3 should not be mistaken for a causal diagram.

Both forms of structural change are accompanied by research problems affecting all aspects of the research process that are hard to solve. Our present research instruments are designed predominantly to examine a set of properties in a *constant* structural frame.

However, regarding the next hierarchical level, there appeared within the last decades some approaches by which trajectories in the case of variable parameters can be examined. This type of structural change concerns the change in operational mechanisms. A change in contraception behavior is an example of this type. The reaction of the trajectory on these changes can be examined by the systematic variation of parameters, which is also one research aim of catastrophe theory. A specially difficult case which normally belongs to the aforementioned second level is that of a structural change affecting the *existence* of a causal relation.

However, even if all three stated structures are invariant, 'sudden' new behavioral figures can appear in the case of non-linear coupling of features. If certain characteristics combine, a qualitatively different development can be initiated. Let this be called *critical combinations of features*. Because each point in the state space corresponds to one combination of features, there can be *critical zones* in the state space. If a trajectory reaches such a zone, even insignificantly small variations are often sufficient to create the transition to another behavior figure. These effects are called *synenergetic* HAKEN [41], see also WEIDLICH/HAAG [135]. One could also say that such zones are *locally chaotic*. Such a process is shown in fig. 3.4. In fig. 3.4, the spiral first turns inward, then outward. In model MUE & SYN in Vol. 2 it is shown how a population rapidly declines owing to such a synergetic effect. The modelled social unit had stayed in a critical zone for some time without dramatic change. The reason for this is the 'good-natured' state of a driving force, climate in this case. If, however, one of the usual climatic fluctuations occurred, a rapid decline of population resulted, while a comparable climatic fluctuation in a former population state outside the critical zone did not have this dramatic consequence. Max WEBER and Gunnar HEINSOHN take the view that the emergence of capitalism can be considered as the consequence of a synergetic effect from the historical and so far unique coincidence of capital and free workers in England.

Branchings at a level can induce branchings at another, or at the same level. Branchings can also concern several branches simultaneously. If morphogenetic self-referentiality is ascribed to social units, these social systems can reach such a high complexity that one must wonder whether these systems should not be characterized by an ubiquitary branching. Finally, their state space would have to be overcrowded with critical zones, so that at

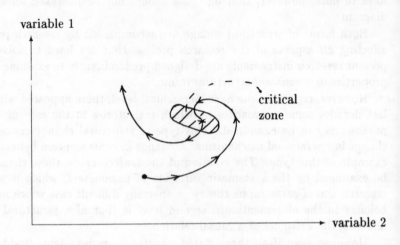

Figure 3.4: Structural rupture in a critical zone

sometime a situation of global chaos must arise. However, we have at present so little knowledge about the operation of social units that we cannot make clear statements on it. The former reflections are rather to be understood in a metaphoric sense.

3.2.3   Civilization development as evolutionary process: some speculations

In the following, we will speculatively try to make some reflections on civilization development.

A civilization tree

In particular, the branchings are of interest to us. The development between two temporally neighbouring branchings shall be called a *civilizational path*. In the most global consideration, civilization can be regarded as an evolutionary process that has branches of various types (civilizational subpopulations), for instance, the Chinese or the middle American type. Within these types further branchings appear, for example the Jewish or the Roman type within the occidental branch. Thus, we arrive at a tree structure as shown in fig. 3.5. Since we know little about the origins of the paths, they have been excluded in fig. 3.5.

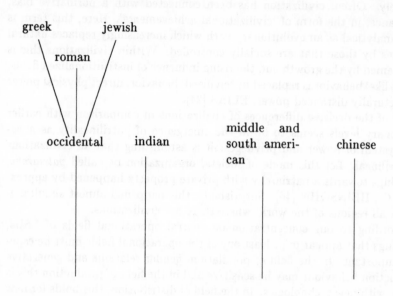

Figure 3.5: Civilization tree

If we go far enough back the selection in favor of cerebral enlargement can be identified as the prehistoric original branching in social evolution. It starts about 5 mio. B.C., presumably in East Africa; as an interesting hypothesis see TANNER [127]. The first branchings concerning organized human societies took the form of the emergence of hunter and gatherer societies (approx. 1 mio. B.C.). The next global branching referred to the beginning of a settled life in the form of horticultural societies: a prominent hypothesis is that a large part of these societies was matrilineally organized. The horticultural epoch lasted until approx. 10.000 B.C. The next global branching appeared with the emergence of agricultural societies and lasted until approx. 1700 A.D., with manifold internal differentiations. The transition to industrial societies is the next global branching. The civilizational path here seems to have reached a critical zone and many indications show that the occidental civilizational path has been in a new branching situation in present decades.

Further branchings seem to have happened in the 3rd and 11th century. At any rate, the duration of a civilizational path from one global to another global branching decreases in orders of magnitude by powers of ten. This would be no surprise, if the above hypothesis is presumed to be right that in the course of time critical zones are more and more narrowly arranged in the state space.

Up to now, we talked about *civilization* without defining this concept more concretely. Often, civilization has been connected with a normative bias, for instance, in the form of 'civilizational achievements'. Here, this term is purely analytical as an evolutionary path which increasingly replaces natural influences by those that are socially controlled. Within civilizations this is accompanied by the growth and the rising influence of institutionalized fields. 'Nature-like' behavior is replaced by 'civilized' behavior, direct physical power by structurally distanced power, ELIAS [24].

One of the decisive differences of civilizations in comparison with earlier evolutionary levels seems to lie in the emergence of patrilineality as a *political* system of power and privileges: it is astonishing that all civilizations are patrilineal. Let this mode of societal organization be called *patriarchy*. Branchings towards a patriarchy with private property happened by approx. 1500 B.C., HEINSOHN [46]. Surprisingly, this happened almost simultaneously in all regions of the world where there are civilizations.

According to our concentration on central operational fields of LSUs, branchings that appear in at least one of the operational fields must be especially important. In the field of population, gender relations and generative reproduction behaviour may be sensitive and in the field of production this is the case with new technologies. In the field of distribution, this holds for new distribution mechanisms (for instance debt or money), in the field of power additional hierarchical levels, just to state a few. Global branchings must then be characterized by the fact that structural change happens in several of these fields simultaneously, or in rapid succession. As an example for this simultaneity, the beginning of the industrial society coincides with a new definition of marriage as the institutionalization of romantic love. Further examples can be seen in the decline in the birth-rate caused among other things by contraceptive methods, the emergence of a new class of women since the mid-fifties being indicators of a branching in the population field, immediately followed by the third industrial 'revolution'.

A new subpopulation of women

For the first time in the some ten thousand years of civilizational development of human societies, there is a large age group of women, namely the age span of approx. 35 to 50 in which there are women who on the average are

- physically sound,

- enjoy a high life expectancy,

- relieved from the task of child rearing (whether because there are no or few children, because the children have reached maturity, have already left the family, or because the task of child rearing has been delegated to institutions or other persons),

- in a position to provide for themselves and are mobile,

- and this is a particularly important factor: able to take measures of contraception.

If we add that in the age between 30 and 40 the personality formation (*individuation*, C.G. JUNG) comes to a certain ending and the professional career as a rule takes its course continually on the reached level in the stated age phase between 35 and 50 years, so that influential positions(if existent) are held in this age phase, there are − perhaps for the first time in the history of civilized societies − millions of self-confident and relatively independent women. It has to be considered that this change is a very recent phenomenon starting approx. 25 years ago. Thus, while for several thousands of years, because of their low life expectancy nearly without exception women did not survive the 'nest building phase', suddenly there are now millions of individualized female personalities. The scale order of this new female population segment alone can, due to the resulting mass effect, cause a branching in the evolution of civilized human societies. Taking political elections in the F.R.G. as an example, approx. 30 % of these women are sufficient to keep a party above the 5 %-margin. Perhaps it is not accidental that environment protection and womens' liberation appear together, that the party of the 'Greens' show an especially high female organizational content. There are indications that there is a new subpopulation of women also from an institutional view, e.g. in self-care-groups, in political parties (in the F.R.G. especially with the Greens), at high schools (women studies), just to state some of them. Moreover, the growing number of petitions for divorce lodged by women, and cultural-artistic trends [3] can be taken as evidence in favor of the stated female subpopulation emergence. Just the indications of cultural-artistic kind direct to the hypothesis of SHERFEY [116]: that an erotic overcharge of the mass of men who are traditional sexual partners of women in the stated age phase is added to the five mentioned factors. From this, a not uncomplicated age relation between men and women can result: while women in the 'nest building phase', hence in the age of approx. between 18 and 35, prefer older men, it could be possible that they rather prefer younger men in the age phase between 35 and 50.

If we follow SHERFEY, all these factors together would lead to a dramatic structural change of civilizations which are, without exception, patriarchalistic after all. Can something like a collective reaction 'of the patriarchy' be possible? Will this be intimidation by wars or threat of war, so to speak the dig out of the symbolic spear (phallic symbol!), a 'men's rite' in some simple societies? Or does the 'mathematization of the society' by 'artificial

---

[3] We can think, for instance, of the championship of voluntary exercise in ice skating (bolero of Ravel) 1983/84, the fascination of some movie roles, e.g. Carmen (the erotically initiative, men-annihilating woman which was also the theme of both the East and West favorites in olympic women skating competition in 1988) or Gudrun Landgrebe in her movie role as the "flamed woman" (witch burning), "the erotic symbol of the 80th" (HÖRZU) and certain make-up idols.

intelligence' lead back to a durable dominance of men? In the present electronic innovation process 'artificial' is talked about, as it seems, in contrast to natural intelligence.

Let us speculate in a more feuilletonistic form, that there would be differences between men and women with regard to brain architecture and information processing, and this is what some recent findings of endocrine and brain research are pointing to especially in regard to mathematic thinking. Incontestably, computer intelligence and artificial intelligence in their foreseeable forms have much to do with mathematics. Let us assume that artificial intelligence could indeed be realized up to some degree. Would this be the highest form of the patriarchy regarding the enforcement of masculine information processing forms, or would this be the transition to a totally new form of society, a 'society of machines'? Is bio-technology finally directed to bringing genetic reproduction from nature dependence to the control of technical civilization? Is the triumphant march of the patriarchy to be continued here, too?

Competition between civilizational paths

All aspects as stated stem predominantly from the occidental civilizational path. This creates the question of the differences between civilizational paths. The South-American (e.g. Incas) disappeared as the result of the contact with the occidental civilization. It is a long time since the Indian branch played any role. Within that of the occidental there are two different paths, the Jewish-Greek-Christian and the Islamic. Presently it looks like the former being the dominant. Indisputably, this branch has been the harbinger of technical civilization for some hundred years, see also LAUE [65]. In that path, the world-wide standards of technique and science are fixed. The intellectual élite recruits significantly from the Jewish subpopulation, and this is evident from the volume of Nobel Prices distributed, see also FISHMAN [28]. DRIESSLER (personal communication) propounded the theory, that this is the consequence of a coevolutionary process: due to their persecution for centuries the Jews have systematically been selected in favor of a high rate of intelligence. [4] Therefore, the two dominant existent civilizational paths can roughly be characterized as Christian-Jewish and Chinese. I would like to make a conjecture that the decades to come will be marked by the 'struggle' of these two civilizational paths and the contact between both could lead to a massive branching. Is that the reason why mention is made of a pacific era: Can such interaction effects in a prototype manner already be made out in the U.S. today? How the super power Soviet Union will behave in this branching, and what of West Europe?

---

[4]That such genetic selection mechanisms work can be seen in the Joh.S. Bach family: Having confined their marriage partners to those possessing high musical talent it resulted after a period of 200 years that all children of Joh.S. Bach were musical geniuses.

It has already become clear that the contact between different civilizational paths can be an important initiator of branchings. There are many examples for this in history. However, this is not at all the only provocator of branchings. Now as before – despite all efforts, especially in occidental civilization branches – natural disasters like climate fluctuations, germs etc. are provocators of branchings. Here, special importance is attached to cosmic catastrophies by collision with big meteorites. Indeed, this is a seldom appearing event, but the effect on branching can be extraordinary large. HEINSOHN maintains that a cosmic catastrophy by 1500 B.C. (perhaps the Deluge) initiated massive civilizational branchings on the whole world which is documented by excavations, fossil records and geological evidence.

In this connection, the growing capability of civilizations to initiate branchings themselves is interesting. A prominent example is the ability to provoke nuclear catastrophies. Actually war is an initiator of branchings and evolutional accelerator on the top level (subpopulative branchings). It is not said for nothing that war is the father (!) of everything. This self-referential structural change raises fundamental methodological and epistemological questions, which I have referred to elsewhere, [87], chap. 2.2.2.

Here, I see three solutions which possibly complement each other:

1. Cognitions are only able relative to a civilizational path, i.e. the trajectory can only be determined between two neighbouring branchings. This is presupposing that enough time is available in such a path to perform the necessary analyses. If the branchings are too close together, objective cognition becomes impossible (recall section 3.2.1).

2. The self-referentiality leads to the designability of trajectories by social units themselves. By this, knowledge is constructed, too. This may work on a local level: for instance, in such a way that deciders who determine the behavior of subjects, subsequently forecast behavior determined that way. Globally, however, this 'solution' arrives at an antinomy: the constructors of the trajectories have to know the determinants of their own actions. Since the global trajectory must be constructed and thus the stated determinants also, the behavior of the constructors must have to be defined by other constructors, etc., etc.. Of course, the subsequent arbitrariness of the trajectory can be hidden from the dominated people. This, however, is a cold comfort for the constructors. They can never be sure whether they themselves will not fall into the 'trap they built'. However, as long as they are in a position to shift the consequences to the subordinates they don't have to worry about that possibility, and perhaps they themselves will not be able to distinguish ideology from truth. Because of lack of alternative information they are safe to follow this way as true and to define this ideology. The constructors can, nevertheless, not be sure that their trajectory would not end globally in a zone where disadvantages cannot be shifted to others, and, hence also would be affected. It becomes obvious that we must recognize the bitter truth that we do not know enough about ourselves.

3. There are structures that are withdrawn from the self-referential manipulation, so-called deep structures. If these structures are evolutionary relevant, one must be in a position to explore knowledge about such principles. In certain respects an evolutionary 'program' proceeds which cannot be stopped from the inside. Then it would be a question whether developments appearing as branchings are in fact not branchings in reality, but that within them evolution is forced back to the programmed path. [5] Thus, evolution would irrevocably aim at a certain zone, for instance, a maximal number of secondary contexts [88], that perhaps can be related to maximal possible energy flow. The final state of a nuclear catastrophe or a transition to a machine intelligence is also imaginable. It is an interesting question whether artificial intelligence and biotechnology are in a position to change deep structures and whether this is admitted in the human system.

Presumably, a combination of the three solutions will render possible an adequate analysis of civilizational processes: deep structures are existent (3), which only change very slowly (1), whereby in the course of the civilizational process the capability to construct trajectories rises (2). From an epistemological point of view it appears of high priority to regard deep structures as explorational orientation and model kernels.

The knowledge about deep structures has a high value, because if deep structures are existent there is nothing better to do than orient to them. With growing self-referentiality, especially, the opinion can be raised that everything is realizable. However, programmes that ignore deep structures have to fail. If we consider that, in critical zones, small deviations can lead to a crash of the system and if we presume that critical zones in the course of the civilizational evolution are overcrowding the state space (recall section 3.2.2), the explosiveness of the failing of those programmes becomes feasible.

The maintained existence of deep structures refers us back again to the beginning of this chapter. If these structures are existent it could also be fruitful to use the corresponding knowledge for coping with the self-referentiality problem that the social operation of *homo sapiens* is examined by *homo sapiens*. However, the self-referentiality problem is so basic that it cannot be discussed within the scope of this book. Previous attempts to tackle these problems have always ended in endless regressions, antinomies etc. We do not propose to deal with the mathematic discussion on this theme (for instance the type-logic of RUSSEL, the undecidability theorem of GÖDEL).

In connection with social-epistemological self-referentialities we have to deal with the question of how social units cope with these problems, i.e. it could be interesting to tackle these problems evolution-theoretically by referring to deep structures. In the beginning of this chapter   intuitively a

---

[5]Is the knowledge about this evolutionary program recorded in the Torah? Do the Jews as the chosen (selected) people most consistently realize this program? Has Jesus possibly in vain died against this program? Will the program be stopped only by (cosmic) catastrophies – as described in the Relevations of St. John?

relation to the doublings of labor productivity π_A was posited. For the social coping with the self-referentiality problematique a connection could possibly be set up as is displayed in tab. 3.5. From this table, some structural con-

π_A	quota of DC-determination of social processes	time approx.	level of self-referentiality
2	.167	2,000 B.C.	1 – begin of historical records
4	.500	1,700 A.D.	2 – begin of sociology
8	.750	1,980 A.D.	3 – begin of artificial intelligence
16	.85	?	4 – begin of ?

Table 3.5: Labor productivity, DC-determination share and self- referentiality levels

clusions can be drawn. If we define **PT** formation ('institutionalization') and its influence on social 'operations' as an indicator of the state of traditional civilizational evolution, the second column shows that for π_A values greater than 8, this process enters the saturation phase, while according to column 1 the technical progress still continues unbroken.

Thus, the evolutionary path that started in the emergence of a settled society comes to an end here and a pure technical evolutionary path possibly begins. Anticipating section 4.2 it is also possible that in reaching the saturation zone, **PT** systems enter a turbulent zone in which different developmental paths can be taken, e.g. system collapse or phase transfer into a strong technologically oriented development.

At present, we can only speculate on the development beyond $\pi_A = 8$. One reason for this is that it is not clear where the final limit of labor productivity has to be drawn.

Just as with the perspective of a human control over technical evolution, as well as for the development of artificial intelligence itself, such speculations could be fruitful, as far as they can be substantiated: as an example see LEM [67]. Perhaps wise principles on intelligent information processing are existent that can be copied from the mechanisms of information processing in natural brains (e.g. of the dolphin or *homo sapiens*). We have to notice that, with a growing DC-share in the determination of social processes, the degree of designability of social development becomes greater and leads to an obligation to take careful advantage of these design capabilities. To answer these questions the pragmatological philosophy on how it has been developed by STACHOWIAK [122,123], or ALISCH [2] is perhaps of high relevance. In our context the question arises as to how this can be integrated with the operation of **PTs** and **PT** systems. Viewing the fact that the occidental civilization presently lives in the neighbourhood of $\pi_A = 8$, a comprehensive and effective discussion seems at any rate pressing.

3.3   Neglect of substantial orientation

As pointed out in the introduction, this book focuses on the question of how far a pure structural approach is useful, i.e. to what extent the dynamics of LSUs can be described by the indicators

$$\Omega_t = \{(\alpha_t, V_t, N_t, D_t, E_t) \mid t \in T\}.$$

Thus, in this approach an abstraction is made from substantial aspects of outcomes that **PTs** furnish to their clients. Especially is it presumed that formation, development and decline of **PTs** would be to such a far-reaching extent dependent on structural determinants that substantial aspects could be neglected. This means that operation fields can arbitrarily be defined, unless structural restrictions are absent, which means, for instance, that a sufficient number of clients and a large enough surplus are available. In doing so, it is implicitly presumed irrelevant that **PTs** settle with priority in certain operation fields and that relevant determinants for the dynamics of LSUs stem from the features of these operation fields.

If the process of LSU differentiation is considered, at least two operation fields seem to exist which could falsify this approach: religion and military. Before entering into a closer inspection of these two fields let us recall some principles of simple societal organization and of primary contexts (PRIM).

3.3.1   Family, territory and primary contexts

We may presume that *homo sapiens* organizes himself socially at least in the form of familial social units in nearly all developing phases and independent of natural or social environmental structures. At first glance, the Kibbuz seems to be an exception which, however, becomes relativated in a differentiated analysis, TALMON [126]. Solitary males or females, celibate groups etc. may be neglected as being exceptions. It is uncertain whether 'far' developed (a clarification of this term follows) 'societies' could be imaginable without such social units. At any rate, in our consideration, families can be considered as *basic* social units; basic means here that this form of social organization appears in all cultural and civilizational variants. Consequently, family is the most fundamental necessary condition for the social existence of *homo sapiens*.

Principally, families are organized face to face. Hence, according to the notations in section 2.3, the following proposition can be stated:

Proposition 4 *As regards the history of his social development homo sapiens has lived predominantly in primary contexts and has been socialized there; his behavioral repertoire is oriented to a life in such contexts.*

Civilization can now be understood as the successive development of non-primary social contexts by an ever increasing 'restrain' of primary contexts, comp. [88], ELIAS [24]. The more a civilization is called developed, the more comprisingly these non-primary social contexts [6] have developed.

A further feature of social units, which is apparently invariant across all cultures and civilizations, is its territorial behavior, GODELIER [34]. Social units demand a territory for themselves. In the most simple case, a night's lodging or housing is obvious. Certainly, territories like village areas, hunting and gathering grounds are not so obvious, but can be found throughout in simple social units. Even pure nomadic tribes have as a rule fixed migrational routes. However, a territory must not appear exclusively in a topographic form. Quite often, social territories can also be identified, for instance, the family or the tribe in simple social units. As to Primates, an example of a social territory is the harem of a pasha.

For our considerations it is of special interest that social units establish demarcations against other social units. Palisades, drains, poles decorated with birds' feathers are examples of topographic marks; descent rules, traditional costumes and skin decoration are examples for social markings. Thus, each social unit constitutes itself a social territory.

We will summerize as follows:

Proposition 5 *At least one topographic and at least one social territory belongs to each social unit; social units delineate their territories from each other.*

A further apparent invariant feature of large social units is the existence of hierarchies, comp. BOULDING, E. [11]. Some mechanisms that contribute to the durability of this structural feature, are stated in [88]. Hierarchies are characterized by the (voluntary or enforced) subordination of individuals or social units to other individuals or social units on a higher hierarchical level. It can be assumed that this order relation is consistent (e.g. its transitivity is fulfilled) at least locally, i.e. in the neighbourhood of a hierarchical level under consideration. Summarizing:

Proposition 6 *Large social units are hierarchically organized.*

---

[6]If we presume that in the mass of people, women are centered stronger in primary contexts, a restrain of primary context importance must entail a curtailment of women's influence; this is a further support of the argumentation of SHERFEY [116]; comp. also PARKER/PARKER [108].

3.3.2   Military and war

From the connection of propositions 5 and 6 we can immediately make the following conclusion:

Lemma 1 *For each hierarchy an associated territory can be identified. LSUs are thus characterized by territorial-specific rules of dominance.*

Concerning the general behavioral relevance of hierarchies for male primates, McGUIRE et al. [81] furnishes some interesting findings. Monkeys of the same species living in close proximity, but in biotopes of different characteristics, displayed strikingly different hierarchical structures and different territorial behavior, LAWICK-GODALL [66]: Monkeys in the savanna show stricter hierarchies, a stronger male dominance and an offence and defence behavior organized in 'combat units' as well as a more differentiated use of instruments in comparison with members of their species that live in the less stressing biotopes of the trees.

KRUUK [63] compares neighboured hyenas of the same species, one part living in the Serengeti, the other part in the Ngorongoro- crater. The crater can be regarded as a naturally limited territory. The hyenas in the crater show a strong territorial behavior with 'frontier patrols' and aggressive reaction towards hyenas of foreign territories, as well as a relatively strict subordination of males to females. With the hyenas of the Serengeti, these structures and behaviors can only faintly, or not at all, be detected. One is inclined to call the Ngorongoro-hyenas 'resident' and the Serengety-hyenas 'nomadic'.

The connection between being 'settled' and aggression is also underlined by SCHMIDTBAUER [114]. After this evidence from animal behavior research we must raise the question as to what extent such 'human like' structures and features phylogenetically existed long before the emergence of *homo sapiens*; identical EIBL-EIBESFELD [22], who indicates territorial behavior as an archaic factor.

Social units that show the features of the last three propositions must be autocatalytically succesfull against social units without these features ("Kain slays Abel"). If, according to the aforementioned findings, a disposition in favour of these features is assumed, it would be sufficient that at some time even without systematic motivation a settled social unit emerges to spread this type of organization over *TERRA*.

Up to now, it does not seem clear in which way different organizational forms of social units are connected with gender dominance (e.g. nomadic vs. settled). Speculatively it could be assumed that the female endocrine system reacts differently (e.g. with respect to specific nest-building strategies) in different social settings, for instance comparing a settled with a nomadic setting.

A functionalistic derivation of the patriarchate from the ubiquity of war as it is done by HARRIS [43] is, apart from substantial problems, unsatisfying from research logic considerations: since matrilineal tribes also make war, at least two different kinds of war have to be distinguished: this distinction would, however, not appear before, but in the sequel of patriarchal organizations. More interesting under this aspect, even if speculative, are the constructivistic reflections of HEINSOHN [46] who cites an abundance of further literature.

Superiority is directly connected with disposition power over objects or social units or individuals. In simple social units without notable surplus and with polygyneous structure and subordination of women, the disposition power of men extends, besides tools, especially to women and children. As a rule, militant competition by men for women can be observed here. As soon as such social units have reached a certain size and begin to overcrowd territorially, they will, by virtue of the combination of propositions 5 and 6, be in a permanent state of war. Often the competition for women will be the cause of violent quarrels. This can indeed be observed, see e.g. several contributions in CHAGNON/IRONS [16], as to the importance of the abduction of women see HERODOT [49, p. 2] and HUNKE [55].

In the Murdock-sample, we find four societies only to whom war is unknown, see also BOULDING, K.E. [12]. All civilizations are extremely aggressive. Matrilineal societies often practice another kind of war (no intra-societal campaigns but only campaigns against foreign tribes). However, in its violence it is hardly inferior to wars of patrilineal tribes. It has already been mentioned above that war and military promote the patriarchate, HARRIS [43]. Perhaps this is an essential cause for the fact that all civilizations are patriarchal. To my knowledge, however, it has not as yet been demonstrated, why it should be impossible that matrilineal dominance strategies could lead to a matriarchal civilization.

At any rate, we can state that war is a universal operational field and that military **PT** structures arise with priority.

3.3.3 Religion

Societies without religious rites and personnel specialized in these rites are not known to me. This holds for both, matrilineal and patrilineal societies. Societies near the subsistence minimum 'afford', besides a chieftain, a male or female specialized in rites (e.g. a shaman). In times of emergency religious rites and the corresponding institutions gain in importance. The chieftain can still be regarded as (in simple societies as quasi-) **PTR**. However, merely from the structural determinants in Ω it is difficult to elicit why, above all, just the religious operation field is the preserve of hierarchically outstanding personnel. The ubiquity of religiousness suggests a very 'deep', perhaps even a genetic embodiment. It could be the case that a highly complex brain becomes self-referential and that, endogenously, contingency arises from this. The uncertainty and fear evoked by this, especially in view of future-oriented decisions and expectancies, ask for fear reduction procedures. What we label religious rites can perhaps be traced back to this fear reduction effect. It is quite imaginable that operational equivalents, for instance science, see HARRIS [42, p. 546], emerge in the course of time. LEM [67] argues that from a certain level of complexity owing to self-referentiality, each intelligence makes itself an idea of God.

Perhaps further operation fields emerge with priority, e.g. education, health, old-age pensions, and possibly an importance ranking exists among them which, however, may vary in the course of time. Then, this ranking could for example determine the sequence or quotas of the allotment of surplus between these fields. As a result, specific distribution cycles and routines result, for instance, in public budgets. Budgets would then be representatives of a complex queuing distribution system. My analysis of the budget of a small town administration over the period of eight years confirmed the existence of such a structure.

4 Power territory structures and the operation of large-scale social units: attempt at a phenomenological description

In the last chapters we described the (occidental) civilizational process as the progressive replacement of natural structures by structures that are socially controlled. As far as organized control is concerned here it has been labelled as "secondary contexts" (SEC), [88]. Social control stemming from SEC is in particular oriented to social disturbing factors that are localized externally of SEC. Supposing the structures in "primary contexts" (PRIM) to be predominantly 'nature-like' (what must not apply in the case of an increasing determination by SEC, however), the civilizational principle is applied to society itself, comp. LUHMANN [74].

In SEC, **PTs** perform among other things the mentioned social control. Let this be designed as *political power* (more precise in [88]). SEC enlarges with growing production of virtual "heads", i.e. V, and in 3.1 it has been stated that organized behavior in an LSU would be determined from the **PT** sphere, i.e. by **PT** strategies, to an extent of V/P %. In the F.R.G., V/P amounted to approx. .75 in 1980. With regard to this it was concluded that

organized processes $Y(t)$ could as a rule be traced back to $Y_{DC}(t)$ (DC :=
decision centre) to an extent of 75 %, hence, that in the analysis

$$Y(t) = Y_{DC}(t) + Y_{MASS}(t)$$

only 25 % was produced by MASS. The necessary condition for the high
determination share of Y_{DC} is that the distribution of Y is strongly concentrated on few 'output generators'. Indeed, such extreme concentrations can
be found everywhere, whether in asset distribution, telephone fees (in 1987
in the F.R.G., the holders of 2 million commercial telephone lines paid 50 %
of the telephone charges) or the business concentration (in 1982 it reached
from 31 % in the alcohol industry up to 99 % in the type-writer industry –
being the percentage share of inland production of the three concerned leading industries, as quoted in DER SPIEGEL No. 47, 1985, p. 117), of energy
supply, of international debts – as concerns banks as well as debtor nations.
This list could, of course, be greatly extended.

Following 3.1 it would make sense to look for **PTs** and **PT** strategies in
order to describe, or to model, Y_{DC} for all such concentration phenomena. [1]
We will summarize as follows:

Proposition 7 *The development of an LSU is mainly dependent on developments in SEC. Behavior in SEC is predominantly constituted by the relations
between* **PTs**. *Consequently*
- is the development of LSUs above all dependent on **PT** *strategies,*
- can the development of LSUs above all be traced back to
operation mechanisms inside and between **PTs**.

In particular it follows that the operation of an LSU is dependent on the
operation of the corresponding **PT** sphere. The question now arises how the
operation of a **PT** sphere can be imagined. If, as described in the former
chapter, *operation* is understood as the rule-based transformation of inputs
into outputs, the crucial question is whether such an ensemble of **PTs** is
able to operate at all, or, whether chaos or non-functioning is existent or
threatening in this sphere.

In this chapter the above question will, in particular, be subject to a
phenomenological analysis. First, the local operation of one **PT** will be considered, then the operation of a **PT** system of an LSU. In this connection,
special attention is given to the local/global and to the micro/macro problems. In Vol. 2, we shall try to study some detail aspects by using simulation
models.

Such a descriptive analysis of social operation mechanisms is in the tradition of an anthropologic orientation that has been revitalized for the analysis

---

[1] Such an approach has a close reference to the élite research whose problems, in particular in the field of methodology, will not be dealt with here. For a draft of a corresponding
methodology, see [93]. A comparison of élite research methods is worked out by KER-
BER/FAVE [60].

of societies during the recent decades, e.g. by LENSKY [69], CARNEIRO [14], BOULDING [12]. Since strategical decision processes are of central importance in the **PT** sphere, the question can rise why in this book the wide field of normative decision and strategy research is excluded. Neglecting the epistemological problems of such a constructivism, as were stated in section 3.3, my opinion is that the impossibility theorem of ARROW [4] forces us onto the path of a descriptive orientation. For, after ARROW's proof, there is the imperative question: on grounds of which mechanisms do collectives operate, having realized that majority voting, consensus of opinion, welfare economics, discourse where masses of people are involved etc. etc. must be dropped as mechanisms as a consequence of the non-restrictive democracy assumptions of ARROW.

4.1 The micro and meso level

The description of the operation of a **PT** has to begin with its identification. For this purpose operational criteria are necessary. We defined a **PT** as an organized ensemble (we spoke about institutions in the widest sense) in which, predominantly, the mobilization, control and distribution of privileges is dealt with. According to this definition, a **PT** is always located in the redistribution sphere. An identifiable influence territory belongs to each **PT**. Often qua **PT** definition power, this influence territory is considered as an operation field to which outcomes of **PT** operation are defined as useful. To the extent to which **PT** structures are established in the LSU this definition is accepted and hence, the existence and necessity of performance orientation, pertinence impact power (*Sachzwang*) and the like. In the following we will briefly speak of a territory.

For the identification of a **PT** the redistribution aspect can be chosen. A sequential identification strategy can be derived from this. Obviously, in each territory persons must exist who have to execute **PT**-strategical decisions acting under prescribed policies from above, be it towards **PT** personnel or towards clients in the territory. This lowest level is to be designed with $SUB(m)$. In a first approximation we will start from a strict hierarchy. Then, in $SUB(m-1)$ decisions are made on $SUB(m)$ etc. It is equally obvious that a $SUB(1)$ must exist on the top. The exceptional case of a 'two rulers on the top' (*Doppelherrschaft*) leads to very complex relations and is not further elaborated here. As a rule, these m levels are organized in threefold levels as *hierarchical cones* and in the case that the cones do not overlap it must hold that:

$$m_j = 3\tau_j \qquad .$$

τ_j denotes the number of hierarchical levels in the global cone of the territory j. Thus, for each territory there is a global hierarchical cone in which a multiplicity of local hierarchical cones is embedded. An example would be the hierarchical cone of the educational territory reaching from the minister (level $k = 1$) to the teachers (level $k = \tau$). Non-overlapping means that $E(k)$ is 'superior' to $E(k + 1)$, $k = 1, ... \tau - 1$. A global cone can be imaginated as an arrangement of pyramids embedded into pyramids, where each pyramid consists of **PTRs** (E), sub-**PTRs** (S), and subordinates (U). Cones on the lowest level shall be called *operative cones*. In the case of overlapping, if for instance $S(k)$ takes the role of an $E(k)$ for a set of cones below $S(k)$, the relation becomes very complex. It becomes still more complex, if recursive relations like that as displayed in fig. 4.1 appear. In reality, however, we find

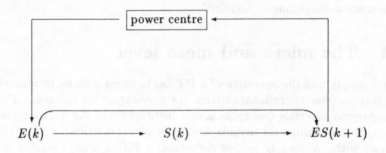

Figure 4.1: Recursive influence relation between hierarchy levels

as a rule non-overlapping threefold hierarchical cones so that we can confine ourselves to the analysis of these.

In the individual case it may be difficult to examine the actual decision structures so exactly that E, S and U can be identified. This is moreover complicated by the existence of informal **PT** structures. The case may appear that e.g. a secretary who perhaps formally belongs to U, is informally established in S. We will not deal with such methodological problems here: in [88] there are some reflections thereon under the key-word *Wallraffie*. At any rate, it is often laborious to identify privilege structures.

Let us assume in the following that local and global hierarchical cones of a territory were identified. With regard to several different territories, three levels of the functional analysis can be distinguished:

1. local cone in a global territorial cone (micro)
2. global cone in a territory (meso)
3. system of global cones in an LSU (macro).

The third aspect will be dealt with in the following section. Here, the micro and meso level shall be examined.

It is obvious to assume that the operation of a local cone is strongly dependent on its position in the global cone. A structure of three hierarchical levels seems to be typical: in this structure there are the 'operative' τ-cone, the middle and the 'leader cone'. In Vol. 2 in the model MUE & HIER, the hierarchy of the four politically defined regions of the F.R.G., i.e. communities, counties, federal state and federation, is examined. At this point, we will consider a typical low, middle and top cone.

4.1.1 The global hierarchy cone of an operation field

We will start with the global cone, because the local is strongly dependent on global operation. Recall fig. 2.3 and the existence and operation conditions of a **PT** as stated in section 2.3.1. Of high priority is a sufficient volume of surplus that is distributed on the territory j under consideration. In a first approximation it can be assumed that the stronger the **PTRs** of j are represented in the **PC** the higher is this share. In the following section we will return to this aspect. A surplus volume shall be called *sufficient* when, in the global cone j, the relative undisturbed ability for a durable mobilization, control and allocation of privileges can be secured. Let us call this *protection of **PT** stability*. We will reserve the case that j is affected by other global cones $j' \neq j$ until the following section. Here only internal operation mechanisms will be considered. In particular we will assume that competences are defined in a manner by which the performance of actors in j are legitimized.

The necessary surplus

The surplus volume necessary for j can be calculated from the demand B_j. This is composed from the contribution to the **PC** budget, which can be labelled the LSU *power protection contribution*, and the internal expenditure, thus

$$B_j = B_{ex_j} + B_{in_j} \qquad (4.1)$$

In turn, B_{in_j} is composed by performance costs towards the clients, personnel costs for E, S and U as well as internal power protection costs H_j, thus

$$B_{in_j} = S_j + P_j + H_j \qquad (4.2)$$

S_j can be related to the annual number of client contacts:

$$S_j = q_j^s K_j \sigma_j \qquad (4.3)$$

with

$q_j^s :$ = rate of clients number K_j, occurring per year

(where "s" indicates that 'performance costs' are meant

and not power protection(*Herrschafts*) costs),

$$q_j^s > 0, \text{mostly} \quad q_j^s \in (0,1].$$

$Kj :$ = number of clients in j,

$\sigma_j :$ = expenditure per client contact measured in $\mathcal{C}$.

On the bottom level, K_j is dependent on the population size and a client factor, unless we exclude artificial clients. The client factor is limited, for instance, from above by the time budget of the individuals. Therefore, there is a certain upper limit of 'client roles'. The clients who are resident above the bottom level are **PT**-members themselves, and virtual clients, i.e. "records" that could be presumed as corresponding to the virtual $\mathcal{C}$. We will denote them as k-clients, and the bottom level clients as τ-clients. Thus, at each level k an

$$S_{jk} = q_{jk}^s K_{jk}\sigma_{jk} \quad ,$$

results, where K_{jk} can be related to the available potential of the k or τ clients respectively.

The personnel depend on the number τ of hierarchical levels. Let us assume that the number of **PTRs** on a certain hierarchy level is 10 times larger than on the next higher hierarchical level, and if we choose

$$S/E = 10 \quad \text{and} \quad U/E = 60,$$

we can posit the following:

$$P_j = \sum_{k=1}^{\tau_j} 10^{k-1}(A_{jek} + s_{jk}A_{jsk} + u_{jk}A_{juk})$$

with

$A_{j.k} :$ = alimentation demand per $E, S, U,$

$s_{jk} :$ = number of sub-**PTRs** per $E,$

$u_{jk} :$ = number of subordinates per $E,$

and $s_{jk} \approx 10$, $u_{jk} \approx 60$. [2] By a more precise inspection the demand does not refer to persons but to positions in the **PT** where, because of interlocking, it holds that the number of positions is greater than the number of persons. Thus, the simplified approach chosen here underestimates the demand. We will make these differentiations in the model MUE & HIER in Vol. 2.

---

[2] In the early phase of a **PT** system development, it is likely that $u = 100$ by scale order; because of the "top heaviness" of the system, and since we hardly find **PT** systems in the early phase, an empirical value of $u < 100$ seems to be more appropriate. 60 was found empiricaly in a regional project, see [97].

Let us posit the following concerning alimentation:

$$A_{uk} = L \quad \text{for all} \quad j, k$$
$$A_{jsk} = a_{js} A_{jek}/2$$
and
$$A_{jek} = a_{je} k L \quad ,$$

thus the k-fold of L on the k-th hierarchical level, where L denotes the average alimentation per productive in the LSU. a_{js}, a_{je} are territorial-specific expenditure parameters. We chose $u = 60$, $s = 10$, $a_{js} = 1$ for all j and thus obtain

$$P_j = .6 L a_{je} \sum_{k=1}^{\tau_j} 10^k k (1 + \frac{10}{k a_{je}}) \quad . \tag{4.4}$$

It is easy for the reader to realize that a number of hierarchical levels can exist in which an additional level necessitates an expenditure that exceeds every realistic surplus. The four regional hierarchical levels of the F.R.G. seem to be the maximal number from the point of view of present financibility.

Assuming that each territory possesses a specific relation

$$u_\tau : \tau\text{-clients},$$

and positing

$$S_\tau = U_\tau/60 \quad \text{and} \quad E_\tau = 10 S_\tau \quad ,$$

the size of the personnel staff can easily be calculated bottom up, if a fixed relation between the hierarchical levels is presumed as before, where it was 10:1. Being trivial it does not require further elaboration here. So long as enough surplus is allocated to j, the relation $u : \tau$-clients can be augmented. However, there is certainly a limit for this procedure. This limit can be set equal to 1 in a first approximation. At any rate it can be posited that the size of the personnel staffs on the hierarchical levels can be determined by the relation between subordinates and k-clients. In this respect,

$$U_\tau : \tau\text{-clients},$$

is of special importance.

However, if a global territory experiences growth pressure there is, in addition to the problem of sufficient financing, the possibility that acquisition of a sufficiently large number of τ-clients becomes critical. By legal enforcement or monopolistic pressure, clients can be conveyed to the territory j. However, there are, to state some aspects, restrictions to this strategy, be it due to time budget restrictions or limited financial resources of clients or the spatial location of the territory under consideration.

Thus, the existence and stability of a **PT** is dependent decisively upon the success of placing allocation activities in the space that is defined by these restrictions. If, for instance, the time of children was fully occupied by school attendance, prescribed social activities etc., a children's television program would not have viewers any longer. In this event, this activity would be subject to legitimation pressure on all other **PTs** that compete for the time budget of the child clients and internally towards programmes aimed at other clients. An alternative would be the introduction of school television. This, however, could only become obligatory for school-children if an agreement had been previously reached with educational **PTRs**.

Nevertheless, there is, at first glance, no hinderance to the growth of the k-clients number so long as financial restrictions are not overspent. This, however, changes immediately if internal personnel and power costs are taken into account. The latter refer on the one hand to τ-clients, for instance, as propaganda costs, and on the other hand to the internal stabilization of a **PT**. With respect to the latter the following conjecture shall be formulated:

Conjecture 3 *With $k \to 1$, there is a growing importance of strategical protection of* **PT**-*positions in the orientation of $E(k)$ behavior.*

As mentioned above, this does not only refer to the acquisition and maintenance of clients, competences and money, but also to the desire to perform **PT**-strategies autonomously. *Autonomy* means in this connection, that disturbances from outside, i.e. from other **PTs**, clients, and especially persons holding positions on lower hierarchical levels, are kept beneath a certain intensity, comp. MEYER/ROWAN [85]. A sufficient number of examples for the before-mentioned conjecture exist. As to an empirical study see [88], chap. 2.

An élite study in a small town which was performed by the author in 1978-80 brought evidence which proved the priority of the securing of **PT** positions. In this study, a list of issues was presented to the political oligarchy sampled by snow ball method combined with positional validation. During the first interviews, these issues were recognized as important by the oligarchs themselves. The issues dealt with the aims of the political 'affairs' in the community under consideration. All persons interviewed stated that the following issue was that with utmost priority; that the positions of "hereditary" operating fields, i.e. such as had been under their predominant influence for a long time, stay under their influence also in the future. Some readers may be astonished that the issue "elections win" came in the middle position of the priority list. Expressed pointedly: so long as the presence in operation fields (via **PTs**) is guaranteed, it is less relevant to win elections.

The strategical protection of **PT** positions, however, must not automatically lead to a 'pertinent' outcome towards the clients in k and particularly in τ. On the contrary, it can quite often be observed that substantial issues are transformed into **PT**-strategic questions on the way from τ to 1. As strategic questions they are decided in 1, and in this form they start their way back to τ.

The Caesar-problematique

From the perspective of the success of this transformation, those $S(k)$ are of high qualification who have an excellent "know how" of this transformation business in both directions. Nevertheless, by virtue of this capability, they become dangerous competitors for $S(k-i)$ and $E(k-i)$, $i = 1, ..., k-1$. As a result **PTRs** on the higher hierarchical levels get into precarious situations. On the one hand, they depend upon the 'expert knowledge' of their sub-**PTRs**, while just because of this they have to fear the competition. We will denote this as the *Caesar-problematique*.

One solution of this problem is to prevent Caesars from getting to such high positions. In the long run, however, this is only successful if all **PTs** proceed that way, since this 'solution' leads to the acquisition of tendentially less qualified suboligarchs. By this lack of qualified leading personnel, **PTs** finally get into a competitive disadvantage vis-a-vis other **PTs**. This strategy creates long cycles in the existence of **PTs** if it is assumed that always one part of the **PTs** does not perform this strategy. Moreover, it can be presumed that Caesars succeed in establishing their own **PTs** independent of established promotion methods. Hence, it must be synchronously maintained that only certain promotional means are existent which are under **PT** control, for instance, in the form of formal educational achievements: for this phenomenon the term *meritocracy* has been formulated.

The dismissal of Caesars is still more dangerous because they are capable of forming their own competitive **PTs** by virtue of their **PT** inside knowledge. In contrast, the elimination of Caesars leads not only to a local discharge of the **PT** but also to the prevention of their later competitive reappearance. The elimination of Caesars, however, has to remain a relatively rare event since, if not, there would soon be no successors at all. Moreover, the probability of a duel is likely to rise, wherein it is decisive who is the first to be killed by whom. This situation seem to have prevailed in the late Roman Empire.

The most effective solution, however, expensive as it may be, is to satisfy a Caesar with his own local **PT**. This is effective because, as a rule, the new **PTR** is totally occupied repulsing or satisfying other Caesars in turn.

Finally, there is the least stressing solution of retirement from **PT** positions by virtue of illness, age or natural death. Vacancies are opened to which the Caesar moves along, and this could be a reason for the fact that predominantly older persons enter into leading positions.

Despite this competition it is observed that leading positions are occupied over a long time. How can this be explained? What are the reasons for the fact that **PT**-mobility is not ubiquitous? I can see five reasons for this:

- as will be shown in the next section, the collapse of the highest **PT** hierarchy level often leads to devolution processes on its lower levels. This seems also to be valid for a single **PT**. If we assume that **PTRs** know this, it can be concluded that that they fear the risk of losing their position by a crisis on the top level. In particular, they may hesitate to initiate such a crisis by too tough competition for a leading position. Perhaps this is a reason for the fact that Caesars generally have no position on the second hierarchy level when starting their revolt but come from the "depth" of the **PT** system.

- competition between **PT** members on a level k for promotion (*divide et impera*). If the relation $E : S$ and $E(k) : E(k+1)$ is 1:10, only one out of 10 can ascend each time. Even if the remaining 9 are quarrelling they can still cooperate in a terminated coalition stemming from a feeling that is shared by all of them: envy.

- defence of Caesars on the level $k + 1, \ldots$

- cyclic collapses of the global **PTs**, or of parts of them, whereby sufficient resources are set free to restart with a reduced impact of restrictions.

- destruction or conversion of global **PTs** or of parts of them initiated by other operation fields, especially by **PC** personnel (preventive strike).

We will return to the two last aspects in section 4.2.

The compensation strategy is confronted not only with financial, but also with personnel restrictions. Additional **PTs** require additional personnel to which there is an obvious limit by the number of persons fit for the task. It is true that the demand for subordinates can be reduced by rationalization, but by this, S would likely decrease as well. Thus, the principle *divide et impera* will tendentially fail. **PTs**, however, will as a rule first reach financial restrictions, so that we may regard the personnel restriction as an exceptional case unless no special qualificational requirements are demanded. In the event that this is the case, very complicated processes can result in **PT** systems the dynamic complexity of which is difficult to describe phenomenologically.

Ideology as a filter mechanism

There remains the aspect of how **PTs** can be protected against claims of clients. As far as records in $k < \tau$ are concerned, we have already handled this problem by the above explanations. Therefore, of interest are the relations to the τ-clients. **PTs** must succeed in convincing these clients that outcomes produced by the **PT** are beneficial to them. For instance, educational **PTs** must convince parents that their children are getting a good education. This is also valid, though to a lesser degree for clients related by force to a **PT**, e.g. prisoners. Since **PT** strategies are not systematically in accordance with this aim, they generally dispose of an *ideology* which externally operates as a screen, also towards external **PTs**. The latter accept this ideology (although the higher their hierarchical location the more frequently with raised eyebrows, in a certain respect like chums). It can become extremely dangerous for the stability of a **PT** if this ideology is internally taken for granted literally, for instance by sub-**PTRs** or **PTRs**, more rarely by subordinates.

The mechanisms that prevent critical impacts on the **PT** in case of a discrepancy between clients' expectations and real **PT** outcomes are stated at the beginning of the section 4.2 because this deals with whole **PT** systems.

Loyalty of PT members

There remains the question as to how such a discrepancy is suffered by position holders, possibly during a whole working life time without resistence. The relevant mechanisms are, in my opinion, founded in hierarchization and in local/global effects. Therefore, we shall now return to the dependence of **PT**-operation on its hierarchical location in a global cone.

The hierarchization ensures that the interaction partners of a **PT** member in k predominantly originate from the environments of k, so that interactively reinforced standard behavior and decision routines are practised. These standard behavior or decision routines are not jeopardized due mostly to the habitual fear of being misunderstood by the interaction partners. Hence, a U or S on the lowest hierarchical level behaves e.g. 'by order'. Since, generally, τ-clients approach the **PT** task-oriented it is plausible to assume that subordinates on the lowest level take over this orientation of their permanent interaction partners. It can be said, as was brought out by a case study of the author [88, chap. 2]: "where a quantification is convincing, there is no scope for politics". In contrast, **PT** members on the highest level interact predominantly with equal-ranking oligarchs. It becomes a matter of course for them to be predominantly engaged in maintaining the stability of the **PT** or the oligarchical sphere.

A central role is played by the **PTRs** on the mid level, e.g. the ministerial board in the federal government. In a certain respect there are "two minds in their hearts". I have to admit that I can only speculate on the reasons for the loyalty of these people. Is it the "march through the institutions" that creates dullness? Is it the lust for power? Or is it the fear of being degraded? Perhaps these persons make frequent lateral changes, the different **PTs** trusting (illusionarily) that it would be better so. Perhaps the timing of compensation by position achievement is systematically arranged so that too big a jam of malcontents can appear only in rare situations. A combination of these mechanisms may be effective and I consider the structural mechanisms such as last stated as dominant.

This would mean that over-proportionally many middle **PTRs** are mainly satisfied with own **PTs**, e.g. obtain their own departments. This would have as a consequence that, unless these new **PTs** are not totally separated (so-called **PT**-partitions, see next section), the cone-structure would become more and more 'top-heavy'.

At some point, however, the relation of thin legs, thick stomachs and small heads will become so unbalanced that the global **PT** will collapse or fall into pieces. However, this partition process is no simple procedure, all conditions necessary for existence, operation and (to lesser degree) stability of a **PT** have to be fulfilled at least twice. In addition, the successful definition of a new operation field belongs to these conditions.

Nevertheless, the total dynamics of a local **PT**, and all the more of a global **PT**, can hardly be described phenomenologically anymore. In Vol. 2 an attempt is made to achieve this by means of simulation models.

Total demand of a global PT cone

Now we will try to make a guess at the total demand B_j of a global cone. For this purpose, the quantities H_j and B_{ex_j} must be known. B_{ex_j} is dependent on the number of all territories, whereas however, the accepted territorial integrity, i.e. a durable mutual demarcation of territories, works as a saving effect. $\sum_{j=1}^{r} B_{ex_j}$ can be interpreted as **PC**-demand. It can be specified as being directly dependent on the number of **PTRs** in the **PC** as was calculated in section 2.3.2. We define briefly:

$$B_{ex_j} = p_j B_{PC}$$

with

$$B_{PC} : = \textbf{PC demand},$$
$$p_j : = \text{contribution quota of territory } j$$
$$\text{to fulfil this demand.}$$

In a collective crisis of a **PT**-system, e.g. in the case of war, peaks of extraordinary costs must be added which we will neglect here. Thus, we will consider the 'normal case' without collective crisis.

H_j refers to the demand for surplus to stabilize **PTs**. These are additional costs not captured by the costs pertaining to the establishment and operation of new **PTs** in order to satisfy certain **PTRs**, because these have already been included in P_j. Hence, costs of all kinds for passing negative consequences over to subordinates, for bribery, corruption and manipulation are included in H_j – provided this is not connected with the foundation of a new **PT**. In the individual case it can be difficult to differentiate between B_{ex_j} and H_j: an operational criterion could be that a demand that refers to positions of sufficient duration is subsumable under B_{ex_j}. Using the results of section 4.3.8 the presumed fundamental period of **PT** dynamics, 8 years, can be proposed as a quantification of "sufficiently durable". But this is, as we will see, still speculative at present. With H_j, too, we will neglect the costs for collective **PT** crisis: in Vol. 2 they will be considered in some simulation models.

In a strict hierarchy, H_j on a level k refers always and exclusively to $k + 1$. In the F.R.G. this would mean that the federal government controls the states, the states control the districts etc. Of course, in reality this is not strictly valid, but this structure can be taken as a first approximation.

There remain the local stabilization costs which already have been discussed under the aspect of the Caesar-problematique, provided they are not included in P_j. Thus, H_j is composed by a global and a local component. Corresponding to the three aspects micro, meso, and macro, three kinds of demand result altogether; local, global and **PC** demand. If we denote the local share in H_j with $H_{lj}(k)$ and the global with $H_{gj}(k)$, H_j can be defined as (the **PC** demand was included in B_{ex_j}):

$$H_j = \sum_{k=1}^{\tau_j} H_{lj}(k) + H_{gj}(k) \quad . \tag{4.5}$$

In its most simple version, $H_{lj}(k)$ depends on the number of possible pairwise contacts between the sub-**PTRs** on the level k, that is on

$$S_{jk}(S_{jk} - 1)/2 \quad .$$

Let us choose again by scale order $S_{jk} = 10$ for all j, k. Then a contact number of 45 results. Using the terms which led to 4.4 we are now in the position to posit:

$$H_{lj}(k) = 10^k 45 q_{ljk} \rho_{ljk} .5 a_{je} (\tau_j - k + 1)L \tag{4.6}$$

with

$$
\begin{aligned}
q_{ljk} : \quad = \quad & \text{quota of contacts which leads} \\
& \text{to a stabilization activity,} \\
\rho_{ljk} : \quad = \quad & \text{multiple of the S-personnel cost} \\
& \text{the latter being posited as} \quad .5 a_{je} kL.
\end{aligned}
$$

L denotes the average alimentation of a productive and $a_{je}k$ that multiple of L which is allotted to the **PTR** on level k.

Presumably, $H_{gj}(k)$ depends on the relation

$$E(k) : E(k + 1) \quad .$$

Hence, we neglect in this specification that, under a global perspective, $S(k+1)$ ordinarily is controlled by $E(k)$, and, under a local perspective, $U(k)$ is controlled by $S(k)$. Assuming complete control, a reference term can be specified as follows:

$$E(k) \cdot E(k + 1) \quad ,$$

hence, for the above-mentioned scale order of 10:

$$10^k 10^{k+1} \quad for \quad k = 0, ..., \tau_j - 1. \quad k = 0, ..., \tau_j - 1 \quad .$$

Analogously to 4.6 we posit:

$$H_{gj}(k) = q_{gjk} 10^{2k-1} \rho_{gjk} a_{je}(\tau_j - k + 1)L \qquad (4.7)$$

with $k = 0, ..., \tau_j - 1$, and q_{gjk}, ρ_{gjk} analogous to 4.6.
The index-function for k results from the index shift in 4.8. $k + 1$ means
that the alimentation of a **PTR** is oriented to the alimentation of the **PTR**
on the next higher level. Altogether we get:

$$
\begin{aligned}
H_j &= 22.5 a_{je} L [\sum_{k=1}^{\tau_j} 10^k q_{ljk} \rho_{ljk} (\tau_j - k + 1) \\
&\quad + .044 \sum_{k=1}^{\tau_j} 10^{2k-1} q_{gjk} \rho_{gjk} (\tau_j - k + 1)] \\
&= 22.5 a_{je} L \sum_{k=1}^{\tau_j} 10^k F(k) \qquad (4.8)
\end{aligned}
$$

with

$$F(k) = q_{ljk} \rho_{ljk} + .0044 q_{gjk} \rho_{gjk} 10^k .$$

By scale order we choose $\rho_{ljk} = \rho_{gjk} = 1$, hence one year-alimentation per
stabilization activity, further

$$q_{ljk} = q_l e^{-\lambda_l (k-1)} , \quad q_{gjk} = q_g e^{-\lambda_g (k-1)} .$$

When choosing $\lambda_l = \lambda_g = 1$, $a_{je} = 2$, $L = 3$, tab. 4.1 displays H_j dependent
on τ, q_l, and q_g. In choosing $q_l = q_g = .1$ as plausible values, i.e. there are

q_l	q_g	τ	H_j 10^6
10^{-2}	10^{-2}	3	.0012
10^{-2}	10^{-2}	4	.0325
10^{-1}	10^{-1}	3	.012
10^{-1}	10^{-1}	4	.325

Table 4.1: **PT** stabilization demand

on the average one stabilization activity per every 10 contacts, the following
can be stated as scale order results:

- H_j is neglectible compared with H_g if $\tau \geq 3$.

- H_j is related with P_j, see 4.4, approximately as 1 : 1, which seems
  plausible.

It remains to determine the **PC** costs B_{ex_j}, which was posited as $p_j B_{PC}$ above. Also in this case we can regard the number of possible contacts in the **PC** as a reference term, so that $\alpha(\alpha - 1)/2$ results. [3] Anticipating the next section, we posit:

$$B_{PC}(\alpha, r, q_{PC}, \rho_{PC}) = \rho_{PC} q_{PC}(\frac{\alpha}{r})(\frac{\alpha}{r} - 1)/2$$

$$= r^{-1}\rho_{PC} q_{PC}(\alpha - r)\alpha/2 \quad . \tag{4.9}$$

with

$$q_{PC}: \quad = \quad \text{quota of stabilization activity contacts}$$
$$\text{related to all possible contacts,}$$
$$\rho_{PC}: \quad = \quad \text{demand per stabilization activity.}$$

When positing $\rho_{PC} = 10 a_{je}\tau L$, tab. 4.2 displays the **PC** costs dependent on α, r, τ, and q_{PC}, where $a_{je} = 2$ and $L = 3$ were chosen. q_{PC} was specified as r^{-1} which means equal distribution. Summing up all costs we get:

$B_{ex_j}^+$ 10^6	B_{PC} 10^6	α	r	τ	q_{PC}
.280	5.60	5,000	20	3	.050
.443	13.30	10,000	30	4	.033
.421	16.83	15,000	40	4	.025
.526	21.00	15,000	40	5	.025

Table 4.2: **PC** costs

+) $p_j = 1/r$

$$B_j = S_j + P_j + H_j + B_{ex_j} \quad , \tag{4.10}$$

and for a parameter constellation that seems plausible for the F.R.G. in 1980, i.e.

$$\alpha = 10,000 \quad , \quad r = 30 \quad , \quad \tau = 4 \quad , \quad q_l = q_g = .1$$

we get

$$B_j = S_j + (.356 + .325 + .443)10^6 \quad ,$$

hence,

$$B_j = S_j + 1.246 \cdot 10^6 \quad .$$

---

[3] ODUM [100] chose a similar specification for the contact complexity of a population in his approach.

Multiplied with the conjectured number of operation fields in the **PC** of the F.R.G., $1.246 \cdot 10^6 \cdot 30$ results for the whole F.R.G., that is $33.72 \cdot 10^6$ C . Let us compare this with the result produced by the approach of section 2.3.2, where the *Herrschafts* protection demand was specified as $.5\alpha^2$. For $\alpha = 10,000$ a demand of $50 \cdot 10^6$, and for the minimal **PC** size of $\alpha = hN = 6,000$ a demand of $18 \cdot 10^6$ results. Hence the result produced with the more differentiated approach of this section is located approximately in the middle of those two extreme values.

4.1.2   Pertinence versus power orientation

Together with 4.4 and 4.8 we are now in the position to guess pertinence and power orientation of the **PC** system in a rough manner. To perform this let us posit that the pertinence fraction of the personnel costs P_j on level k equals

$$\frac{q_{\tau_j}}{\tau_j - k + 1} ,$$

and that H_j as well as B_{ex_j} are completely power oriented. Then we can compare both orientations as is displayed in tab. 4.3, where $P_{jk} :=$ personnel costs due to the sum in 4.4. In the case of $q_{\tau_j} = 1$, that is, for a complete

pertinence orientation	power orientation
S_j	$H_j + B_{ex_j}$
$\sum_{k=1}^{\tau_j} P_{jk} q_{\tau_j}/(\tau_j - k + 1)$	$\sum_{k=1}^{\tau_j} P_{jk}[1 - q_{\tau_j}/(\tau_j - k + 1)]$

Table 4.3: Pertinence and power terms regarding one operation field

pertinence orientation on the lowest level, and choosing the above-mentioned plausible parameter values, we get:

- pertinence oriented $C = S_j + .339 \cdot 10^6$,

- power oriented $C = (.325 + .443 + .017)10^6$.

We can choose the total share of all state activities in the national income of the F.R.G. as a first approximation for the total **PT** system budget of the F.R.G., that is around 40 % of the national income. In section 2.3.2 the latter was calculated as $240 \cdot 10^6$ C in 1980. The result is then that the power orientation fraction is approximately $30 \cdot .785/96$, that is .25, so that the pertinence orientation share would be .75.

Two remarks are necessary here:

- the relatively high pertinence share of 75 % results from the following: there is the hierarchical cone that widens downwards in powers of 10 and in this cone there is the mass of the **PT** members. They are, in accordance with the supposition made, predominantly pertinence-oriented, whilst, at the hierarchy's top the pertinence orientation is only 25 %. Problems that are precarious to oligarchic functioning are as a rule attracted by the highest decision authority and are coped with predominantly in a power-oriented way. Thus, problems of high pertinence would also be coped with in a more power-oriented way when gaining a larger oligarchy critical potential. DEUTSCH [18] has already pointed to this crusting effect. However, his conclusion that oligarchs tend finally to neglect reality seems to be too global as we will see in the following section.

- With growing power orientation, **PT** or oligarchy behavior will be more and more dominated by strategical considerations. If a certain threshold of power predominance is reached the operation of a local or global **PT**, possibly even a **PT** system, can no longer be described adequately without explicit regard to this strategical component. As a result research problems appear which can be said to be unsolved so far. Hopes originally set in game theory did not succeed in coping with situations that correspond to complex, dynamic, many-persons-non-zero-sum-games. Moreover, I presume that in the case of a high power orientation and a certain **PT** structure that could be labelled oligopolistic, the behavior of a global **PT**, or a **PT** system, could suddenly become erratic.

In the period before the electorate (*Kurfürstentum*) in the German Reich such an erratic phase presumably was existent. The sequence First World War, the world economic crisis and the Second World War could be another example of a period of erratic dynamic behavior. The interesting question whether critical zones in the state space or parameter situations leading to erratic behavior can be identified has to be reserved to other researches: recall section 3.2.1.

In view of this pertinence share of approx. 75 % an important aspect of the local **PT** operation is posed, namely, that of the relation of power and pertinence. First, we may presume that **PTs** cope with mass phenomena in their lowest levels in the form of technical processes. The case that a **PT** in τ copes with concentrated phenomena is unknown to me. Exceptionally it could be imaginable that the number of **PTs** in an operation field could become so large that **PTs** would develop whose τ-clients again are **PTs**. However, such a territory does not seem to exist at present. The **PC** could be a systematic exception. If that could be conceived as a virtual **PT**, namely, the oligarchy, its clients would, in fact, be **PTs** from the different operation fields. In the following section we will return to that aspect.

Hence, we may assume that the pertinence is predominantly sited on the lower hierarchical levels at $U(\tau)$, $S(\tau)$ and possibly to a lesser extent at $E(\tau)$. The pertinence is determined by the necessities and restrictions of the applied technical processes, e.g. medical equipment, construction technique prescriptions etc. As these processes permit only a certain performance maximum due to the capacity existent at a time in τ, there is a gate here for impeachment by the τ-clients, namely in the form of the overload of the performance capacity of a **PT** in τ. This overload is tendentially the more dangerous at least for τ, but presumably to a lesser degree also for $k < \tau$, the clearer the discrepancy between requests and outcomes can be perceived.

However, it would be a shortcoming to derive sequentially that from τ to 1, at least in the case of overload, there is a pertinence orientation of the **PTRs**. On the one hand as a rule, a **PT** disposes of definition power with regard to scope and volume of the inputs to be processed, even though not always completely. On the other hand it cannot be ruled out that an overdemand in τ is strategically feigned by **PTRs** in order to strengthen the request for their own **PT**.

An overcharge of the financial resources of a **PT** has nearly always serious impacts on **PT** stability, since in this situation ordinary problem solutions, i.e. the growth of the output regardless of how its usefulness is substantiated and compensation of **PT** aspirants, are excluded.

Altogether, three situation types can be identified which more or less enforce pertinence orientation:

a) outcome oriented overcharge of financial resources,
b) direct linking of **PT** positions
   produced under the responsibility of the position holders,
c) clear coupling that is difficult to conceal
   between request for outcomes and realized outcomes.

As a rule, the amount of pertinence orientation increases from a) to c). In a) **PTRs** are not forced to attack the causes of overdemand. For instance, saving elsewhere, or additional loans, are imaginable substitutes. Hence, taking the school system as an example, it is imaginable that **PTs** from newly defined educational lines emerge and existing educational **PTs** disappear.

Frequently b) will be the result of strategical mistakes, i.e. the mentioned linking between position maintenance and outcome is a strategy in **PT** competition, which can be very effective. Especially, the strategically caused overload of the operation capacity of a **PTR** can be observed in practice (he is stimulated to eat himself out of house and home). A true linking between position maintenance and outcome can be regarded as a sub-case of c).

c) generally needs the **PT** interest in such a clear coupling between outcome request and realized outcome. Since such an interest will be the exception, only in rare cases are operation fields imaginable where the pertinence orientation stems 'from substantial reasons' provided that technical processes (in the widest sense) do not reach objective (e.g. natural) limits to the production of relevant outcomes. We will return to this in the following section.

Thus, any coping with a τ-client's problem can be regarded as a transformation in several steps. In [93] I proposed a coupling of two filter models, a selective and an activity filter model. I specified such a model for the problem of nitrate pollution of drinking water in a region of intensive agriculture. The simulation model with plausible parameter values proved to be in line with the factual development of that region. By this it is demonstrated that a model which contains aspects of **PT** operation shows a considerable appropriateness towards real structures. Recent implementation research also deals with these aspects: in particular see WOLLMANN [137].

4.2   The macro level

By virtue of the above considerations concerning 4.5 we have already entered into the topic of the operation of a **PT** system of an LSU. The result from 4.5 shows that the approach developed in section 2.3.2 is reasonable by scale order. In the previous section we succeeded in guessing in a more differentiated fashion that power demand in the form of $c\alpha^2$ (α denoted the number of the top-**PTRs**) results to a considerable degree from the demand stemming from the target of power protection in the hierarchy cones of the individual territories. This, however, should not induce us to skip the former **PC**-oriented approach. On the contrary, because of the high plausibility of the results in 2.2 we have support for the conjecture that a fixed relation exists between the size of the **PC** and the hierarchy structure of the **PT** system of an LSU; in other words that the scale orders of each hierarchy level size are determined from the top.

4.2.1   Oligarchy size and hierarchy structure

Let us first make an attempt to determine α from the territorial hierarchical cones. For this purpose let us assume that the **PC**-members are recruited from the upper hierarchical levels of the territorial cones. In this connection the proximity to the **PC** will be of special importance. We will return to this aspect below. It can be posited then:

$$\alpha = \sum_{j=1}^{r} \sum_{k=1}^{\tau} [p_{jk}^e E_j(k) + \delta_k p_{jk}^s S_j(k)] \qquad (4.11)$$

with

$$p_{jk}^{e,s} : = \quad \text{quotas of } \textbf{PTRs} \ (E) \text{ or sub-}\textbf{PTRs} \ (S)$$
$$\text{who succeed in promotion into the } \textbf{PC}$$

$$\delta_k : = \quad \left\{ \begin{array}{l} 1 \ for \ k = 1 \\ 0 \ else \end{array} \right. \qquad (4.12)$$

The $p_{jk}^{e,s}$ presumably are reversely proportional functions of k.
Numerical example: For

$$p_{j1}^e = 1 \quad , \quad p_{j2}^e = .75 \quad , \quad p_{j3}^e = .5 \quad , \quad p_{j4}^e = 0$$

and $p_{j1}^s = .33$

$$\alpha = 9,270$$

results if $r = 150$ and choosing a relation of 1:10 for $E : S$. This is in good accord with the results of section 2.3.2.

If it is true that, as far as **PT** influence is concerned, the LSU dynamics heavily depend on the behavior within the **PC**, it can be concluded that, in a first approximation, LSU dynamics could be explainable by **PC** and mass dynamics. Then, with regard to relevant macro variables it would hold:

$$Y(t) = Y_{PC}(t) \square Y_{MASS}(t) \tag{4.13}$$

and $\square$ denotes a functional relation that needs further investigation to be determined more precisely. Here, all members of an LSU are to be included under MASS who inhabit no U, S or E position. If 4.13 has validity, then LSU dynamics could be traced back to the classical relation between the ruling class and the reigned mass.

4.2.2   Autonomy of a power territory system

Hence, the analysis of the operation of a **PT** system of an LSU must first of all begin with the two questions directly suggested by 4.13:

- Which mechanisms have the effect that processes in MASS, as a rule, do not develop a power-critical impact?

- How can we imagine the functioning of a **PT** system even if it is not affected by MASS-influences, i.e. what we can presume *a fortiori*?

The two questions are complementary, because for exerting power two parties are always necessary: those who dominate and those who let themselves be dominated.

Let a **PT** system that is capable of filtering MASS-influences in order to maintain power protection be called *autonomous*. Before dealing in greater detail with this another comment on the term 'system' seems necessary. Up to now we always used the term social unit and not system. However, **PTs** which possess the property of autonomy are able to structure, maintain and control their operational relations durably enough by means of internal strategies. Special mechanisms render external influences compatible with internal operation demands. If these conditions apply, then we will speak of a "system", comp. ZELENY [140], LUHMANN [75]. Notice, that, as a consequence, any cone (e.g. the health 'system') may only then be called a territorial hierarchy system if it is autonomous. This means, especially, that

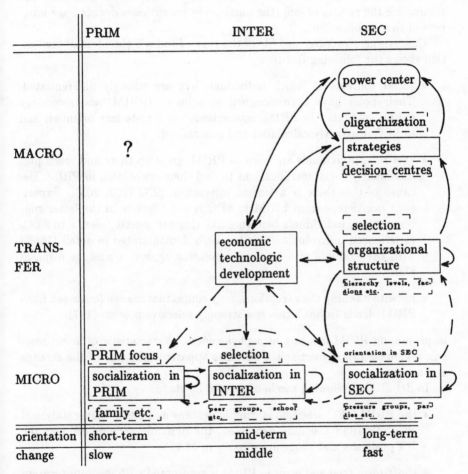

Figure 4.2: Structure and operation of a large scale social unit

Legend: ⟶ := high importance   - - - > := low importance

PC influences are territorially partitioned in a sufficiently durable manner. If we think, for example, of the MISP in the U.S.A. or the "pantouflage" between ministries and big industries/banks in France (just to state two examples), the partitioning hypothesis seems doubtful.

Now we want to show that a **PT** system of an LSU generally is autonomous with regard to influences of MASS. We may be brief here and summarize the results of [88] (the numbers in parentheses denote page numbers of that publication).

Concerning *structure*, an LSU of the type of today's (occidental) civilization shows the following features:

- social contexts in which individuals live are strongly differentiated. Their poles have been designed as primary (PRIM) and secondary (SEC) contexts. In PRIM, interactions are face-to-face oriented, and in SEC abstractly calculated and generalized.

- as a rule, individuals are born in PRIM, grow up there and reach predominantly social qualifications to find their orientation in PRIM. Because of this there is a fear to interact in SEC (203, 205). Experience transferred from PRIM to SEC is not effective in the latter context. Thus, individuals behaving like this are mostly inferior to SEC-experienced individuals. This has been demonstrated in detail (166ff) with the example of a citizens' movement against a wastage disposal plan.

- notwithstanding the exceptions, only contextual change (outbreak from PRIM) leads to SEC; this is a strongly selective process (197).

In presuming PRIM-focusing as a phylogenetic characteristic of *homo sapiens*, a general ruling mechanism becomes apparent: the fear of the strange and unusual.

In detail, the following mechanisms can be stated:

- the PRIM/SEC-selection is complementary and has an autocatalytical effect (207ff). Casually expressed, the dynamic persons conquer the **PT** positions and hence are missing in MASS.

- short-term trial and error in PRIM is confronted with medium-term up to long-term strategies and tactics in SEC (238ff).

- PRIM-focusing is generally connected with pertinent orientation. This orientation, however, is ineffective because of the transformation of pertinent issues into power issues in SEC. A PRIM-oriented critique against power issues, therefore, will generally fail (109ff, 166ff).

Structures and mechanisms are demonstrated in fig. 4.2. By virtue of our **PT**-theory the question mark in fig. 4.2 can now be clarified. The question mark concerned the fact that the combination PRIM/MACRO has not been observed so far. A reason for this seems to be that in LSUs with sufficient surplus, concentrations of behavior and influences, **PT** formation and a high DC determination of the system behavior are deep structures, as to this term see BOULDING, E. [11]. By a *deep structure* a structure is understood which wins through even against the intention of actors. Example: an actor aiming at abolishing **PTs** creates by his/her intention, as far as he/she can convince others, the new **PT**-abolishing-hierarchy-cone immediately.

To prevent always creating new **PTs**, principles of positional rotation have been established. Apparently there are two types, the Kibbuz and the Yugoslavian rotation principle. With the former, the relatively small number of families having the privilege of rotation can be observed for big Kibbuzim (size greater than 10^4). With the latter, the development of a substantial oligarchy appears to have prevented requests for rotation. It would be interesting to examine which type the Greens are following in the F.R.G.

On the basis of the aforementioned reflections, the following proposition can be stated:

Proposition 8 *Let clients from MASS be denoted as τ_m-clients. A* **PT** *system of an LSU is τ_m-autonomous.*

Proof Sketch:
Assumption 1: The overwhelming majority of MASS is is PRIM-focused.
Assumption 2: MASS phenomena result from the behavior of members in MASS. If members from the complementary set

$$\{ \text{LSU} \setminus \text{MASS} \}$$

are participating exceptionally in activities that lead to mass phenomena, they act in PRIM (example: as a rule, children are not begotten by members of cabinet during cabinet meetings; refrigerators are not bought by trade union functionaries while they attend the tariff commission meeting).
Assumption 3: Filtering mechanisms exist that transform the effects of activities in PRIM, directed towards SEC, in such a way that the stability of **PTs** is not endangered; these mechanisms are under control of **PTRs** and are effective.
Assumption 4: Behavior concentrations are DC outputs, DCs are localized in SEC.
Assumption 5: SEC is organized as a **PT** system.

Proof of: assumptions 1-5 are necessary

As a proof the reverse conclusion is drawn here: if an assumption is not fulfilled, the proposition is disproved.
ad assumption 1: Only in the case of the SEC-focusing of the mass of population are the filtering mechanisms in assumption 3 not effective. The proof

of this conjecture shall not be undertaken here. As to plenty of evidence for the PRIM-focusing of MASS, see [88].

ad assumption 2: Mass phenomena in SEC could lead to an overload of oligarchy's control capacity, because by definition, a mass of DCs will be involved in this case. This conjecture, too, would have to be proved. Strictly speaking, one such counter example against assumption 2 would be sufficient. However, it must be examined whether such a SEC-mass-phenomenon is real, i.e. tolerated for a long time by oligarchies. Otherwise, it would be a pseudo SEC-mass-phenomenon. It could be the case that in the field of social infrastructure in the F.R.G., at least temporarily, such pseudo SEC-mass-phenomena exist. For the present we will let it rest that the strong plausibility is that real SEC-mass-phenomena are absolute exceptions.

ad assumption 3: The necessary condition is obvious.

ad assumption 4: This necessary condition is a direct consequence of the existence condition for **PTs** and of the defined influential relevance of concentrations.

ad assumption 5: This necessary condition is trivial.

One problem of this proof sketch, however, is the possible existence of singular events. There can be influences not organized by **PTs** which endanger the structures of **PTs** or of oligarchies (imagine, for instance, the refusal of some farmers to sell urgently needed land for the realization of land use plans). This general problem will not be examined further here.

If one of the five assumptions is not necessary here there remains the still strong proposition that assumptions 1 to 5 are sufficient conditions. The proof of this may be sketched by the following conjecture:

Conjecture 4 *If all 5 assumptions are fulfilled,* **PTRs** *and oligarchies have the power to define, select and control functioning relevant features.*

If this conjecture is right, the proof of the sufficiency of the 5 assumptions is immediately plausible. Some evidence is stated in [88].

If the correctness of this proof sketch is accepted, the research has to concentrate on the empirical examination of the five assumptions. In my view, this has been done adequately elsewhere, e.g. in [88], LASSWELL/LERNER [64], so that details are unnecessary here. [4]

---

[4]If the proposition is right, analytically weak positions are immediately revealed, e.g. the strategy of DUTSCHKE of the "long march through the institutions" or MARCUSE's refusal conception. On the other hand, in emphasizing the intentional aspect of **PT** strategies, PARETO misjudged the quasi-automatism by which the **PT** mechanisms stated in [88] develop their high effectiveness.

Remarks

1. There are LSU-relevant mass processes which presently are not under the control of the **PT** system, e.g. births. Nevertheless, the population size is, at least regionally partly under control of **PT** strategies, for instance, by housing politics.

2. Strategies can be imagined that are located in MASS and at the same time **PT**-critical. One example of this is the *Lysistrate-* [5] strategy of the refusal of a sufficiently large number of women to exert their normal roles (for instance, having children, household care etc.). As demonstrated in JANSSEN/JURREIT [57], there is only one – and moreover simple – society known in which this strategy belonged in the behavioral repertoire. Hence, it is one of the central questions for understanding the operation of LSUs why this strategy is not observed more frequently.

Perhaps the women studies will approach this problematique.

4.2.3   Oligarchic destabilization

The foregoing remarks are hardly in a position to counterargue the proposition 8. The proposition, however, referred to τ_M-clients and is, therefore, relatively weak for it is obvious that τ_M-clients can mobilize very little to counteract a **PT** system of an LSU.

Such helplessness cannot be expected in the case of clients stemming from **PT**s, i.e. in the case of τ_E-clients. **PT** members who go to a hospital, who send their children to school etc., will be able to use their own **PT** experiences to put efficient strategies to combat these "foreign" **PT**s. Examples are to charge the opponent with necessary legal action, the blocking of decisions etc. A whole range of activities is at their disposal, which can effectively disturb the operation of a **PT** and to a lesser degree, however, that of a **PT** system.

I see three **PT** strategies in order to cope with this problem:

- privileged treatment of τ_E-clients (for instance, private patients, reservations and enclaves of all kind),

- in the case of a permanent τ_E-critique the satisfaction of the disturbers with their (possibly time-limited) own **PT**s,

---

[5] The *Lysistrate*-strategy must be considered as extraordinarily efficient because it leads to *faits accompli* in a very short time (within one year). A considerable decline in the birth rate cannot be compensated if migration is neglected. Perhaps the decline of birth numbers in some western civilizations could be interpreted as a systematic *Lysistrate* effect stemming from socio-structural conditions.

- to exert pressure on τ_E-clients in their **PTs**; e.g. through initiating surveillance by the next higher hierarchy level.

With a growing number of **PTs**, however, none of these strategies can be maintained in the long run since the first two strategies require considerably additional expenditure and the third strategy finally leads to a situation in which many **PTs** threaten themselves mutually. Thus, for this reason, the LSU-oligarchy has to care for a permanent very large $MASS$ size in comparison to E. It is an interesting question how this can be practised despite a growing production of virtual C . We will not deal with this question here, however.

Already at this point, though under the client aspect, we enter into the second question area: how can the operation of a **PT** system of an LSU be imagined? The consequences for the stability of the **PT** system will be dealt with in section 4.3.

Let us presume that the **PT** system operates on the micro and meso level so demonstrated in the foregoing section. In addition, let us assume that the **PT** system of an LSU be τ_M- *autonomous* and possesses no τ_E-critical scale order. We will call this a normal **PT** system of an LSU and will ask ourselves how this is able to operate. For this purpose we have to differentiate at least two dimensions: the position of single **PTs** towards the **PC** and the hierarchical structure of the **PT** system. As mentioned in section 2.3.2, that ensemble of **PT** positions is labelled **PC**, on which predominantly the conditions of existence and operation of **PTs** are determinated strategically. Thus, to identify the **PC**, principally the methods of the identification of DCs can be adopted; to this see [93]. This should not lead to the shortcoming that it will be simple to identify the **PC** in detail. We will not go deeper into these empirical-methodological questions but will proceed from the assumption that the **PC** can be identified.

The central conditions of existence and operation of a **PT** have already been stated in sections 2.3.1, 4.1.1. and its subsections. Because of the over-proportional alimentational demand of the **PTs**, the acquisition of a sufficiently large surplus volume is the overwhelmingly important condition concerning existence as well as operation of **PTs**. This requires that a sufficiently large quantity of virtual C is produced and that distributional strategies to allocate surplus to the **PT** system do function.

Therefore, we must search first for the **PC** members in such areas where the subject to be dealt with is the securing of a sufficient production volume. Because of the demand dynamics stemming from the request for alimentation of the **PTs**, production processes cannot be stationary. On the contrary, the establishment of appropriate growth conditions must be of high priority. It is obvious that with a sufficiently high production growth no redistribution problems will appear. If, however, the previous considerations, especially those of sections 2.3.1, 4.1.1. and its subsections are true, new **PTs** will squat immediately in the volume of additionally produced virtual C . These **PTs** in turn create an overproportional (namely square) growth pressure etc. When extrapolating these dynamics towards a very large volume of virtual C a situation will sometime appear in which additional production is absorbed immediately by **PT** demand. Sooner or later, the **PT** dynamics, therefore, lead always to redistribution problems.

Notice, that redistribution in favor of **PTs**, for instance, by duties or high prices has no effect other than described previously. **PTs** will squat also in this alimentation volume.

As we elaborated in section 2.4 and its subsections, machines, technologies and energy are the essential determinants of production and hence corresponding **PT** positions definitively establish in the **PC**. Looking at the F.R.G., the RWE (electricity trust) is an example of a DC whose **PTRs** hold positions in the energy sector of the **PC**. Further **PC** positions must be devoted to the creation and securing of redistribution mechanisms. Therefore, DCs especially in the following fields are concerned: revenues, insurances, banks, subsidies etc.; important receivers of assistance can possibly be added.

Finally, the internal and external safe-guarding of production and distribution is a relevant **PC** field. Since, in the case of violence against **PT** members and assets, the existence of **PTs** can be directly affected, the technologies of psychic manipulation, violence exertion and killing must represent a priority **PC**-field.

Thus, each territory is specifically represented in the **PC**. This representation, however, can change in the course of time. A detailed analysis of the **PT**-system of an LSU would have to arrange the territories in their position relative to the **PC**. It would surely be elucidative to demonstrate topographically the development and migration of **PTs** relative to the **PC** in the course of time. This, however, requires hardware and software instruments so far available only in a rudimentary form, that topologic analyses with their manifold aspects and problems will have to be left aside here. An exemplary sketch of a distribution algorithm oriented thereto has been elaborated in section 2.3.2. Specific stability aspects of some corresponding dynamics are discussed in the following section.

A **PT** system is systematically short of finance. Since it disposes of designing power in the finance field and is able to grab with priority on the money market, debt [6] is a very obvious strategy to overcome such situations. In the case of external funding of machines and technology the result is an additional increase in debt. However, we have to consider that **PTs** also squat in this alimentation volume so that the debt process can also be autocatalytic. By growing debt, the **PT** positions from the banks and insurance companies involved also become parts of the **PC**. Activities of the **PC** referring to investments, production and technology will reduce with a

---

[6]Hence, it seems in no way out of place, if HEINSOHN [46] explains the emergence of money from debt.

growing number of virtual C , because the **PC-PTRs'** time budget will be absorbed by power protection activities. This will be reflected immediately in the corresponding shares in the **PC** budget for investments etc. and power protection respectively. Thus, the **PC** will extend over-proportionally in the redistribution sphere itself and be occupied with its protection. Here, growth-theoretical reflections of OLSON [105] come into play, but at least with the present scale order of the number of virtual C it does not seem to be clear whether processes of **PT** confinement, tendentially contra innovation, are not compensated, or even overcompensated by the **PT** growth dynamics described.

However, it can be attractive for people with decision power in an enterprise to receive fundings to a considerable extent from redistribution, be it in the form of subsidies, governmental orders or insurance benefits, just to state some aspects. Since the procuring of such redistribution money is generally dependent on the presence of the enterprise in the **PT** system, large enterprises are mostly advantaged here. Short-termedly, a debt financing of this redistribution is possible; in the long run, however, the necessity to produce this redistribution mass is indispensable. If the production, which is 'blown up' in its value by means of the redistribution, increases then the case may be that there are too few productive enterprises in the substructure of the **PT** system to care constantly for a sufficiently large production volume. Frequently, however, this becomes evident only in a crisis where enterprises of the **PT**-type collapse. In history this can be observed with the example of the Spanish textile industry in the absence of the former Latin American treasures (OTTEN, personal communication): perhaps, Great Britain is another example during the period of 1975–80. There is the interesting question (which will not be scrutinized, here) whether, possibly, each **PT** system, if it evolves long enough without structural ruptures, will run into this critical zone.

The priorities in the **PC** stated here are analoguously valid for the top areas of the **PT** cones. Recall, that **PC** personnel recruits from the **PT** system. In the **PC**, however, certain operational fields are more important than others, as was stated before.

Thus, we have to return again to the question raised in section 3.3 whether it is admissible to neglect operational substance when describing the **PT** dynamics. We had argued there and in the former section that operational fields can be defined relatively arbitrarily if enough surplus is available. Hence, we should assume that this arbitrariness increases with the distance from the **PC**. In a first approximation it may be presumed that, genealogically, **PT** structures develop first of all in the mentioned fields that are relevant for existence and operation. However, it remains to be explained how religious **PTs** have settled in the **PC** over milleniums. Fear-creating and fear-destroying rites, legitimations for power and redistribution, control over behavioral dispositions endangering civilization, are imaginable reasons for the relevance of religious structures, but are they sufficient to explain the presence in the **PC** over such a long period of time? We have to reserve the clarification of this question to other studies.

During the differentiation process of a **PT** system, new type **PTs** establish first and preponderantly at the periphery. A complex centre/periphery -problematique results from this. A growing **PT** system seems to create autonomous systems at its borders ("playing meadow" effect). Thus, it has possibly become clear belatedly that too many resources are spent in the periphery and, therefore, cannot short-termedly be allocated to the **PC**. This seems to have been at least one important mechanism for the ruin of the Roman Empire.

By such system formations at the periphery, a **PC** shift can be the consequence. If such peripheral systems are (possibly temporary) attractors of resources, the pertinence-power transformations, ideologies etc. established there may throughout have an opinion-shaping influence in the **LSU**. Thus, collectively shared opinions of an extra-ordinary manner can emerge, as, for instance, in the late medieval period, that children's crusades could save the Occident.

As a matter of fact, such processes can also be observed in **PT** cones. Obviously, operation and differentiation of a **PT** system are mutually interdependent, so that we have to deal with this more intensely. However, before this the intruding question of pertinence orientation in the **PC** has to be discussed. If the explanations elaborated so far in this book are transferred to the **PC**, the power orientation here must be expected to be particularly strong. A precarious relation exists, however, between the protection strategies concerning privilege structures and redistribution, on the one hand and the technical-economic aspects of production on the other. This can hardly lead to a crisis in the **LSU** under consideration, because the **PC** is to a certain extent blind to such crisis indications owing to its definition power. Only in the 'emergency case' of the confrontation or competition with other **LSUs** or **PT** systems does it become evident whether in **PT** strategies, technological-economic force and competence have been sacrified. As already mentioned above, the Shuttle explosion in February 1986 can be regarded as an example of such an efficiency-diminishing pertinence-power transformation, SPIEGEL 11/19865, p. 271 ff "They switched their brains off".

An 'intelligent' **PC** strategy will thus subordinate privilege structures and redistribution strategies to technological-economic aspects and anticipate emergencies. However, does a concentration of surplus in the MISP not lead immediately to the process, that also in this alimentation volume **PTs** squat, again erecting their own privileged structure etc.? Recall the analysis, relevant to this, of the SDI program in section 2.4.4. Certainly there are differences between LSUs in that some LSUs are more inclined towards opulent **PT** structures than others. As strange as it may sound, within certain boundaries, limited budgets seem to be more effective than high budgets.

However, how can it be achieved that the **PC** does not serve itself, when it systematically has access to surplus and definition power? Solutions of these problems are so vague at present that they shall not be the subject of these deliberations.

4.2.4   Evolution of power territory systems

Now, we return to the question of the differentiation of a **PT** system of an LSU. In the following we will try to describe this process phenomenologically in the form of a rough model. This model can only depict the typical differentiation process, but not the manifold variations. A **PT** system – topologically illustrated – can be imagined as mountains that are permanently in motion (in which even **PC** structures can appear having several cones) with a varying mass centre (= **PC**). Because of this variability the typical differentiation process as a model result will empirically, only rarely, be observed. Thus, what is dealt with is a theoretical construction.

In section 3.2 the difficulties one has to cope with have been shown in order to describe the nonlinear **PT** dynamics in a high- dimesional state space. This complexity grows remarkably in case of competing LSUs, which must be considered as the normal case. It would be extremely difficult to describe the trajectory produced by the **PT** dynamics in this case and its forecasting would be even more complicated. Due to this nonlinear complexity we should not implicitly assume the functioning of a **PT** system when studying its operation, as it happens, for instance, in the traditional functionalism. Nevertheless, we have to postulate some basic operation mechanisms in order to have a theoretical basis at all. The theoretical reflections, scale order calculations and empirical evidence produced so far in this book give us the justification to set up such a conjecture.

The early phase

Let us first consider an LSU wherein there is so much surplus available that already a **PC** exists consisting of military, priests and office clerks. Such LSUs where some **PTs** were already established, i.e. in which population size and surplus are large enough, emerged in the early phase of the (occidental) civilization (before approx. 2000 b.C.) isolated on *TERRA*. In this phase, extraordinary favorable environmental conditions for agriculture could locally make such "LSU-islands" develop. For that reason it is in no way surprising that early civilizations appeared at fertile, climatically preferred sites, for instance, along the Nile or in the Euphratus and Tigres region. As long as the distances between these "islands" were great enough, the corresponding **PT** systems of the LSUs evolved 'autochtonously' in their relevant operation fields. Thus, the study of this early civilizational phase could be very fruitful for an understanding of the basic operational mechanisms of **PT** systems of an LSU.

In the early phase, the square term $c\alpha^2$ (where c may, of course, vary) had not yet developed a strong autocatalytic effect. Moreover, the agricultural technologies evolved very slowly between the innovation advancements.

However, climatically favorable conditions, high fertility of the soil and irrigation systems permitted a considerable population size throughout. Under these circumstances, from a scale order view, it must be expected that some centuries elapsed before the number of **PTs** came to its limit due to lack of finance. During this time, some operation fields developed; predominantly these were regional fiefs which were given, for instance, to officials.

Let us first consider the unrestricted development of a **PT** system. At the beginning a number of **PTs** exists, hence a number of **PTRs**, sub-**PTRs** and subordinates. In the course of time, these position holders drop out of their positions for different reasons and are replaced by persons from the waiting chain. As long as no surplus shortage exists and we may proceed on this assumption in the case of unrestricted evolution, we are justified to presume that population grows faster than **PT** vacancies. Moreover, in the case of no surplus shortage, sub-**PTRs** in particular can hardly be kept from their desire for promotion.

The career jam of aspirants for promotion

A double overdemand for **PT** positions arises on the one hand out of the younger generation and on the other hand from the **PT** system itself and there particularly by sub-**PTRs**. This overdemand, however, meets with already occupied positions. In the case of an easy availability, or mobilization of additional surplus, it is relatively simple to fulfil these desires for promotion by new positions or operational fields. However, territories in agricultural societies are attractive only if they deliver sufficient biomass. We can assume that the most fertile territories are given first so that the attractiveness of this **PT** compensation strategy decreases very slowly in the beginning and finally very rapidly. In this situation, only social territories remain as compensation offering. Since existing social territories are already defined, new operational fields must be defined. Because of the definition power of **PT** members there must be a sufficiently large number of sub-**PTRs** agreeing on the 'promotion' of a new operational field for it to be successful in that definition process. Hence, we can make the conjecture that it is this *career jam* that is responsible for the definition of new operation fields with all the corresponding ideological aspects, e.g. value system, life style, fashion etc.. Since this career jam is more or less completely absorbed by the development of a new territory, such definition peaks will appear cyclically, so long as the **PT** system is not too complex. New value systems will not emerge in each event of such a definition; there may also appear cyclical motions between traditional value systems (e.g. East Roman versus West Roman position, left versus right).

Under this aspect it would be interesting to examine the movement of the Youth, the 68ths, the alternatives' movement etc. If new career aspiring subpopulations emerge, the corresponding definition processes will, of course, be more differentiated, as we presently observe it in the women's lib movement, which shall not mean that there could be no other than career reasons for this movement.

In the course of this section we will elaborate some mechanisms which generally prevent a **PT** system becoming so complex that the **PT** mobility gets 'smoothed' by virtue of a large number of new definitions and becomes, as a consequence, a continous process. At first sight, there are no limits to the variety of definitions; thus career aspirations based on the slogan 'no career' or 'abundance of **PTs**' are imaginable. However, we repeatedly elaborated that 'anti-**PTs**' – at least in the structures of the (occidental) civilizations – cannot be durably established.

Owing to the modest autocatalytical effect of the **PT** number in the early phase of civilizations, the problem of the absorption of **PT** aspirants of the subpopulation of sub-**PTRs** must have been of less significance compared with the problem of the absorption of aspirants stemming from the younger generation. From this the question arises, how the career jam, fed from the non- **PT** population, could be coped with in the case of a **PT** system being slowly differentiated and slowly evolving. Perhaps, the monuments that can be found everywhere give an answer? Perhaps, collective tension phenomena have been reduced, possibly also in view of the described labile **PT** system structure? At any rate there must have been success in defining this activity which made sense over a long period of time. Notice, that a **PT** system stabilizes itself autocatalytically by a such a strategy, because the career aspirant power is absorbed from the basis and **PTs** can proclaim just this achievement as their success.

Approaching the saturation

Nevertheless, sooner or later the typical **PT** system moves inevitably into a saturation zone, unless no natural catastrophies or destruction from outside happens. In this saturation zone, **PT** aspirants can no longer be compensated by new operation fields or **PTs**. As a result the system enters into a critical zone in which different branchings are possible. One solution is expansion, be it territorially by occupation of foreign territories, be it temporarily by debt, i.e. by passing **PT** costs over to future generations. It seems plausible to presume that the latter leads to the creation of money (see HEINSOHN [46]). The former leads to an instantaneous increase in military importance. Now at last, the power structures shift in favour of the male.

Expansion, however, can also appear locally inside an LSU, by the occupation of **PTs**, or the redefinition of operational fields by fractions of **PT** systems of an LSU. Plausibly, this must have been the predominant strategy in situations where expansion was ruled out for geographical reasons, e.g. in the case of islands like Madagaskar, or Japan. In fact, we observe for these countries a centuries-lasting process of militant LSU-internal **PT** competition. In these processes, the elimination of **PT** competitors leads to a temporary relief so long as the raided additional surplus is consumed again by new **PT**s. Then the process restarts. Thus, internal wars have to appear cyclically here, as they are well documented for Madagaskar by BLOCH [8].

Expansion to the outside can also postpone the entrance into the saturation zone only temporarily, because new **PT**s establish from the surplus set free by the elimination of foreign **PT**s. The **PT** number can even grow stronger than before, when the defeated survive. [7] That is, the problematique aggravates in the course of time. One consequence is that internal **PT** quarrels arise: empires collapse into partitioned territories. By this process they are weakened further so that new **PT** structures can emerge at the border regions. Losses at the border regions weaken the legitimation of the **PC**, so that the border regions become more autonomous etc. Thus, this process is autocatalytical.

Notice, that allotment of surplus in an agriculture within the technological saturation zone can proceed only by redistribution. The production of surplus by debt in the saturation zone can, only by imports, lead to a real increase in consumable goods. Hence, this strategy requires a functioning trade system. If not, this strategy must lead to inflation. However, since the coinage power was held by the government and the ordinary population was hardly in a position to refuse the usage of the official currency, this strategy could be forced successfully by the state upon its population in the medium run.

It is a suggestive strategy to enlarge or modernize the military by loans in order to be able to maintain order and to expand to the outside. In this expansion strategy, creditors would have to be a preferred object for elimination. Surely, this strategy has contributed to the persecution of the Jews as prominent creditors.

Upheaval and collapse

If this strategy is not successful, famine and **PT** bankruptcy are the inevitable consequence in an agricultural society. In such crisis, **PT**s collapse and even disappear, so that surplus is set free again for distribution and the process can restart. It is one of the most important aims of the independence of the national bank from government in today's civilizations to avoid, or at least to delay, this process.

The periodical collapses of parts of the **PT** system is an important reason for the fact that – at least in agricultural societies – **PT** systems cannot become very large. Below we will discuss how this behaves in industrial

---

[7]Does the elimination command in the Torah concerning occupied neighbouring populations have its roots herein?

societies. In section 2.3.2 we have already performed calculations on the number of financable **PTs**. However, we neglected debt in this calculation. In Vol. 2 we will consider debt in some simulation models.

At least in the saturation zone, **PTs** will try to mobilize surplus by redistribution up to the maximal limit. Obviously this limit is reached at the subsistence minimum of the non-**PT** members. The more the consumable mass income approaches this minimum, the more difficult it becomes to mobilize additional surplus. This leads to an enlargement of the career jam of the sub-**PTRs**, so that militant **PT** quarrels become very likely. Unlike MARX, I maintain that it is the career jam in the **PT** system that leads to structural changes; this seems to be the more universal mechanism. That this may coincide with mass exploitation is a particular, even if at times a serious, phenomenon.

The upheavals in the **PT** system described here must have been particularly heavy in agricultural societies, after nature-conditioned circumstances having led to a temporary growth in surplus.

Some historical reflections

In Central Europe this case appeared during the period of warm climate at the turn of the millenium. This entailed a strong growth in population; there are estimations that state a quadruplication during the period of 1000–1150 A.D. According to 2.23 the number of **PTs** would have to grow proportionally as the financing conditions are fulfilled, hence, they also must have quadruplicated, and the **PT** system demand must have had to increase sixteenfold with constant c. The chism between state and church could be one of the forms in which this growth of the **PT** system revealed itself. But here, too, there was soon the necessity to absorb the **PT** aspirants from the younger generation. The crusades can be interpreted as a strategy that would simultaneously have solved a great part of these problems. A considerable part of younger men could be absorbed in them and in addition, could serve for expansion and for the acquisition of further surplus (e.g. the raid of the Byzantine treasures). They are the scene on which the **PT** quarrels between the State and the Church could materialize. The successful crusaders, however, reappeared as **PT** aspirants of a grown importance on account of their booty, even if this was modest in comparison with the booty allotted to the **PTs**. Moreover, the traditional expansion towards East Europe was complicated by the successful defense on part of the Slavs. Thus, the crusades could only bring a short-term reduction of strain.

The emergence of new ecclesiastical orders can be regarded as a consequence in this shortage situation. However, this strategy could only then have a strain-reducing effect, if these orders did not create a **PT** demand. Especially advantageous must have been orders with the programmatic of poverty movements. Indeed, such orders arise in this period. History has shown, however, that after a while these anti-**PTs** underwent a process of **PT** formation. Whether this interpretation holds for granted must be shown in detailed analyses which will not be made here.

In an agricultural society, human manpower is of outstanding importance. If favorable climatic conditions like the afore-mentioned period appear, the surplus that may be achieved can only be realized if enough manpower is available. It is well known, that, under agricultural circumstances, families adapt the number of their children to the disposability of sustenance for their support in old age. This is a further indicator of the relevance of manpower. Thus, *ceteris paribus* they raise more children under favorable natural conditions. Whether this adaptation has been accelerated by the cestercian monks in the period considered above, as e.g. HEINSOHN/KNIEPER/STEIGER (1979), OTTEN (1987) [45,107] maintain, is an interesting question. In order to examine this question and the former considerations a detailed analysis of the social situation in the 11th century in Europe in all its aspects would be necessary. However, no historical analyses shall be made in this book.

At any rate, we can presume that in the late 13th century a great number of new territories was established at a high population level, and the **PT** system had approached at least the next saturation zone. In this situation the so-called short interim ice age and later on the plague epidemics penetrate. The first event led to a chaotic process that did not disappear in Germany before the development of the "Electorate" (*Kurfürstentum*). Due to the latter there were regions that were depopulated by 50 % by these epidemics within one year. The strange situation appeared that there existed positions and also **PTRs** due to selective mortality from the epidemics in a time when the surplus producing capacities were already broken down. The consequence must have been an extreme **PT** competition, exploitation of the productives, manifold famines etc., which can indeed be observed.

Nevertheless, it may have happened that the favorable circumstances in the 11th and 12th century led to a productivity level beyond a take-off threshold and innovations having become realizable which finally led to the industrial society, see fig. 4.3 from LENSKY [69].

At least in a saturation zone, demand for inventions and innovations rise dramatically and **PTRs** will undertake great efforts in order to support the establishment of productivity-enlarging technologies. To the extent at which chances for external expansion diminishes and debt strategies become less legitimate, the procurement of new production forms becomes more and more compelling. It is obvious that necessary innovations happen particularly in those times. Thus, the question arises whether there are objective limits to innovations. In section 2.4 and its subsections we discussed approaches to examine this problem field, in the following section we will return to these approaches.

With the transition to machine-oriented production, productivity increases rapidly. Phenomena similar to those in the 10th - 13th century must be

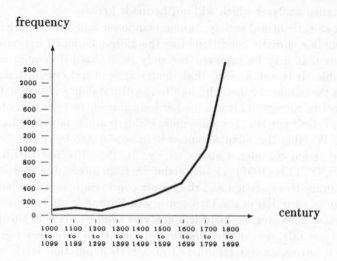

Figure 4.3: Frequency of important innovations and discoveries

expected here. Indeed, new **PTs** developed that established not without violence. The French revolution and the wars of Napoleon seem to be the form in which these upheavals were manifested. After that period three aspects are of high importance for the development of Europe up to the First World War, which in their interdependence, can only roughly be sketched here:

- The wars of Napoleon cleared the '**PT** landscape', so that, stimulated also by growing productivity, the **PT** systems of various LSUs could evolve without great frictions.

- The new production form required big markets, in addition the production volume was so enlarged now that nation-wide **PT** formations could be financed. The German unification, however, was, after the centuries-long split in its territory, an alien element in the European state system.

- The victory over Napoleon, the rapid **PT** formation, partial refeudalization in France, led to a continuation of feudal **PT** structures. However, feudal **PTRs** mostly did not succeed in establishing in civil operation fields so that the feudal/burgois differentiation of the PT system continued.

After the intermezzo of the German-French war at the beginning of the 20th century a situation arose in which a mutual blocking of **PTs** or **PT** systems emerged. This situation is conditioned by the growth in population and **PT** systems in combination with the traditional **PT** structures. It required two world wars to enable the **PT** dynamics to enter into the areas opened by the enlarged productivity. Those states are advantaged which had to bear the lowest burden of old-fashioned **PT** structures at the given technological know-how. In a certain respect they can restart at a *tabula rasa*: Japan and Germany. In these states it takes more time until **PT** systems reach a size at which blocking effects reappear. [8] Today, the expansion of the **PT** system appears predominantly in the form of social territories. If the control over some raw materials is left out of consideration, the classical territorial expansion has entirely receded. The expansion dynamics concentrate predominantly on the new bearers of productivity: machine-oriented technologies. Consequently, **PT** competition must be expected to happen predominantly in this field. Quarrels for technology access must be the consequence, see MAHR [78]. In the U.S.A., this became clear in the McNamara era. Today, SDI is the form in which this confrontation appears. It cannot be excluded that such technological quarrels take the form of a new type of world war that affects great parts of LSUs, recall section 2.4 together with its subsections and the previous section. By this, the outstanding relevance of possible limits to technological expansion are again shown clearly. In the following section we will return to this question quasi-speculatively.

PT systems are hierarchically structured, i.e. each operation field shows hierachical levels and a **PC** exists that predominantly recruits from top-**PTRs**. The operation of a **PT** is characterized by the feature that power issues are generally decided at the upper hierachical levels. In particular decisions on militant **PT** competition are as a rule made at the top level. If a **PT** system develops an additional hierachical level at the top, this generally leads to peace on the lower levels. An extension of the hierachy cone below the top, however, will lead to an intensification of fierce **PT** quarrels. History is full of examples for peace-making effects of the first differentiation, e.g. the American, German or European unification. For the second type of differentiation there are fewer examples. Perhaps, the reformation and the religious wars that were marked by extreme violence are such examples. Notice, that there could also be a top level quarrel between economic and political **PTs**. We shall return to this in Vol. 2.

It must be of utmost turbulence when more than one hierarchy top exists in a **PT** system, e.g. two **PCs**. The investiture quarrel between emperor

---

[8] In the Soviet Union, revolution and second World War produced such a large mass of **PT**-ruin that this state must have evolved without great frictions for a very long period of time. However, the more prolonged such an evolution the more immobile are the established **PT** structures. The attempts at a revision under Gorbatschow can be interpreted as a "revolution from the top" to break open this immobilization.

and pope could be an example of such a situation. Recall what we mentioned just before with regard to a competition between political and economic oligarchies.

4.2.5   Some evolutionary mechanisms

We will regard the first differentiation process as the typical. Let us make the following conjecture concerning this differentiation process:

Conjecture 5 *The number of* **PTs** *in an operational field increases so long as enough surplus can be allocated. If the* **PT** *number in such a field is too large, the hierachy cone splits and new operational fields emerge. If the number of* **PTs** *becomes too large at the top, a new hierarchy level will develop there.*

Both, the cone partition and the new level, entails an increased **PT** demand provided that the number of positions in the operation fields remains unaffected by this partitioning process. It can be assumed, at least soon after a cone partition, that the number of positions is below the average. The possibly considerable conflict costs are also lowered, so that temporarily a remarkable reduction of strain can emerge. After a short time, however, the **PT** demand will be considerably larger than before owing to the existence of a new operation field.

Restrictions

Three types of restrictions limit this process of structurally unlimited growth:

1. Demographic restrictions: Sufficient staff of the **PT** system must be available, be it **PT** members, productives or technologists. Here, complicated allocation problems can appear which we have discussed in section 2.4.4.

2. Natural restrictions: shortage of energy and/or raw materials, physical limitations on *TERRA* (for instance, its specific gravitation), pollution sustenance, limits to biomass production etc.

3. Internal restrictions: mutually blocking **PTs**, **PT** formation processes in areas relevant for societal development (e.g. technology), **PT** demand exceeding reasonable thresholds, scale order of **PT** systems that can hardly be controlled any more.

To 1   Shortage of productive staff can, up to a certain degree, be compensated by increase in productivity; this is also valid for shortage of technology, but to a considerably less degree. The decrease in number of clients below a critical limit, however, can hardly be compensated, but this is unlikely in a world-wide over- population and sufficiently unrestricted mobility. Producers and technological staff as well as technology can also be imported by foreign LSUs. Clients can be replaced by records.

More important is the problem, whether all **PT** positions can still be occupied adequately in case of a decreasing population size. At any rate, the problem of appropriate allocation of the personnel defined as qualified becomes more and more critical. It could be a possible solution to unite several LSUs in order to reach a sufficiently large potential of human beings. Perhaps this aspect, too, is an aspect of the European integration.

No matter how it is, as shown in section 2.4.6.2 the innovation speed cannot be maintained in the long run without the creation of artificial intelligence because the population can only increase with a certain speed (not to speak of the physical limitations on *TERRA*). In other words, without the creation of artificial C , the **PT** system dynamics of an LSU will in the long run inevitably enter the first restriction. How quickly this restriction will be reached depends on the size and growth of population, the starting time of the machine-oriented production, the innovation speed, the allocation of personnel and the propensity towards **PT** formation. A monography would be necessary to examine the complexity of these conditions and to describe possible developmental paths of LSUs. It would be beyond this book simply to discuss the interesting question whether and how – also in normal demographic situations – it will succeed in mobilizing enough personnel for the relevant operational fields of an LSU.

To 2 | It is trivial, that the **PT** dynamics will, because of the physical limitations on *TERRA*, finally reach natural limits.

To 3 | The mechanisms have already been described sufficiently. It is of interest here, whether the effects of these mechanisms can be compensated by productivity growth. With small amplitudes of the business cycles, hence with approximately monotonous growth of production, this may locally, i.e. for one LSU, hold. However, in the case of larger business cycles when oscillations can be caused or amplified by inert **PT** systems or when there is competition between LSUs in relevant operational fields, much then depends on the flexible reaction of a **PT** system. It cannot be excluded that long before approaching the restriction 1. or 2., LSUs decline in this process, because their **PT** systems have become too inefficient.

Power territory partition

Up to now, we examined the process in which a **PT** system gets into tension from the basis, be it by maturing population or by promotion oriented sub-

PTRs, [9] and finally how it declines due to competition between **PTs.** This decline may be accompanied by a large structural decay. As a rule, the extent of a decay is smaller in the case of a **PT** partition which is the usual case when a sufficiently large amount of surplus is available. Let us label the mentioned ruin process as the ruin of a **PT** system *bottom up* and consider it as the typical course of process. But there are also cases in which the **PT** system partitions *top down*. Such events happened after the break-down of the Roman Empire, in which great parts of oligarchies disappeared rapidly within several regions: HODGES/CHERRY [52] mention this procedure for England and found out that, in the 5th century, England partitioned rapidly into many competing territories. A devolution process was the consequence, from which England did not recover until centuries had elapsed. In this perspective it would be interesting to examine Spain after the loss of the Latin-American treasures or South-American states after their independence declaration.

The extent of the cleavage effect could be dependent on the number of hierarchy levels affected by this top down ruin process. Of course, this is dependent on the number of hierarchy levels and this, in turn, is dependent on the development state of the LSU at the time of the partition. It must be presumed that devolution processes appear above all with the ruin top down, because ruin bottom up is part of the 'normal' differentiation process.

In examinations and observations I repeatedly discovered out that the non-**PT** members of an LSU regard a destabilization of the **PT** system with grave concern ("Now we are without support and leadership"). One reason for this might be the selection effect, that self-confidence is a bonus for promotion success towards **PT** positons. [10] The manifold restrictions, partition phenomena and hierarchization effects lead to the following: in the known history of the occidental civilization, **PT** systems have partitioned again and again before they have become very large. A **PT** system is labelled *very large*, if its **PC** possesses more than 10^4 **PTRs** since in this case the **PC** itself would again by scale order be an LSU. Such a **PT** system thus meets with one of the three restrictions, i.e. is dissolved from the borders by competing LSUs, or establishes a further hierarchy level, so that the **PC** size decreases remarkably below 10^4.

With a growing population size and strongly growing productivity, however, so many virtual C are produced that very large LSUs can be imagined in which the **PC** size is considerably above 10^4 without the development of further hierarchy levels. The U.S.A. and the Soviet Union can be examples of this. If this is right, new branchings in new evolution paths must be expected here. We could speculate that in the U.S.A. strong status and racial cleav-

---

[9] The aspect that one **PTR** holds or pursues further positions was neglected by us here. In Vol. 2, these interlocking aspects will be considered.

[10] It would be interesting to examine whether a destabilization of social hierarchies produce endocrine reactions with the human beings concerned.

ages serve as differentiation mechanisms. This analysis cannot be deepened here.

A generation cycle of power territory formation and decline

Now we can again take up the reflection that **PT** systems evolve cyclically. For the purpose of clarification we will start from the extreme case that a **PT** system has collapsed to a far-reaching extent. Persons of a certain age class comprising predominantly people between 30–50 years of age, then start to occupy or define **PT** positions. First, the generation of the 29, 28, ... old people obviously grow up in this context. They develop the recruitment reservoir for new **PT** members, but only a few people can reach positions here, since the old **PT** members are still 'in charge' and only a few of them leave the system. Some of the aspirants can become subordinates or sub-**PTRs**. After a number of years, the career jam has become so large that new operation fields have to be defined. The **PT** aspirants are in a dynamic phase of life and are willing to be promoted, some of them dispose of **PT** experience. In that set of **PT** aspirants there sometimes develops an informal hierarchical cone (shadow cabinet), in which new top-**PTRs** are already reflecting. By this, an attraction towards a still latent operation field arises, certain values, fashions etc. are shared by more and more aspirants. The dynamics and the novelty of this process lead to increased attention in the non-**PT**-population. If additional surplus can be mobilized, a new formal hierarchical cone will now emerge. Only if no established competences have been affected by this new operation field, it will, as a rule, develop without violence.

A part of the career jam will be absorbed in this new operation field, the remainder is, in the ideal case, so small that it can achieve on the traditional **PT** positions by vacancy chain promotion. Of course, a new operation field can also attract promotion-oriented sub-**PTRs** from other territories. As is familiar, promotion is not only a matter of a higher salary, but also and perhaps more important of a proper field of influence.

Now a long cycle begins here concerning the younger generation. The greater the number of operation fields that are existent, the stronger is the natural absorption capacity of the **PT** system. Thus, concerning this generation cycle it has to be expected that the periods will advance up to a "next critical jam extent". However, there are new **PTRs** and sub-**PTRs** with every new territory. Additional **PTR**-aspirants recruit from the sub-**PTRs**. Thus, with growing differentiation of the **PT** system the reservoir of the **PT** aspirants is to a growing extent filled by sub-**PTRs**. Since these possess **PT**-strategical experiences from their previously occupied positions, it becomes more likely that **PT** partitions will happen, or that the top of the hierarchical cone will grow larger. The relation $S : U$ shows the tendency to become greater than 1 : 10. Despite the absorption of sub-**PTRs** we must expect that in the case of **PT** system growth the number of those sub-**PTRs**, who want to "do something totally different" will increase.

Concerning the set of **PT** aspirants, if the process continues the situation must be arrived at that, at some time, the number of non-compensated sub-**PTRs** will exceed the number of aspirants stemming from the younger generation. The increased absorption capacity of a growing **PT** system, therefore, does not automatically lead to a prolongation of the time periods between two critical career jams. When the **PT** system of an LSU has entered into a critical zone, they can even get shorter.

The predominance of **PT**-experienced sub-**PTRs** in the set of promotion aspirants is especially critical, because these persons are **PT**-strategically qualified. Moreover, as a quadratic growth of **PT** demand ensues from **PT** growth, the situation is likely to arise that **PTs** are mutually blocking within and between territories and finally the **PT** system will more or less be ruined by internally induced collapses or by external aggression. This blocking will be especially strong in situations when many operation fields are involved, or when **PT** strategic know-how is needed simultaneously in many operation fields. The blocking effects can lead finally to problem solutions hardly distinguishable from random outcomes. Here, a new dimension arises in the conflict between pertinence and power orientation. But we will not elaborate on this here.

Since these blocking effects typically appear in a state of far developed differentiation of **PT** systems, they will frequently be accompanied by other crisis aspects, as for instance, debt overload, inflation etc.

If in such a situation a more or less comprehensive decline appears in the **PT** system, new **PTs** can develop in the destroyed territories, i.e. the long cycle restarts from the beginning. The dynamics of the **PT** system is so complex that it can hardly be described more precisely phenomenologically than by what is said here. Under the hierarchy aspect alone, a model in which position holders and aspirants and interlockings would be specified, would contain approx. $4 \cdot 10^4$ stock and flow terms, as we will show further below. By the parameterization of the interlocking and array formalization of hierarchicy levels we shall however succeed in the specification of the quite surveyable model MUE & HIER in Vol 2.

In a comprehensive **PT** system model it must be described how in each territory

- **PT** personnel is recruited,

- clients are defined,

- hierarchies of subordinates, sub-**PTRs** and **PTRs** differentiate,

- surplus is received,

- **PTs** emerge and disappear,

- inputs are transformed into outcomes and

- interaction with other territories is organized.

In this process, the specific routines and organization principles of each territory and their pertinence-power tranformations must be considered. In my view, it is presently impossible to specify a valid and manageable model of this complexity. In Vol. 2, a way is followed in which several models are constructed each of them focusing on one aspect leaving the remaining aspects only roughly specified.

Sociologically, the following fact is interesting: **PTs** define social interests, or, are such contexts themselves, where life events or individual biographies can be located. **PTs** can be designed as attractors of biographies, i.e. **PT** existence depends on allocating biographies towards their territory. In this sense it may be said that **PTs** operate on the set of possible biographies. [11] The life-tree approach developed in [89] is perhaps an instrument that could be used, in the case of appropriate further development, in an integrated **PT**-biography model. The elaboration of this approach, however, is beset with great difficulties: so, for instance, a hierarchical morphogenesis must be specified, for the solution of which, in my view, specific software is required which at present is only in its conceptual stage. In addition, the modelling of the dynamics of a tree structure still presents great difficulties. Solution attempts in this research field must be reserved to future examinations.

As mentioned above, career jams stimulate orientation towards social value structures. This orientation will be attractive provided they are covered by **PT** structures. It would be interesting under this perspective to examine some prominent socio-political issues like the alleged dysfunctioning of the education system (*"Bildungskatastrophe"*), the ecological movements or the women's movement in recent history of the F.R.G. In my opinion the 68 movement was a generation jam in the post-war generation sequences. It will be interesting to observe whether the generation jam expected in the 90ies will, due to the large-size cohorts, again bring about new value orientations.

In an industrial civilization, however, a situation can also be imagined in which, by stagnating or even falling birth rates and high productivity growth, a **PT** system can evolve for a long time without collapsing. In this system, aspirants diffuse into the position system and existing operation fields can grow according to a queuing principle. In such an LSU orientation problems are likely to result in which people will finally no longer know "why they are living at all". If then this 'anomic potential' establishes itself

---

[11]It is known that institutions take biographical aspects into account in their personnel recruitment. This is one of the most important criteria for American firms in respect of leading personnel. An enterprise director told me that men in the 'nest-building phase' are preferred to men in the 'midlife crisis' in his firm.

as **PT** aspirants, extremely dangerous situations can appear. This will be scrutinized in section 4.4 and its subsections.

As a rule, a **PT** system will not enter into critical zones in all its territories simultaneously. Rather it has to be expected that this is first the case with a few territories. With a growing number of territories, however, the likelihood will grow that at least one of them will enter into a critical zone. As a result, the important question arises as to how such turbulences, which occur at a hierarchy level or in a hierarchal cone, are spread over the **PT** system. This question will be discussed in the following section in connection with the local-global problematique.

4.3   Operation and stability of large-scale social units

In the previous chapters, questions on the operation and stability of **PT**s or **PT** system have repeatedly been raised. We drew attention that mere operation should not be confused with permanent sustainability. *Operation* has already been defined as the rule-based transformation of inputs into outputs, or technically, as the identifiability of behavior figures in the state space of a system. The epistemological problems connected with this approach have been stated in previous sections, above all in section 3.2.

4.3.1   Some topological considerations

We will call a system model *stable* if the behavior of its state variables and parameters is restricted to non-trivial behavior channels in the state space spanned by the variables and parameters. For instance, a trivial channel for the variable population is $[0, \infty)$. The stability of a system can be characterized by being not overcharged. In other words that it will not get into situations in which it collapses totally or partly. The world model WORLD II of FORRESTER, for instance, describes, with regard to population development, an unstable system, provided that the behavior channel for this variable is appropriately chosen: population collapses approx. by the year 2050. On the other hand, it is non-chaotic, since if the model continues to run, it becomes evident that growth and collapse repeat cyclically, and therefore, that a behavior figure is identifiable.

A situation of a non-sustainable operation shall be called non-functioning. *Non-functioning* can be characterized by the feature that unexpected movements appear in the system behavior, that small influences have great effects, that turbulences, i.e. erratic ups and downs can be observed. Let us call such a behavior and the corresponding system *chaotic*. Now we are in the position to define non-functioning in an operational manner: If such ups and downs go beyond a pre- defined border the system under consideration shall be called non-functioning. Notice, that a stable system can be non-functioning and a non-functioning system can be stable. Notice further, that a chaotic system can be functioning and stable so long as the chaotic behavior is restricted to specified channels. Each unstable system must in the long run become non-functioning. In this general consideration, a relation beween chaos and instability exists in chaotic systems merely in that they are as a rule more difficult to stabilize than functioning systems. Thus, the general chaos consideration is less fruitful for our investigation. Of greater interest is the problem of local chaos or non-functioning and global instability or non-functioning and the local/global problematique connected: that a system changes, for instance, from a 'smooth' to an erratic behavior, and then goes beyond a threshold and collapses, see fig. 4.4. Or topologically:

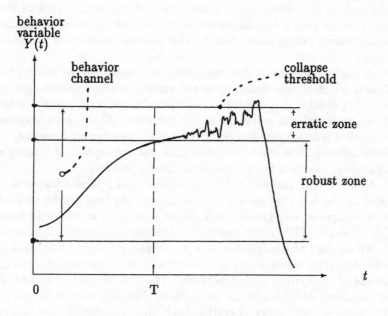

Figure 4.4: Erratic zone and collapse

whether and how chaos and collapse in a part of the state space diffuse into the remainder of the state space. Domains in the state space where a system changes its behavior figure (e.g. by transfer from smooth to erratic behavior, or reversely, by branchings of all kinds, or collapses) will be labelled *critical zones*: recall section 3.2.1. Frequently, critical zones are located at the limits of the system operation capacity; in the following we will also speak of reaching a *saturation* or *shortage* zone. In this zone there is a high likelihood, that small sysenergetic effects are sufficient to let the system collapse. [12] A particular problem results from operation mechanisms proving unfit in the critical zone, although being fit in the robust zone, see fig. 4.4. In this connection it is interesting to what extent the system state space is occupied by critical zones. As a rule, **PT** formation leads in the case of a crisis to the maintenance of such unfit mechanisms.

Because a system behavior can empirically be observed always in finite time periods only, it generally cannot definitively be made out whether a system functions, or is stable. If we were observers in fig. 4.4, say, at time point T, the system seems well describable by a classic saturation model and, therefore, will be characterized as a functioning stable system.

In such situations empirical knowledge on past system behavior is frequently misleading: we have to proceed constructively and identify the chaos or instability creating mechanisms and constellations, and validation must be based on the examination of the 'real' systems with regard to the question whether such mechanisms are established within them or whether such constellations can appear. Just for this purpose, simulation models can be useful.

It must be presumed that conflicting system properties leading to situations in which an 'amelioration' in one variable is accompanied by a 'deterioration' in another variable (in economy, the 'magic quadrangle' can be taken for an example) can result in chaotic behavior. Also (possibly systematic) protracted reaction times of regulations may cause erratic behavior. Competition between social units or individuals who are capable of shaping system parameters can be a further chaos producing potential.

However, the analysis of the consequences of a local collapse is complicated by the fact that such a collapse may in the long run be useful for the more comprehensive system, as it is, for example the case with forest fires GROSSMANN [37]. Local instability thus may ameliorate global stability.

An attempt at a solution of this problematique could be again to analyse basic operation mechanisms and conditions in elementary operation fields instead of the system output behavior. Thus, in the case of an LSU it must be examined, whether and due to which mechanisms and conditions, relevant structures in elementary operation fields (i.e. population, production etc.) collapse. Concerning **PTs** and **PT** systems it must be elucidated whether basic conditions of existence or functioning are affected.

Having this in mind we are now in the position to formulate, at least for single LSUs, working hypotheses concerning the identification of relevant study objects. In a more comprehensive analysis, however, the relativism problem of local instability/global stability appears again: large parts of **PT** systems, even whole LSUs can collapse in order to increase stability in the long run, or for the 'world society'. Whether the reference to a world society

---

[12] Such processes are well known with technical equipments of all kind. Their construction has to make sure that running near complete capacity is sited in a robust zone.

as one LSU is appropriate depends on whether an adequate hierarchization or scale order of **PT** systems is possible. We will return to this question soon. Recall also the speculations in section 3.2.3.

The detection of mechanisms and constellations in connection with stability analyses is one of the particular application fields of computer simulation. However, we are far away from understanding the operation of **PTs**, or even **PT**, systems, so exactly that their operation or stability can be analyzed in detail. We will try to eleborate some few mechanisms and have to restrict to rough guesses. More complex non-linear interdependencies of variables, as they are characteristic for **PTs** systems, can only be analyzed in sufficient detail by using simulation models. This has to be reserved to Vol. 2.

Summarizing, chaos taken alone is of secondary importance for our stability considerations. Of higher interest is the question whether turbulences or phase transfers will reach critical zones in which the system or system parts can 'collapse'. The connection between chaos and stability becomes closer, however, if the structure of thresholds, beyond which a system collapse will happen, is in turn influenced by such turbulences. With increasing duration or intensity of chaos these structural changes can even mutually enforce, as exemplified in fig. 4.5. Such structures are 'malicious', because, from inside

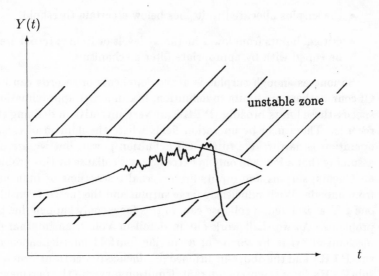

Figure 4.5: Turbulences and stability

the system, it cannot be recognized that the process approaches the chasm: people become accustomed to the erratic behavior, and not before the synergetic coupling with the deteriorating 'external' existence conditions does the system collapse appear.

According to the working hypothesis formulated earlier we will deal with existence and operation conditions of **PTs** and **PT** systems and ask whether mechanisms and constellations can be identified that may entail collapses. Owing to the great importance of the functioning and stability of **PT** systems for the functioning and stability of the LSU under consideration, a considerable part of the operation and stability analysis concerning the LSU is done with the former analysis. We will confine ourselves to this **PT** perspective and not enter into an analysis of mass phenomena, like population development.

4.3.2   Stability of a single power territory

We will start with the consideration of one single **PT**. Its existence and operation conditions are known and its 'normal' operation has been analyzed in section 4.1. From this, indications on the operation and stability problems result immediately. A **PT** gets into functioning troubles if

- its capacity usage goes below a lower boundary of client claims or records,

- the surplus allocated to it goes below a certain threshold,

- critical inputs from lower hierarchy levels or from external areas cannot be coped with by appropriate filter mechanisms.

So long as enough surplus is available, clients or records can be defined. Of course, there are limits to definition, but in a first approximation we may specify these limits broadly. **PTRs** are very inventive in defining clients and records. There may be operation fields where the domain of existence and operation is narrow due to the **PT** definition power, but we are justified in assuming that a **PT** will only in extreme cases collapse by this problematique.

Clients, surplus and inputs are external restrictions or influences acting from outside. With sufficiently large surplus and the (fictive) consideration of one **PT** as isolated, a collapse can, in this focus, only happen due to internal problems. As we shall work out in detail in Vol. 2, an internal precarious mechanism exists by virtue of a specific fourfold interdependence between sub-**PTRs** and the above-mentioned pertinence-power transformation. Since sub-**PTRs** have the preponderant definition power in the pertinent field and the **PTRs** are dependent on sub-**PTRs** expert knowledge, there is always the opportunity for sub-**PTRs** to define objects in the pertinent field such that the corresponding power oriented decisions show a large discrepancy to these objects. These 'malicious' pertinent objects are especially difficult to cope with and, therefore, are taken seriously within the **PT**. A sub-**PTR** able to define his competence in such a critical field, must appear as an indispensable expert of high qualification. Even if the sub-**PTR** are presumed not to have a usurping intention the autocatalytic effect of this mechanism leads to the following: by growing duration of stable existence of a **PT** without the appearance of turbulences and structural ruptures, the likelihood increases that islands of such critical factual issues emerge in an operation field. The relevance of these issues is strengthened autocatalytically. At the end of this process, the **PTR** is powerless in his confrontation with a new power territory in which an additional oligarchy has established itself, unless he does not succeed in satisfying the critical sub-**PTRs** with their own **PTs**. It is even imaginable that those islands of critical factual issues will be defined as new operation fields. In the case of several such emerging territories, it may for a certain time be successful in neutralizing the impacts of their competition by the strategy *divide et impera*, but the likelihood is very large that the **PT** collapses, or partitions in this constellation.

This mechanism becomes effective more probably the younger the **PTR** is when entering his position and the longer is the duration of his career – depending upon pension age, life expectancy etc. Reversely, a natural change in mobility increases the likelihood of a stable process. This could be one reason that predominantly older people enter onto **PT** positions.

PTs differ with respect to the pertinence orientation of their internal definition of the outcome at which they are aiming. The greater the extent of pertinence orientation, the stronger is the effect of the afore-mentioned mechanism. Thus, **PTs** having a high pertinence orientation will more frequently show fashion fluctuations, turbulences etc. than **PTs** with a low pertinence orientation. The long office period of **PTRs** in the political field, e.g. in parties or trade unions, and the higher positional mobility in enterprises could be evidence for the correctness of this hypothesis. [13] Hence, in the economic system there seems to be a more urgent need to decouple an orientational change from firm collapse: this happened by the establishment of limited companies.

Notice, that, in the political sphere, elections can have effects on positional mobility of **PTRs** only to the extent to which their positions are affected by election results. After all that we have elaborated so far, only a small number of **PTRs** will be affected by elections. Nevertheless, if political fields are directly related to important LSU operation fields, such as surplus generation, there can be a stricter binding of position holding to the acceptance of **PT** outcomes by other, for instance, economic **PTRs**. Due to the competence structure, **PT** personnel on higher hierarchy levels are more dependent on this acceptance. Thus, staying in the **PC** depends on being in line with the consensus established in the **PC**. Whether, and under which circumstances, a pertinent orientation from one part of the **PC**, for instance, concerning certain economic issues, can spread over a large part of the **PC**

---

[13] Reversely, a low positional mobility in an economic field may be an indicator of the extent to which this field has become a part of the political sphere.

is an interesting question which, however, must be a subject of other studies.

As concerns the central existence and operation conditions, there cannot be much said in considering one **PT** only, except for the internal mechanisms just mentioned. Since **PTs** compete for clients and surplus, these conditions can be examined only if whole operation fields, i.e. a global cone of **PTs** (see above) are considered. Since clients and surplus are distributed on operation fields, an analysis even on the level of the **PT** system of an LSU can be necessary.

Competition of several **PTs** in one operation field must be of special functioning and stability criticalness, since in this case the same types of clients and records are subjects of competition and, therefore, experiences made in one **PT** can be transferred to other **PTs**. This can be used strategically against competitive **PTs**. If such a territory gets into a shortage of clients or surplus, a transfer to turbulent behavior seems inevitable. In this turbulence, even the collapse of a **PT** can happen. The greater the number of equal ranking **PTs** in the operation field, the more vehement will be this turbulence, and the greater will, as a consequence, be the likelihood that the operation field is affected as a whole. Since acquisition of clients and surplus is of central importance and since, as we know, **PT** demand increases quadratic with the number of **PTs**, we may formulate in a first approximation the following proposition:

Proposition 9 PTs *located in an operation field which is occupied by a large enough number of competitive equal ranking* **PTs** *are unstable.*

Equal ranking means here, that **PTs** dispose of approximately the same number of clients and surplus volume.

In a detailed examination it would now be essential to identify the critical values of **PT** number, as well as clients' and surplus volume shortage. It is not proposed to make such an examination here.

If the proposition 9 is right, we have to presume that **PTRs** are conscious of this problem and that they are searching for solutions. An obvious solution is to care that enough clients and surplus are acquired, so that the behavior space becomes broadened. By this strategy, however, the territory enters into a distribution competition with other territories that we will deal with in the following.

A further solution is for agreements to be made by the oligarchy of an operation field. Notice that in doing this, in the extreme case the number of **PTs** in an operation field is informally reduced to 1, albeit with several top rulers. Such agreements and cooperations can be established, whilst, in their relation to other operation fields, to the non-**PT** population and even to members of own **PTs**, the oligarchy of the operation field under consideration can pretend the existence of competition and a variety of pertinent outcomes.

However, the oligarchy cannot avoid acceptance of the entrance into the oligarchy of some of those persons who succeeded in the promotion into a

PTR position. However, the repeatedly described constancy of the relation between the number of heads and **PC** members indicates that this strategy can be at least locally or temporarily successful. One important reason for this could be that it is often advantageous for oligarchs to join non-cooperative coalitions (which can also consist of single persons).

After all, the propensity towards **PT** formation can be lowered by oligarchization, but it must be taken for granted that the quadratic **PT** demand cannot be abolished, i.e. by oligarchization, the term c can be lowered in $c\alpha^2$ but finally α^2 will dominate. In addition, too large a growth of the oligarchy entails the danger that **PTs** decline from the top. Serious devolution processes can result from this.

Taking all this together we can formulate the following

Conjecture 6 *Operation fields without a sufficient number of clients or surplus volume are unstable. The clients' shortage is of lower importance.*

4.3.3 Stability of a power territory system

This, however, does not mean that the **PT** system of an LSU must also be unstable because the ruin mass of a collapsed territory can be reallocated in favor of other territories so that a pulsating **PT** system is quite possible. If such collapses are non-cyclical, the pulsation may be erratic. Thus, a **PT** system may be chaotic without getting unstable.

We can assume that **PTs** will predominantly collapse at the boundaries, i.e. far apart from the **PC**. Examples are **PTs** occupied with the care of old people or with the raising of children. In decline the associated outcomes are often reduced or even vanish. The redistributable surplus volume originating from such declines will, with priority, be allocated to operation fields near the **PC**. As a consequence, a **PT** system will likely undergo a transformation process towards a larger concentration around the **PC** when approaching client or surplus shortages. The serious problems in connection with a restricted variety and creativity that may result from such a development, have already been indicated.

It is also of great interest to us to analyse a situation in which the collapse of a **PT** may have impacts on the **PT** system of an LSU as a whole and, in particular, because of the affect upon the **PC** itself. With growing concentration around the **PC** this will happen with increasing probablilty. On the other hand, a concentration around the **PC** can increase the striking power of the **PT** system, since it is in a better position to solve its problems by external expansion. In such an expansion, it gains a new periphery. Therefore, this is also a growth process. Altogether we can formulate the

Conjecture 7 *A **PT** system of an LSU is growth-stable.*

Growth-stability of the system means that collapse can only be prevented by permanent (i.e. by trend) growth. The immediate result from this is the following

Lemma 2 *A* **PT** *system evolving free of disturbance is unstable in the long run if there is a finite client mass or surplus.*

This is a pure theoretical formulation. In concrete cases, the finite limits of client and surplus masses may be so high that this case of instability will not appear. Moreover, the lemma 2 holds for a single **PT** system. In reality, however, **PT** systems evolve in a world of competitive **PT** systems and LSUs. In addition there are external causes for instability such as disease and natural catastrophies.

The lack of clients can be replaced by records. For instance, kindergardens can be closed and the available personnel can be occupied with the care of outcasts, or, recreation zones for industrial robots. However, such luxurious operation fields are of low priority compared with **PC** demands, and, especially by virtue of LSU competition, available surplus will be put into **PC**-near operation fields. If **PT** expansion would become impossible on *TERRA*, be it by virtue of a too strong striking power of **PC**s (for instance, nuclear equilibrium) or by the fact that the periphery to be incorporated is burdensome rather than useful (for example, what help would it be to the U.S.A. to incorporate a developing country), the situation may appear that *TERRA* gets too 'scarce' for the possible and desired growth. Perhaps this is a deeper reason for SDI.

The interesting side question results whether a global oligarchy, hence the emergence of a new hierarchy level for LSUs, is possible world-wide and whether **PT** dynamics can slow down. After all we have elaborated so far, such a global oligarchy would again quickly collapse by reason of its size, so that this way of coping effectively with instability seems unlikely.

The question of a possible slow down of **PT** dynamics is also a question concerning the existence of constellations in which forces balance which enhance and damp dynamics. In other words: whether there are equilibria paths. This question can hardly be answered phenomenologically because the **PT** dynamics are too complex. What we can conclude as an obvious conjecture is that an enduringly stagnating or declining population size can finally lead to the situation that no persons can be found to occupy **PT** positions. By virtue of the resulting vacancies, surplus is set free. A decreasing number of **PT** aspirants and **PT** members can, therefore, lead to a surplus situation, in which there is so much surplus per **PTR**, that no instabilities will occur, provided productivity is not reduced by that decline of **PT**s. This, indeed, is the decisive question:

Can productivity be kept on its level in a process of decreasing **PT** *dynamics?*

The desire for the acquisition of scarce territories surely is a strong achievement stimulus in (occidental) civilizations. Perhaps the decline of Venice can partly be explained by such a slow-down of PT dynamics.

In a system of competitive LSUs, the survival of an LSU whose PT system dynamics has declined is certainly imaginable only at the periphery of the world societal system. Moreover, anomia problems can result from such a constellation.

Internal expansion, i.e. growth of production, is finally restricted by natural limits (e.g. scarcity of resources) and the physical limits of technical progress. Because saving of resources can also be achieved in part by appropriate technologies, an evolving PT system will get more and more dependent on technology and the PC will incorporate more and more technological features. It depends decisively on the propensity towards PT formation how far the growth potentials stemming from this rationalization will be used.

If the attempt at a selective (i.e. PT, not MASS oriented) take off to the orbit will not succeed, the natural limits on TERRA must sometime be reached. It is highly probable that these limits will be reached particularly by those LSUs whose PT systems are located within or near critical zones. Hence, we must expect that PT systems reaching the natural (e.g. ecological) limits will collapse in violent turbulences.

Thus, the question arises whether stable evolutionary paths exist at all in the mainstream development of PT systems. To underline it again: stability with regard to PT system operation does not mean non-existence of violence, or, absence of PT collapse; it means that the PT system predominantly, in particular in the PC, evolves without collapse. [14] We elaborated two possibilities of stable development paths, stagnation or slight diminution of population on the one hand, permanent expansion, possibly beyond TERRA, on the other hand. However, stable expansion to the orbit is possible only if adequate technologies are available, the volume of production is large enough and if the timing of the take off is appropriate: expansion must resort to extra-terrestrian resources before the 'exodus' will fail when confronted with natural limits on TERRA. If the 'exodus-PTs' are sufficiently present in the PC, the redistribution of surplus on the corresponding (orbital) operation fields will be realised. To the exodus-problematique see O'NEILL, HEPPENHEIMER [106,48].

---

[14]However, the internal expansion by virtue of production is generally less violent inside an LSU than an evolution without this growth potential, because many fierce competitions can be mitigated by surplus distribution. Perhaps this mechanism answers the open question posed by LENSKI [70] concerning the reasons rendering the relation

$$growing\ production \rightarrow growing\ violence$$

no longer valid with the beginning of machine-oriented production.

However, both types of stable paths are extreme types that will be observed only in rare cases. Thus, the question arises whether there can be stable evolutionary paths in the case of normal operation of an LSU. [15] A stable evolutionary path implies that there exists a combination of population development, number of clients, territorial, hierachical and centre-periphery-specific differentiation of productivity and technology development as well as production in the **PT** system such that neither the **PT** system collapses by internal competition, nor endogeneous or exogeneous shortages appear systematically. This constellation is so complex that it cannot be answered phenomenologically. Even in the simulation models that will be elaborated in Vol. 2, only partial analyses are possible.

It must be presumed, however, that, if such a path should exist at all, it is a labile equilibrium path; in a certain respect, a tour of mountain ridges by which the system can be led on an unstable path by small disturbances. In a system of competitive highly civilized LSUs, in which disturbances are produced permanently, it can be excepted that no path of that kind can appear that lasts for a historical time period of, say, 500 years. Thus, only those paths remain which we characterized as growth-stable paths. If competition between LSUs were non-existent, the stable surplus-path would be enticing. The 'exodus-path' corresponds to a tunnel-through strategy which, however, will fail if its intended route reveals as a blind alley. See fig. 4.6. In the case of a blind alley, tunnel-through seems to be an adequate concept, because the blind alley does not exist independently from **PT** strategies. If a return in the tunnel is connected with too great risks, a situation can arise in which many **PT** systems are ready to make large sacrifices (preferentially on account of the periphery), in order to avert the vast catastrophe.

Concerning, for instance, the SDI program, it appears rational if as many LSUs as possible participate in it. As already shown in section 2.4.4, this would, in addition, spread **PT** formation over a larger number of LSUs, and, therefore, reduce **PT** formation in the single LSUs. It could be rational for an opposing **PT** system to create exactly so much competitive pressure that the exodus strategy would be maintained and then defensively wait to see how the exodus-LSUs enter into a turbulent zone. We will not go into details of these strategical reflections.

Therefore, as a normal case of possible stable paths the growth-stable case remains, in which it is attempted to create a sufficient surplus volume all the time so that an unstable development is avoided when being confronted with new **PTs**, operation fields, clients or records. As already mentioned, surplus can be procured by means of loans. Growth problems, however, are not solved by this strategy but are passed over to the future LSU.

Indeed, most development problems of **PT** systems are solved by passing problems over to other units, be it territorially on foreign LSUs (e.g. de-

---

[15]The case that an LSU is stable because it has suffered a devolution process shall be neglected as trivial.

functional
condition 2

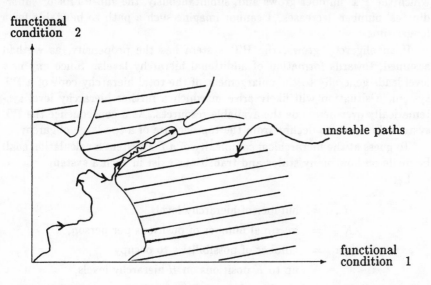

unstable paths

functional
condition 1

Figure 4.6: Topological structure of an exodus-path

velopment countries), hierarchically on subordinates and non-**PT** members
(e.g. redistribution), sectorally on non-LSU sectors (e.g. depletion of natural
systems) or, as mentioned, temporarily on the future development of LSUs
or **PT** systems.

In a world of competitive LSUs, important sequential problems result in
this *pass-over* strategy: which LSU **PT** system will win the complex pass-
over game. If violent pass-over strategies are non-performable, oligarchies
of various LSUs will try to come to agreement. The decree on environment
assessment of the European Community can be regarded as such an agreement.

4.3.4   Hierarchization and power territory formation

Hence how long a **PT** system of an LSU can be growth-stable depends on
so many variables that phenomenologically no general results can be yielded.
Here, we will merely point to the structural problem that a **PT** system evolving over a long time without collapsing will finally over-exceed all realistic
limits of available population or production. Since **PTs** are located in the
surplus domain they are always in need of productive members who can create
the surplus. Also, with higher productivity it is always only a part of the
employable people who can be **PT** members. Thus, the situation appears in

which the **PT** number grows and, simultaneously, the sub-PTRs or subordinates' number decreases. I cannot imagine such a path to be stable for a longer time.

If an oligarchy grows, the **PT** system has the propensity, as we had assumed, towards formation of additional hierarchy levels. Since any new level leads generally to the enlargement of the total hierarchy cone of a **PT** system, a situation will likely arise in which a further hierarchy level systematically over-demands the available resources. As a consequence the **PT** system threatens to decline from the top because of a too large oligarchy.

To guess at the hierarchical complexity of a **PT** system a calculation shall be made on how many states and transitions exist in such a system.

Let

$$H : \quad = \quad \text{number of hierarchy levels,}$$
$$K : \quad = \quad \text{maximal number of positions per person,}$$
$$n(.) : \quad = \quad \text{number of possibilities to occupy}$$
$$\text{up to } K \text{ positions on } H \text{ hierarchy levels,}$$
$$m(.) : \quad = \quad \text{number of possibilities to occupy}$$
$$\text{exactly } k \text{ positions on } H \text{ hierarchy levels,}$$
$$k \quad = \quad 0, 1, \ldots, K \quad .$$

Then it holds:

$$n(H, K) = \sum_{k=0}^{K} m(k/H) \qquad . \tag{4.14}$$

Recursively it can be calculated:

$$m(H, K) = \begin{pmatrix} H + k - 1 \\ k \end{pmatrix} \qquad . \tag{4.15}$$

Inserting this into 4.14 it results:

$$n(H, K) = \sum_{k=0}^{K} \begin{pmatrix} H + k - 1 \\ k \end{pmatrix} \qquad . \tag{4.16}$$

Let us choose $H \leq 4$ and $K \leq 4$. Notice, that H and K are equifunctional, i.e.

$$n(H + a, K) = n(H, K + a)$$

with

$$a \in \{-\max(H, K), \ldots, 0, 1, 2, \ldots\} \quad .$$

However, K is restricted by the time budget of the **PT** members under consideration. Let us distinguish between the following types of individuals:

$$E : = \textbf{PTRs},$$
$$S : = \text{sub-}\textbf{PTRs},$$
$$W : = \textbf{PT} \text{ aspirants},$$

and the following types of positions

$$PE : = \textbf{PTR} \text{ positions},$$
$$PS : = \text{sub-}\textbf{PTR} \text{ positions},$$
$$PV : = \text{vacancies} \quad .$$

The complexity of such a **PT** system can be indicated by the number of states and of possible transitions between them. A lower bound guess at the complexity is based on the assumption that there exist only the following transitions for individuals:

$$E \to E \ , \ E \to S \ , \ S \to E \ , \ S \to S \ , \ E \to W \ , \ S \to W \ ,$$
$$W \to E \ , \ W \to S$$

and the following transitions between positions:

$$PE \to PE \ , \ PS \to PS \ , \ PE \to PV \ , \ PS \to PV \ , \ PV \to PE \ ,$$
$$PV \to PS \ , \ PS \to PE \quad .$$

Let as make the additional assumptions:

1. PS $\to$ PE represents a **PT** partition,

2. PE $\to$ PS is excluded,

3. there are no relations between persons and positions that are of complexity relevance,

4. the before-mentioned transitions can be specified as mutual independent.

Then the complexity indicator C results as:

$$C = L + R \tag{4.17}$$

with

$L : = $ number of states,

$R : = $ number of transitions .

– – –

$$L = L_i + L_p \quad , \tag{4.18}$$

with

$$i : = \text{individual index},$$
$$p : = \text{position index} \quad .$$

$- - -$

$$L_i = 3n(H, K)$$
$$\text{with} \quad n(H, K) \quad \text{from 4.16,}$$
$$\text{``3'' because of} \quad E, S, W \quad \text{and assumption 4,}$$
$$L_p = 3H \quad . \tag{4.19}$$

$- - -$

$$R_i = R_{E \to E} + \ldots + R_{W \to S}$$
$$R_p = R_{PE \to PE} + \ldots + R_{PS \to PE} \tag{4.20}$$

$- - -$

$$R_i = 8[n(H, K)]^2 \quad ,$$
$$\text{since all 8 processes are equivalent,}$$
$$R_p = 7H^2 \tag{4.21}$$

$- - -$

Altogether we get :
$$C = 3n(H, K) + 3H + 8[n(H, K)]^2 + 7H^2 \quad . \tag{4.22}$$

Numerical example: For $H = 4$ and $K = 4$ we get:

$$C = 3 \cdot 70 + 3 \cdot 4 + 8 \cdot 4900 + 7 \cdot 16 = 39,534 \approx 4 \cdot 10^4 \quad .$$

If we now assume that 2.23 is valid and choose

$$E : S = 1 : 10 \quad ,$$

and interpret hN as the (minimal) natural **PTR** reservoir in an LSU, then we can equate:

$$\alpha + 10\alpha = 11hN \quad .$$

Let us now posit the hypothesis, that an LSU must be so large that every transition according to 4.21 can be performed, i.e. that there is for each transition an E or S. Hence,

$$8[n(H, K)]^2$$

persons are required. From this the necessary population size N to realize all (H, K) - combinations can be calculated, namely:

$$N^*(H, K) = 8[n(H, K)]^2 h^{-1}/11 \quad . \tag{4.23}$$

With $K_{max} = 4$ it results:

$$N^*(H = 1) = 181,818$$
$$N^*(H = 2) = 1.64 \cdot 10^6$$
$$N^*(H = 3) = 8.9 \cdot 10^6$$
$$N^*(H = 4) = 35.64 \cdot 10^6$$

For $H = 4$ we reach the scale order of the population size of the F.R.G, whereas for $H = 5$ we get

$$N^*(H = 5) = 115.5 \cdot 10^6$$

which already surmounts the scale order of the F.R.G. population size and reaches the magnitude order of the population size of the European Community.

Notice, that in a detailed model all terms must be specified explicitly, hence in our example approx. $4 \cdot 10^4$. Models of such a complexity are neither overseeable nor manageable. In the model MUE & HIER in Vol. 2 we arrive at a remarkable reduction of model complexity by introducing the terms $k_E = PE/E$ and $k_S = PS/S$. The reduction of model complexity, hence, is achieved by a parameterization of interlocking. Perhaps also in reality, interlocking leads to a reduction of **PT** system complexity?

However, the development of **PTs** and **PT** systems is restricted not only by the population size of the LSU under consideration, but also by the volume of production. In recalling section (2.3) we can posit the **PTR** number in an LSU as

$$\alpha \approx hV = h(P - N)$$

and the total **PT** demand as $c\alpha^2$, where α denoted the **PTR** number in the **PC**, P the production in the LSU per year measured in $\mathcal{C}$, and N population size. If we choose the labor productivity π_A as a simplified productivity indicator, it results:

$$P = qN\pi_A$$

with $q :=$ quota of productives.

Since a part of production, denoted with $1 - \beta$, is reserved for non-**PT** members,

$$\rho = 10^{-8}c(\pi_A q - 1)^2 N/(\beta\pi_A q) \leq 1 \tag{4.24}$$

results as the restriction to the number of **PTRs** due to the limited production. Notice, that from this a reference value for N can be derived, namely 10^8. Maybe 10^8 can be interpreted as the threshold beyond which we can speak of *very large social units*.

If we choose $\beta = .4$, $c = .5$, and $q = .4$ (these are plausible values for the F.R.G. in 1980), then it results for $\pi_A = 8$ (again the situation of the

F.R.G. in 1980) a $\rho = 1.13$, that is already an overdemand compared with production which must be fulfilled by other means, for instance, by debt.

In the case of a critical ρ, i.e. $\rho > 1$, each production growth leads to an aggravation of the situation. Here we see once again how important is the parameter c, which can be interpreted as an opulence parameter. But even in the case of $c = .25$, $N = 50 \cdot 10^6$, $q = .4$ and $\beta = .5$, it may be a future plausible constellation for the F.R.G., a $\pi_A = 15$ leads to a critical ρ, and at $\pi_A = 17$ it even results a $\rho = 1.24$, a scale order which certainly cannot be compensated by debt.

These considerations, of course, are simplified since the interdependencies beween the terms and with additional relevant variables are neglected. This will be specified in some models in Vol. 2. The systematic overcharge of economic potentials, however, should become clear even in this simplified specification.

LSUs will be different with regard to parameters and structures. In particular, from this there result selective advantages and disadvantages in a world system of competitive LSUs. However, we will not enter into a world-wide analytic perspective.

4.3.5   Spreading of a local instability over the system

Since the **PT** system of an LSU more often will show instability than stability a local/global question becomes relevant: whether and how instabilities or turbulences occurring in one **PT** or operation field spread over the **PT** system. This cannot be answered with universal validity because spreading depends on the specific organization of the **PT** system under consideration. Damaging effects will in any case be produced by mechanisms which support that spreading. LUHMANN has repeatedly pointed out that "universal media" can be such dangerous mechanisms, for instance, "justice" or "money" or "scientific truth". Such mechanisms can entail mutual amplifications of damage processes. However, it must be noticed as mentioned above, that such turbulences can be desired strategically. For instance, a law for data privacy protection can be invented to divert from other issues. It may even happen that a **PT** is tranquilized by rendering it stable, so that fruitful turbulences are prevented (*"Friedhofsruhe"*). Thus, stability considerations are not very informative unless mechanisms are not worked out concretely and, especially, unless it is analyzed [16] whether **PTs** close to the **PC** are affected. For instance, ubiquitous turbulence in the **PT** system periphery combined simultaneously with a minimization of universal media effects on the **PC** can lead to a remarkable discharge of the **PC** despite the fact that instability is

---

[16]Hence, in the **PT** system theory, neither LUHMANN's position is shared that there is no rank order or operation fields nor can we accept his opinion that there is no direction in societal evolution. LUHMANN's position concerning the self-referentiality of social systems, however, is largely accepted: recall section 3. and 3.2.

predominant in the system. In the periphery and on lower hierarchy levels of the **PT** system a stressing work blocks the time budget of **PT** aspirants. Territorial and centre/periphery differentiation, as well as hierarchization and oligarchization, will in the normal case be sufficient to prevent the **PC** from those disturbances, or, to filter them out during their passage through the hierarchical system, provided the **PT** system does not operate in a critical zone. If, however, several **PTs** or even parts of the **PC** are operating in a critical zone the problem aggravates considerably. In such cases disturbances can spread over the system and can even lead to its collapse. In any case, functioning and stability of the **PT** system strongly depend on the functioning and stability of its oligarchy. We will return to this aspect in section 4.4 and its subsections.

Even if we suppose that turbulences can be restricted to one operation field, the question must be raised, whether the surplus necessary to reach that aim does not surpass the capacity of a **PT** system to mobilize surplus. We are justified in assuming that, in a local perspective, i.e. for each **PT**, there is the propensity to maximize the demand for surplus, whereas the oligarchy is engaged [17] in minimizing the disturbing consequences stemming from that behavior. We see that micro and macro levels are opposed. [18]

4.3.6 Power territory system functioning: the parameters of the total demand equation

In the foregoing we did elaborate upon the general problematique of **PT** system functioning that resource potentials of all kinds are systematically overdemanded by the propensity towards **PT** formation. Therefore, we have now to pose the question whether parameters influencing **PT** demand, i.e. c and especially ϵ in 2.26 which denoted **PT** formation propensity, can be subject to variation in order to achieve at stable development paths, at least for time periods covering several generations.

So long as V is small compared with N, surplus is spent almost completely for financing the obligatory hierarchical system so that there is no scope for such variations. This seems to be one main reason for the tragedy of agricultural societies: On the one hand productivity is already so large that N can become considerably large, on the other hand scope barely exists to escape from the law $\alpha = hN$. Due to the overproportional **PT** demand $c\alpha^2$ this must lead to a permanent competition for territories.

What happens, however, if V is large compared with N? To examine this situation let a v be defined by virtue of which we can combine V with the minimum hN:

---

[17]To the homogeneity of the oligarchy see USEEM [132].

[18]Perhaps this is the reason for aggregation difficulties. If we are right in this speculation, the aggregation problematique would be no methodological but a deep theoretical problem, see [97].

$$\alpha = hN + v(hV - hN) \quad ,$$

where $V \geq N$ shall be assumed.

Thus, a possible scope for influencing **PT** formation propensity is opened only if $P \geq 2N$, which refers to a labor productivity of $\pi_A \approx 5$. Inserting $V = P - N$, we get the following linear combination:

$$\alpha = (1 - v)hN + vh(P - N) \quad . \tag{4.25}$$

P in turn depends on α via

$$P = [N - (1 + s + u)\alpha]q\pi_A$$

with

$$s : \quad = \quad \text{sub-}\textbf{PTRs} \text{ per } \textbf{PTR},$$
$$u : \quad = \quad \text{subordinates per } \textbf{PTR},$$
$$q : \quad = \quad \text{quota of productives},$$
$$\pi_A : \quad = \quad \text{labor productivity} \quad .$$

Inserting this yields:

$$\alpha = \frac{1 + v(q\pi_A - 2)}{1 + vh(1 + s + u)q\pi_A}hN \quad . \tag{4.26}$$

For $v = .5$, $q = .4$, $\pi_A = 8$, $N = 60 \cdot 10^6$, that is, approx. the constellation for the F.R.G. in 1980, the result is:

$$\alpha = 9,492 \quad .$$

$v = 1$ results in $\alpha = 12,907$, and $v = 0$ in $\alpha = 6,000$ (i.e. $= hN$). Hence, the scope is

$$\frac{12,907}{6,000} = 2.15, \text{ that is, } 115 \text{ \%}.$$

Let us insert v into 2.27 after the parameterization

$$v = \tilde{v}\,\beta\gamma \quad , \tag{4.27}$$

where

$$\gamma : \quad = \quad \text{saving effect}$$
$$\text{due to territorial differentiation,}$$
$$\beta : \quad = \quad \text{cost effect due to hierarchization,}$$
$$\tilde{v} : \quad = \quad \text{LSU-specific } \textbf{PT} \text{ propensity.}$$

Notice, that $\tilde{v} = 1$ held in 2.27.

$\tilde{v}$, β and γ will vary from LSU to LSU. Due to this variation, LSUs will gain specific selective advantages and disadvantages in the world system of competitive LSUs. A minimized **PT** formation propensity is by no means favorable in this respect in all cases because we are justified in assuming that a remarkable reduction of **PT** formation coincides with a slow-down of aggressiveness and it is known that a minimal aggressiveness is necessary for survival. Reversely, a too strong **PT** formation will be disadvantageous due to the resulting mutual blocking effects between **PTs** and the above-mentioned overdemand of resource potentials.

4.27 is a rough simplification, because interdependencies between territorial differentiation, hierarchization, and **PT** formation propensity are neglected in this specification. However, we know little about this, and the corresponding models must be very complex and non-linear, since already in the case of one LSU, distribution algorithms and a multiplicity of restrictions must be taken into account. A detailed analysis of these problems must, therefore, be reserved to future researches.

Since, however, γ is limited from above and β from below, $\tilde{v}$ must be the decisive parameter. However, as argued before, due to lack of knowledge in this field we cannot do much more than to assume a maximal **PT** formation propensity, i.e. $v = 1$, as was done in 2.27. This seems to be justified when we reflect upon the results of political activities concerning reforms of all kind, reduction of subsidies etc.: in fact, there seems to be no great opportunity to alter the propensity towards **PT** formation.

Thus, what is left over, is the variation of c. Concerning this parameter, oligarchization via interlocking can have saving effects, as we have already mentioned. We posited that the effect of c is proportional with the interlocking coefficient

$$k = P_E/\alpha \qquad ,$$

where $P_E :=$ number of **PTR** positions.
Hence,

$$c = c_1 k \qquad ,$$

with c_1 as the proportionality constant.
Since $\alpha = P_E/k$ we get for the **PT** demand in an LSU:

$$B_E = c_1 k (P_E/k)^2 = c_1 P_E^2/k \quad .$$

For $P_E = 10^4$ and $c_1 = 1$ for growing k a falling **PT** demand results, as is shown in tab. 4.4. The time budget of **PTRs**, however, leads to a restriction of k within narrow limits. So a $k > 1.5$ will be impossible in the **PC**. Thus finally, there is only the proportionality constant c_1 to be investigated. Is there something like Prussian saving and mediterranean opulence? Maybe there is a corresponding h for each civilizational path. For instance, the

α	10,000	6,667	5,000	4,000	3,333
B_E $10^6\,C$	100.0	66.7	50.0	40.0	33.3
k	1.0	1.5	2.0	2.5	3.0

Table 4.4: Interlocking and **PT** demand

$h = 10^{-4}$ in the case of the occidental civilization can possibly be traced back to the fact that in this civilization the hiearchy levels are occupied with positions by powers of ten, i.e. 10^0 on the top of one **PT**, 10^1 on the next level etc.. These relations were practised in the military organization of the Roman Empire. We need then only to assume four hiearchy levels in the **PT** system to get $10^{-4}N$ as an approximation of the **PTRs** number on the top level of the **PT** system, i.e. the **PC**. This means that the non-**PT** members, i.e. the remaining population, is located on the lowest (the fourth) level, so that on the third level there are

$$(\mid PC \mid \cdot 10^3)^{-1} N$$

persons under the control of one **PT** member. Assuming that the Roman Empire at some time had approximately $60 \cdot 10^6$ inhabitants the result would be

$$\mid PC \mid = 6,000$$

and 100 persons was the control span of a **PT** member on the third level. The whole **PT** system contained 600,000 members. All that seems to be in plausible scale order.

An application of 2.23 on the Peoples Republic of China would have the result, if we suppose an $N = 10^9$, that $\mid PC \mid = 100,000$, an exorbitantly large number if we take into regard, that $\mid PC \mid$ is of scale order of

$$10 \cdot \mid LSU \mid_{\min} \quad .$$

According to the theory elaborated in this book, that is, applying occidental circumstances to the Peoples Republic, a **PT** system of such a scale order must depict properties of a system in a critical zone, for instance overdebt, striving for expansion, **PT** collapses etc. Perhaps the Cultural Revolution was such a collapse resulting in a volume of **PT** ruin mass which allowed for a new cycle of **PT** system development. Otherwise, the Peoples Republic must possess a significantly smaller h than that of the occidental civilization or be characterized by completely different operation mechanisms. Both features could be subjects of a program "learning from China". Reversely, if the theory developed in this book also held for China, the recent strategy of internal expansion, i.e. economic growth, in China must lead to considerable stability problems.

REICH [110] pointed out after a comparison between the U.S. and other industrial societies, that in Japan and several European countries the difference between management and labor costs are smaller than in the U.S. He described the case of a Japanese firm running into a critical situation in which the salaries of personnel were subject to a bigger reduction, the higher the positional rank they held.

This leads us to a further aspect in our analysis of **PT** formation consequences: the amount of alimentation of the **PTRs** and the sub-PTRs which was denoted by E and S in 2.31. Recall the explicit derivation of the **PT** demand from a hierarchy model in section 4.1. Only in this explicit formulation did the relevance of these aspects, especially of E, become evident, since we assumed with some justification that the **PT** demand for a compensation activity in favor of a **PT** aspirant orientates itself towards E. From the equation system 4.3, 4.4, ... , therefore, it results that the total **PT** system demand ca^2 is directly affected by E.

Thus, despite an equal number of **PTRs** the **PT** system demand can vary significantly. Of course, at sometime the quadratic demand will become the dominant factor in every **PT** system, but this *sometime* can make remarkable differences between **PT** systems. This is particularly relevant for the strategic position of an LSU in a system of competitive LSUs, since in this case much depends on the sequence of running into critical zones. Trivially the last one will win the competition. At present, however, such strategic analyses cannot be performed in detail due to the absence of an adequate methodology so we must be satisfied with structural considerations for the moment.

We can summarize that the typical evolutionary path of a **PT** system of an LSU will enter into a saturation zone where turbulences of system behavior will appear with high probability. Due to the short and sometimes mid-term discharging effect of debting, this strategy is compelling. Cyclical overcharge with debt must, therefore, be the normal case. From this it appears fruitful to use debt as an indicator of the **PT** system state. Thus, a **PT** system would operate further away from a critical zone the lower its total debt.

4.3.7 Large scale social unit wide functioning problems of power territory systems

So far the local/global problematique was related to the process of turbulences or collapse consequences from one operation field spreading over the **PT** system, and thereby, over the LSU under consideration. Not so evident is the reverse case that due to a bad constellation of properties in one operation field, turbulences or instabilities are initiated in other operation fields. This, however, can happen only if interdependencies between the operation fields under consideration are strong enough. Generally, such horizontal interdependencies are weak or non-existent. To exemplify this, there is no direct interdependence between the educational and the sanitarian system.

Vertically, however, this can not be excluded: an operation field can be affected from another operation field through a chain of consequences which contains the **PC**, i.e. there is a chain

turbulences in an operation field A

↓

turbulences in the **PC**

↓

turbulences in an operation field B.

As an example, imagine the intricate situation of a strong permanent agriculture oligarchy in opposition to an environment protection oligarchy, aggravated by the establishment in the first-mentioned oligarchy of a sub-oligarchy in the newly defined operation field of an agriculture oriented to ecologically sustainable production.

Especially precarious are synergetic effects such that situations as aforementioned are unproblematic in single operation fields and gain their deterrent characteristics as a consequence of their combination in the **PC**. That is, in such cases sleeping crisis situations can exist which awake in the case of specific properties in several operation fields. In contrast to the afore- mentioned example of ecological agriculture such a crisis is *principally* incapable of being anticipated in the traditional modes of perceptional and information processing routines in **PT** systems. If reaction time periods for adaptation to such problematic situations are long enough then collapse can generally be prevented by structural changes in the **PT** system. In highly complex **PT** systems, however, situations can emerge in which the number of critical constellations becomes so large that a systematic overload of the **PC** adaptation capacity results. Then it can happen that an adaptation to one problem amplifies critical constellations in other operation fields of the LSU. This leads with high likelihood to a decline of reaction times. If this situation is reached not enough time for error correction remains in the event of an adaptation failure and this can occur even in a situation of an uncharged operation capacity of a **PT** system: then, in extreme cases, one failure will be sufficient to prompt a complex crisis constellation. Briefly, what is hypothesized here is that **PT** systems have a tendency to become chaotic with growing complexity.

Such phenomena can only be described vividly by making use of complex dynamic topological simulations, an approach to which, so far, there are remarkable blanks of software as well as of hardware.

The aforementioned chaotic scenario has described the late stage of a **PT** system. Recall our conjecture that **PT** systems try to solve their problems by pass-over strategies (passing problems over to lower hierarchical levels, foreign LSUs, future generations, nature). If we could succeed in the specification of 'reservoirs' to be filled by 'matter' in these pass-over strategies, then we could make the approach of indicating crisis intensity by the extent to which these reservoirs are filled. The late stage of a **PT** system would then be characterized by the fact that at least one reservoir goes to zero, see fig. 4.7. The vertical and horizontal lines in S_{t_i} in fig. 4.7 indicate that a backwards

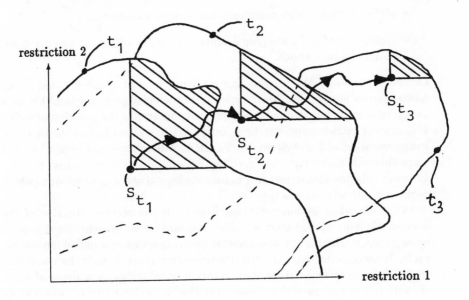

Figure 4.7: Niche reduction in the developmental path of a **PT** system
\ \ \ \   remaining scope for development

directed development (devolution) is designed as impossible.

An extreme crisis stemming from a slow down of the potential to the pass-over strategy arises if:

- no further scope is available for internal expansion (i.e. economic growth),

- in the case of further passing over of problems to foreign LSUs, these will collapse,

- serious damages occur in the natural environment of the LSU under consideration,

- a debt overcharge occurs,

- capabilities of redistribution from bottom up to higher hierarchical levels have vanished.

If such a constellation exists simultaneously in many LSUs then the capacity limit of *TERRA* is reached so that a branching situation emerges in which the following paths of development are possible:

- selective take off to the orbit,

- global collapse, with massive devolution consequences,

- emergence of so far sleeping evolutionary paths which can become dominant in a new epoch.

Of course, the probability that many LSUs enter into such a situation simultaneously is not high. More probable is the collapse of single LSUs, as a sequence of local catastrophes. Notice, that this entails the question of which **PT** system (which must not be a national **PT** system but could be every conglomeration of **PT** systems on *TERRA*) will collapse as the last but one since this will determine the surviving **PT** system. Notice further, that by virtue of this possible sequence a hidden ecological war can break out (which perhaps is already underway).

After all, what we have elaborated so far is the present situation of the occidental civilization characterized by a turning phase in technology. It is an open question whether it can succeed in entering into a new global innovation cycle. If we consider tab. 3.5 the determination share of social behavior due to DC influences approaches its saturation zone: trivially a share of more than 100 % is not possible). From this the 'smoothing effects' which stem from the large number of actors involved in mass phenomena are reduced. [19] However, an LSU characterized by a very low mass phenomena influence, i.e. by a predominant oligarchization, will be confronted with completely new situations. [20] In any case, it could be a tragic error to trace the shortage and saturation characteristics of the present development phase back to aspects of productivity and technology alone and to overlook thereby the dysfunctions in the **PT** systems. Tab. 3.5 could even justify the interpretation that the essential shortcomings have to be probed in the **PT** system. SDI, for example, would then be something like an escape-hatch.

It would be urgent also to contemplate inventions and innovations in the field of **PT** system operational mechanisms. However, in this field serious

---

[19] In this argumentation **PTs** and DCs are equated, which is an approximation. For our considerations at this point, however, this is acceptable because of the strong correspondence between **PTs** and DCs.

[20] Perhaps artificial "heads" can be defined in the further technological development also as social "heads" or units. The problem could then be solved by the emergence of artificial mass phenomena. Or, LSUs together with their **PT** systems will themselves be rendered objects of a machine intelligence, in which event the problem would vanish. We cannot cope with possible structures of such new societal types at this stage.

scientific, particularly epistemological problems exist, which predominantly stem from the self-referentiality problematique. How, for instance, could it be prevented that the operational field of "innovation of **PT** operational mechanisms" would not again be the subject of **PT** formation? [21] If problem solutions exist at all in this field they will not be found in traditional ways of scientific discovery. However, more cannot be said in the scope of this elaboration.

4.3.8 A basic crisis period of eight years?

Finally, a property of **PT** or **PT** system operation shall be sketched, which is eventually related with the above-mentioned career cycles in **PTs** and **PT** systems. This property could support the recently developed hypothesis that contra-intentional reactions systematically occur in LSUs, BOUDON [10]. However, existence and explanation of this property is so far a matter of speculation whose substantiation must be left for future study.

What is meant here is the presumption that crisis situations in a **PT**, an operational field or a **PT** system occur at the end of time intervals whose lengths are full divisors or multiples of 8, provided that the operation of the system under consideration is not interrupted or terminated by an extreme structural rupture, for example, by a collapse of the complete system. Hence, crisis time points will appear in the years 2, 4, 8, 16, 24, ... after a restructure or a structural rupture. Possibly, this time structure is ruled by a doubling phenomenon so that powers of two are of relevance.

Even if I could be accused of number mystics I want to list a series of examples showing the time characteristic of 8 years. In doing so I will focus on recent history. A systematic analysis of past epochs must be left to historical studies.

- in the F.R.G. in 1977 the new divorce act became effective, in 1985 it was revised,

- in South Africa in 1976 there was a peak of revolts, in 1984 the new riots began which last up to now,

- Schleyer was murdered in 1977, Zimmermann in 1985,

- the period of the military regime in Panama terminated after 16 years,

- the military regime in Argentina terminated after 8 years,

- general Zia cancelled the war law (*Kriegsrecht*) in Pakistan after 8.5 years,

---

[21] In the neglect of this problematique could reside a conceptional error of "constructivism" (construction of desired social structures) which we pointed to already in section 3.2.

- the Greek colonels' regime terminated after 7.5 years,

- the dynamite attack of the Lower Saxony intelligence agency in Celle in 1978 led 8 years later to an éclat,

- Iraq and Syria came to a reconciliation after a conflict period of 8 years,

- Iran showed willingness to terminate the war with Iraq after the war having lasted 8 years,

- the West-German feminist journal Courage gave up after 8 years of existence,

- in Poland there was a strike peak in 1980 and in 1988,

- the German Greens entered into a crisis after 8 years of presence on the federal level,

- India entered into serious national cleavage conflicts 40 years after the independence declaration,

- Austrian state industry entered into serious financial problems after 40 years of existence (1946–86),

- electric power lines reopened from East to West Berlin after a period of 40 years.

It must be expected that if such crisis periodicity exists, LSUs have invented organizational principles to cope with that challenge. Maybe the period between successive olympic games in ancient Greece, which was 8 years, was such a principle. Also the 4 year period of today could be such a device. Nearly all parliamentary democracies have an electoral period of 4 years. In the U.S.A. the tenure of the president's office expires by law after a maximal period of 8 years. Perhaps also business cycle lengths depend on this periodicity?

There could be a relation between two successive restructures in a **PT** or **PT** system as is shown in fig. 4.8. To explain that periodicity I will propose the following

Conjecture 8 *Pertinence-power transformations, horizontal and vertical* **PT** *competition as well as career cycles interact such that, after a restructure, a certain time elapses until a contra-constellation has established itself with the consequence that this structure is rearranged again.*

Supposing that **PTs** or **PT** systems operate predominantly near their saturation zones, and, that restructures entail a limited amount of newly available redistribution mass then a specific *"eigen-time"* of the process could be the result: periodic peaks are localized in the years 2, 4, 8, 16, 24, ... after a

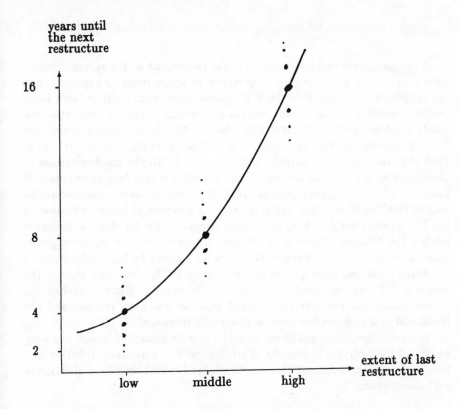

Figure 4.8: Restructure and crisis periods: an exemplary scattergram

restructure. Periods greater than 8 years must result from a larger redistribution mass at the beginning of the process, or from large growth potentials.

Such dynamics can be well demonstrated by a scenario concerning the
career jam periodicity of **PTR** aspirants:

| 2nd year after restructure | The absorption of the old career jam is finished,
new shortages are not yet existent. However, the initial promotional euphoria
has vanished: a motivational gap appears.

| 4th year after restructure | The new career jam is in its first formation stage.
In favourable cases, aspirants can, in this stage, be satisfied from existing reserves. If this is impossible, new debt is necessary, but often uncritical.

| 8th year after restructure | The career jam has been enlarged and is aggra-
vated by additional problems, for instance, overdebt. Illegitimate practices
such as corruption increase. The credibility of the **PTRs** decreases.

| ... etc. |

If the aforementioned description of the periodicity of **PT** system dynamics is correct and if this were a deep structure which must be expected then any long-term orientation in the **PT** system must be in contrast with these contra-dynamics. That is, only after a restructure could an orientation towards a longer period be successful. Maybe this is the deeper reason for Ludwig Erhard who said approximately 16 years after the currency reform of 1948 that the "post-war period" had terminated. Maybe the Perestroika of Gorbatschow is such a restructure necessary after a very long time period of undisturbed development (approximately 40 years). However, the Perestroika will be confronted with the self-referentiality problem of being addressed to the **PT** system itself if there is the real intention of a top-down restructure leaving the existent oligarchy unaffected. Concerning self-referentiality, the establishment of a new "Perestroika-oligarchy" would be less problematic.

Notice that the time period orientation of **PTRs** becomes shorter the longer a **PT** system operates without a restructure. Having reached the 2-year period the shortest time period possible has been reached and the likelihood of a collapse has been dramatically increased.

However, operation problems in LSUs can be imagined which can only be solved by a certain continuity of strategical **PT** activities. Whether and how in modern civilizations this can be realized would then be a question of high importance.

4.4   Social catastrophes

A sudden structural change shall be called a *catastrophe*. Referring to LSUs, two types of catastrophes can be distinguished: natural and social catastrophes. Natural catastrophes have at all times led to evolution branchings in LSU development. Let us focus at this point on social catastrophes. Under *social catastrophes* all kinds of structural ruptures are comprehended which are initiated or strategically pursued by social units or individuals.

Some kinds of social catastrophes are regular components of **PTs** and **PT** systems, as has been elaborated above, for instance, such that stem from **PT** or **PT** system competition. From an evolutionary perspective such a structural change is nothing extraordinary. Therefore, if we assign the term "catastrophe" to extraordinary events then that type is of subordinate interest. Of high interest are structural ruptures which occur beyond the every day operation of LSUs, but nevertheless, are related systematically to structures and operation mechanisms of LSUs and **PT** systems. These are the real social catastrophes.

Let us first analyse catastrophes which are called so in every day language, i.e. such that endanger the functioning of a system through destruction.

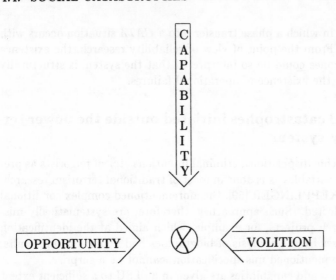

Figure 4.9: Coupling of necessary conditions to initiate a social catastrophe

Hence, the question is: are there such destruction potentials in LSUs and how are they related to **PT** and **PT** system operation. As we shall soon see this question goes far beyond the narrow perspective of the terrorism aspect. However, we cannot cope with this problem in detail in this elaboration and must confine ourselves to some basic considerations.

When choosing the **PT** system as the research subject, two kinds of real social catastrophes can be distinguished: such that are initiated or strategically pursued by social units or individuals who are not **PT** members, and such that are initiated or strategically pursued in the **PT** system itself. Let us call the first type *catastrophes from below*, $CATA$ (U), and the latter *catastrophes from above*, $CATA(O)$. Terrorism is generally related to $CATA$ (U). For both types a set of obviously necessary conditions can be worked out:

Volition, opportunity, and capability

of initiating or strategically pursuing catastrophes which must occur in an appropriate combination, as is shown in fig. 4.9. Only in a synergetic coupling of these three conditions can a transfer to $CATA$ result. It is the neglect of this complex structure of conditions that renders a large part of traditional terrorism research ineffective.

Under the perspective of LSU or **PT** system operation and functioning it must, therefore, be analyzed whether there are critical combinations of the three conditions in which a phase transfer into a $CATA$ situation occurs with high likelihood. From the point of view of reliability research, the existence of such critical zones could be so interpreted that the system is structurally characterized by the existence of operational failures.

4.4.1   Social catastrophes initiated outside the power territory system

In regarding psychic dispositions, criminal intentions etc. of terrorists as predominant causal variables as is done in most of traditional terrorism research, see for instance KEPPLINGER [59], the aforementioned complex conditional structure is neglected. Such approaches, therefore, are systematically mis-specified. Research projects, for example, which aimed at the identification of terrorism causes by the analysis of biographies had no convincing results, which due to the mentioned mis-specification, cannot be a surprise.

If opportunities and capabilities are given in an LSU to a sufficient extent then volition is in an LSU of the scale order of the F.R.G., i.e. $20 \cdot 10^6$ non-**PT** members of active age, of low importance. In such a mass there always will be some people who make the engineers' wisdom become factual: "What can happen, will happen." The consideration of knowledge from the fields of security and reliablity, however, is not common in terrorism research presumably because it is undesirable to reveal whether and how an LSU surrenders itself structurally to such $CATA$ potentials. Consequently it was recently alleged that terrorism must be attacked in international cooperation instead of confining oneself to the above-mentioned conditional structure. This orientation likely aims at shifting responsibility to a higher hierarchy level in order to prevent one's own **PT** or **PT** system from legitimation problems. Hence, this is a classic **PT** strategy.

Notice, that there is a complex net of factors behind the three components displayed in fig. 4.9 so that a detailed analysis requires the nonlinear linkage of three complex models. Problems of such a complexity can rarely be studied phenomenologically. We must, therefore, restrict our analysis at this point to an introductory level. In Vol. 2 we shall make an attempt to perform at least a rough structural analysis by making use of a simulation model.

Following the above-mentioned reflections on $CATA(U)$, its probability and effect depend on the components "opportunity" and "capability" if a certain threshold of population size is transferred. With an increasing opportunity of an LSU to be the subject of injury from $CATA$ activities and with growing logistic capabilities of $CATA$ actors such $CATA$ events becomes more probable and more effective. Effectiveness, however, also depends on the target of $CATA(U)$. So long as $CATA(U)$ is directed on single **PTRs** as, for instance, in the SCHLEYER case, effectiveness remains low, since violent **PTR** mobility adhered at all times to the normal repertoire of **PT** competition. In other words, **PTs** are accustomed to coping with that disturbance.

If such *CATAs* are rare events they are absorbed in the mass of competitive **PTR** mobility. Moreover, they stimulate the creation of additional operation fields, for example, the field of terrorist attack. Altogether, at most the relative position of the **PC** in the **PT** system may change insignificantly.

A *CATA*(U) of the mentioned type can be dangerous, however, if it occurs in a situation where the **PT** system operates in a critical zone. We have elaborated that in such a situation small disturbances can be sufficient to lead to a collapse of the system. Without going into details we must also capture that this instability is not by virtue of terrorism but is a consequence of a structural defect of the system.

Hence, if necessary preventive reactions do not exist in the behavior repertoire of **PT** systems, then *CATA*(U) is of systematic danger to a **PT** system and, therefore, also to the LSU under consideration. This most dangerous form of *CATA*(U), which was suggested in [88], will possibly occur in the future, because the above-mentioned conditions move further in the corresponding dangerous direction.

4.4.2 MABUSE catastrophes

Let us call this *MABUSE catastrophes*, [22] and distinguish again *MABU*(U) and *MABU*(O). *MABUs* occur in concentrated areas or sensitive installations of LSUs. Some examples of *MABU*(U) can already be identified:

- attacks of the *action directe* in France,

- the "black friday" (Nov. 29, 1985) in Japan, initiated by city-guerilla,

- the attack on the railway station of Bologna.

Regarding this *CATA* type, the focus on the *MABU actors* alone is completely inapt. One way, and in my view the only way, to counteract *MABU*(U) would be a radical decentralization of LSUs. Maybe certain electronic developments can support such a decentralization strategy. An inappropriate usage of such devices can, however, even increase the *MABU*(U) potential. Above all this, since LSUs are dynamic systems, is a matter of the right timing and sequencing also. Frankly speaking: Are those decentralized structures created in time?

The question remains, how in an LSU which has evolved further in favor of *CATA* and *MABU* risks, can the emerging destructive potential be kept under control. This is a matter of adequate technology and of the availability of the necessary surplus. It must be doubted that *MABU* potentials particularly can be got under control by technical means alone. This requires additional detailed studies which cannot be undertaken here. In any case,

---

[22] Labelled after the German movie "Dr. MABUSE" directed by Fritz LANG.

the money needed for such a control surpasses all reasonable economic limits. We can guess at this sum from a case study of *MABU* control activities performed in Japan on the occasion of the world economic summit of May 4, 1986 in Tokyo. These control activities required a budget of 10^8 DM as was reported in "Die Zeit". Calculated analogously for the the F.R.G. this budget corresponds to $5 \cdot 10^{-5}$ of its national income. When performing 18,000 such controls per year the total national income would be spent for these activities. The neighbourhood of such conference places, however, contains only a small fraction of the total number of sensitive elements of an LSU. It shall be noticed besides, that the control measures in Japan could not prevent the *MABU* activities, i.e. the launching of rockets towards the conference building. The rockets did not cause a *MABU* only because of having missed their target. Altogether, we are justified in formulating the following

Conjecture 9 *Large LSUs with strong operational concentrations and many sensitive elememts cannot be safeguarded against CATA and even less against MABU.*

After all there could be the impression that $CATA(U)$ and $MABU(U)$ were, despite the above-mentioned counter argumentation in section 4.4, terrorist activities. This conclusion would be incorrect since in a highly concentrated operation field, that is unstable in addition, $CATA(U)$ and $MABU(U)$ can also be initiated by mass behavior, accidents, mental disturbance, slipshoddery etc. with equal destructive effects. [23] Notice, that in case of a nonlinear coupling of the three components, possibly even with feedback, displayed in fig. 4.9 situations can emerge in which accidents traditionally recognized as harmless suddenly can have collapse impacts.

4.4.3   Social catastrophes initiated inside the power territory system and a reliability analysis

All we described so far for $CATA(U)$ holds also for $CATA(O)$. $CATA(O)$ means that catastrophes are initiated or strategically pursued by **PT** members. In the case of $MABU(O)$ concentrations or sensitive elements of the LSU are targets of the action.

It appears extremely surprising that $MABU(O)$ has not been observed more frequently in LSUs, since **PT** members have privileged access to sensitive installations by competence, and by this very fact, possess the necessary capability. If it is true that Nero set Rome on fire, then that was a prominent example of a $MABU(O)$.

---

[23]Examples are the break down of electric power in north-east France some years ago caused by mass switching on of electric appliances, traffic accidents where trucks are involved which carry dangerous material, the tanker accident caused by a drunken pilot near Brusnbüttel on Jan. 3, 1986.

An incurably insane leading statesman, for instance, could be mad enough to order that as many people as possible must die with him [24] and order a military action by which a $CATA(O)$ would be initiated. We have the example of a Chinese officer on a warship who, having the responsibility for the chamber of explosives, went into the magazine and blew the ship up presumably because of having quarrelled with his wife the night before, as was reported. This was an example of a $MABU(O)$.

To analyse the rareness of such events more precisely let us make use of a reliability approach and take the F.R.G. as reference. Let us assume that there are 10^5 sensitive installations in the F.R.G. From that we can guess that on $TERRA$ we have

$$\frac{\text{world popoulation size}}{\text{F.R.G. population size}} \cdot .5 \cdot 10^5 \approx 4 \cdot 10^6$$

sensitive installations, where .5 has been chosen as a development lag parameter of the average society compared with the F.R.G.

Now we can pose the question how great the reliability of a system of $4 \cdot 10^6$ components must be so that only *one* $MABU(O)$ per year can be observed. Let us assume that the *Poisson*-model is adequate to provide the corresponding calculations and that the one year period is admissible. The latter means: personnel having privileged access to the installations, job duration and the necessary $MABU$ preparation time mutually depend on each other, such that the one year period makes sense as the $MABU$ event period. Then we can formulate:

$$\text{Prob(up to 1 } KATAs \text{ per year)} = \sum_{i=0}^{1}(\lambda^i e^{-\lambda}/i!) \qquad , \lambda = np$$

$$= (1 + np)e^{-np} \qquad (4.28)$$

with

$$n : = \text{number of installations,}$$
$$p : = \text{failure probability } (= 1 \text{ - reliability).}$$

Now we have to search for that p which results in a Prob(.) near 1 (for instance, .995). Tab. 4.5 displays that p as dependent on the number of installations for which Prob(1) = .995 is reached. Hence, in the case of 4 million sensitive installations opportunity, capability, and volition must be combined such that, on the average, there occurs only one failure, i.e. $MABU(O)$, per year among the 40 millions of personnel having privileged access to those plants. In the case of 10 million sensitive installations there must only be one failure per year among 100 millions of personnel to keep the number of $MABU(O)$ below 2 per year. Compared with air traffic: according to statements by *Lufthansa* there is at most one severe accident per 10^9

---

[24]Dying with the ruler was routine in Pharao's empire.

p 10^{-8}	number of sensitive installations on *TERRA* 10^6
2.50	4
2.06	5
1.38	7.5
1.04	10

Table 4.5: Admissible failure probability of personnel having privileged access to sensitive installations

flights. Thus, the reliability of personnel having privileged access to sensitive installations must approach the reliability of those extremely safe-guarded machines up to one order of magnitude.

Let us assume that the three components of fig. 4.9 are multipicatively combined probabilities being stochastically independent, which is a remarkable simplification. Then we get the result:

$$1 - z = \text{Prob(opportunity)}$$
$$\cdot \text{Prob(capability)}$$
$$\cdot \text{Prob(volition)} \quad , \qquad (4.29)$$

where

$$z : = \text{reliability} \quad . \qquad (4.30)$$

Then regarding the first row of tab. 4.5 it mus hold:

$$1 - z \leq 2.5 \cdot 10^{-8} \quad .$$

Alone due to the specific qualification of the personnel having privileged access to sensitive installations we are justified to assume that Prob(capability) is near 1. Privileged access means that Prob(opportunity) will also not be small. Notice, that even automatic controls let the privileged personnel pass by definition. Only by cross-controls can Prob(opportunity) be reduced significantly. Whether such principles could be implemented durably for all sensitive installations must be doubted. Moreover, we have to consider that the number of access opportunities increases combinatorially with the number of privileged persons. For the purpose of calculation this can be handled by augmenting the number of installations, since this is equivalent to the number of access opportunities. That can be read off in tab. 4.5.

If we assume that we get any knowledge at all upon $CATA(O)/MABU(O)$ events which is *not* unconditionally plausible from **PT** strategical considerations, and, hence, in fact there are not more than 1 $MABU(O)$ per year world-wide, then there is nothing else than to assume Prob(volition) as the dominant factor.

Fear of punishment, career aspirations etc. cannot result in an order of magnitude of 10^{-8}. Therefore, deeper mechanisms must exist such as stemming from long-lasting selection pressure, presumably with coevolutionary caused genetic fixation. We cannot go into details in this elaboration. However, without such details we are still in the position to perform some structural considerations.

Above all it must be noticed that in the case of a nonlinear coupling of the components of fig. 4.9,

$$\text{Prob}(MABU)(t), \ t := \text{time} \qquad ,$$

can be malicious, and this all the more if there are feedbacks between the components. That means that the system looks reliable over a long time period and instantaneously shows a phase transfer into a situation of multiple social catastrophes. In particular, it cannot be concluded from the rareness of such $MABU$ or $CATA$ events to date that this will also be the case in future.

The world-wide analysis just performed was done as a guess at reliability. Since there is so far no world-wide LSU it is of greater interest to analyse one LSU with regard to $MABU$ probability. Again taking the F.R.G. as an example, we calculate from 4.28 that in the case of 10^5 sensitive installations a reliability of $1 - 10^{-6}$ must exist to exclude more than one $MABU(O)$ per year with a probability of .995.

In the case of very large LSUs with many sensitive installations like the U.S. it cannot be excluded that scale orders are reached which are $MABU$ critical. These large LSUs especially are, however, characterized by a high development of structures in favor of $MABU$. From this circumstance the serious conclusion must be drawn that LSUs where $MABU$ can have serious destructive impacts are particularly those with an increased $MABU$ probability. The $MABU$ scenario becomes really dramatic if there is the special case of

$$\text{Prob}(\text{volition}) = 1$$

in 4.29. This, however, must be assumed in the case of conscious $MABU$ strategies, i.e. when $MABU$ is not initiated in derangement, as in the example of the Chinese officer. According to BÖHRET's opinion (privat communication) six **PTRs** would be sufficient to throw a state like the F.R.G. into chaos, if they initiated appropriate $MABUs$ in a coordinated strategy. The main reasons for this are the erratic reactions in the **PT** system having the consequence of mutual amplification, and not the $MABUs$ alone as such.

It is, however, extremely improbable that six **PTRs** will occur all having Prob(volition) = 1. [25] In a world system of competitive LSUs and **PT**

---

[25]If we are right in assuming deep rooted selection pressures for providing the above-mentioned reliability, then there could, consequently, be posed the question, what would

systems it is more probable that such activities are undercover strategies initiated by hostile **PTs**. Who will doubt the possibility that six such positions are already held by such undercover agents?

If we have focused on terroristic $CATA(O)$ and $MABU(O)$ this should not lead to the conclusion that this is the only variant. On the contrary, as in $CATA(U)$ and $MABU(U)$ we have a multiplicity of possibilities to cause $CATA(O)$ and $MABU(O)$ stemming from accidents etc. Such events are by no means fictional, as we can observe. That great parts of an LSU can collapse due to one such accident is quite imaginable today, for instance, imagine a fire in a plant where biological weapons are produced. We are justified in assuming that this variant has a much greater probability than the terroristic variant. Of further interest is the question, under which conditions $CATA(.)$ or $MABU(.)$ chains can occur in an LSU. Notice that concentration *ceteris paribus* increases the probability of such chains.

4.4.4   Interaction of different types of social catastrophes

Presumably the most dangerous constellation exists when $CATA(U)$ and $CATA(O)$ and/or $MABU(U)$ and $MABU(O)$ interact. For instance, imagine that an anomic potential is defined as an operation field, so that anomic **PTs** can establish, or, even more dangerous, $CATAs(U)$ and $MABUs(O)$ are strategically related by a conspiratory association consisting of **PT** members from different operation fields (recall, e.g. the *propaganda due* in Italy). To capture the dramatic impacts on LSU functioning, imagine scenarios in which the period 1930–35 in Germany is shifted into present time.

Let such an interaction be denoted by $CATA(U,O)$. So long as the determinants which increase the probability of a coupling of $CATA(U)$ and $CATA(O)$ develop unrelatedly, the probablility of a $CATA(U,O)$ will be small. However, situations can appear in which critical non-**PT** and **PT** processes suddenly interact. Structural ruptures stemming from such an interaction could be labelled revolutionary because non-**PT** members are involved. [26] In fig. 4.10 a scenario of a CATA(U,O) is displayed. In this scenario the relation between

$$CATA/MABU(U) \text{ and } CATA/MABU(O) \text{ potentials}$$

becomes closer and closer during time and finally leads into a

$$CATA/MABU(U,O) \text{ situation.}$$

---

happen if those selection mechanisms would not work any longer, and, whether there could be constellations in civilizational evolution that could destroy those mechanisms. We must let it be enough with this question in the present elaboration.

[26] However, we cannot elaborate further on the idea to regard a revolution as a synergetic branching effect.

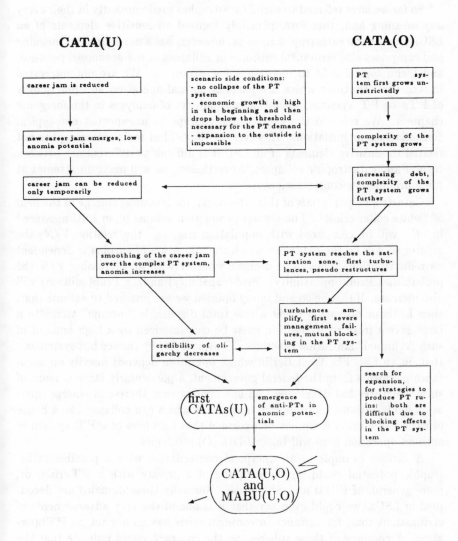

Figure 4.10: A scenario of the coupling of top-down and bottom-up social catastrophes

Let this scenario suffice at this point: in Vol. 2 in the simulation model MUE & MABU, an attempt is made to analyse this problem more precisely.

So far we have referred to social catastrophes predominantly in their every day meaning and, therefore, plausibly focused on sensitive elements of an LSU. The general catastrophe concept, however, has a much broader meaning and comprises also structural ruptures or collapses in the economic, political, and technological field to mention a few examples. We are not interested in structural ruptures which are parts of normal operation and functioning of **PTs** or **PT** systems, since that was subject of analyses in the foregoing chapters. We referred the catastrophe concept to unexpected non-typical constellations or initiations. However, in the field of social catastrophes not related to sensitive elements of an LSU it is difficult to differentiate between regular and catastrophic collapses. Nevertheless, we will make an attempt at some preliminary considerations.

Catastrophe potentials of this type could, for instance, emerge in the field of "white collar crime". The greater production volume in an LSU measured in C will be compared with population size, i.e. the relation V/N, the greater so will be the extent to which the allocation of surplus is dependent on redistribution. Thus, it is decisive whether with an increasing V/N the probabilties Prob(opportunity), Prob(capability) and/or Prob(volition) will also increase. If this be so and in my opinion we are justified to assume that, then LSUs or operation fields whose total disposable "income" stems to a large extent from redistribution must be characterized by a high amount of such "criminal" allocation practices. Thus, it is not by chance but systematic that, in an LSU like West Berlin whose operation depends heavily on assistance payments from the federal government, a particularly large amount of such structures has developed. As one consequence there can emerge operation fields without a productive fundament which can collapse like a house of cards. In a crisis it cannot be excluded that members of a **PT** system in such an operation field will take $MABU(O)$ strategies.

A further example of an untypical constellation with a possible catastrophic potential could be the coupling of a private with a **PT** crisis, or, more general, of PRIM and SEC crisis. Normally these domains are decoupled in LSUs: we could even say that it is one of the very advancements of civilizations that, for instance, a conjugal crisis has no impact on **PT** operation. A coupling of these spheres, on the contrary, could indicate that the **PT** system or the LSU under consideration has entered into a critical operation zone. The Perrot affair in France (DER SPIEGEL 3(1986) pp. 113) is a good example of such a critical coupling.

Taken altogether, due to the ubiquity of such private crisis phenomena, the growing 'criminal' allocation of surplus, the increasing number and complexity of sensitive LSU elements, and the collapse mechanisms ordinarily implanted in **PT** systems, not to speak of a synergetic coupling of all these features, there must be an increasing probabilty that LSUs enter into a critical operation zone in the course of time. Owing to these risks the neglect of a systematic analysis of such potentials of social catastrophes can be revealed, perhaps in the near future, as a serious shortcoming.

Can there be an awareness of these risks in **PT** systems? Can a decentralization, if ever possible in the evolutionary path of civilizations, be realized in time? Is there a strategy of a selective take off to the orbit, a "solution" of extreme consistency within the civilizational problem solving repertoire? Can there emerge on *TERRA* a fundamental conflict between natural and civilizational evolutionary principles?

Bibliography

[1] ALBERTIN, L./MÜLLER, N. (1981): *Umfassende Modellierung regionaler Systeme — Probleme, Modelle, Praxisbezug* — Köln: Verlag TÜV Rheinland, ISR

[2] ALISCH, L.-M. (1986): *Bemerkungen zur strukturalistischen Theorienlogik und Logik der Praxis*, in: MÜLLER /STACHOWIAK (eds.)

[3] ARMINGER, G. (1987): *Einige Gründe für die Irrelevanz sozialwissenschaftlicher Modelle: Fehlspezifikation, mangelnde Dynamik und unbeobachtete Heterogenität*, in: MÜLLER /STACHOWIAK (eds.)

[4] ARROW, K.J. (1963): *Social Choice and Individual Values*, New York: Wiley

[5] BACON, R./ELTIS, W. (1978): *Britain's Economic Problems: Too Few Producers*, 2nd ed., London: Macmillan

[6] BATES, D.G./LEES, S.H. (1979):   *The Myth of Population Regula-
     tion,* in: CHAGNON/IRONS (eds.)

[7] BENARD, Ch./SCHLAFFER, E. (1985):   *Viel erlebt und nichts be-
     griffen — Die Männer und die Frauenbewegung,* Hamburg: Rowohlt

[8] BLOCH, M. (1978):   *The Disconnection Between Power and Rank
     as a Process: An outline of the development of kingdoms in Central
     Madagascar,* in: FRIEDMAN/ROWLANDS (eds.)

[9] BODGANY, F.J. (1980):   *Soziobiologie — Möglichkeiten und Grenzen
     der "Neuen Synthese",* in: Kölner Ztschr. f. Soz. u. Sozialpsych. 32,
     312–324

[10] BOUDON, R. (1982):   *The Unintended Consequences of Social Action,*
     London: Macmillan

[11] BOULDING, E. (1979):   *Deep Structures and Sociological Analysis:
     Some Reflections,* in:Amer. Sociologist 14, 70–73

[12] BOULDING, K.E. (1978):   *Ecodynamics — A New Theory of Societal
     Evolution,* Beverly Hills: Sage

[13] BROUWER, F.M. (1986):   *Integrated Environmental Modelling,* Am-
     sterdam: Free University, PhD Thesis

[14] CARNEIRO, C. (1967):   *On the Relation between Size of Population
     and Complexity of Social Organization,*
     in: South Western J. of Anthropology 23, 234–243

[15] CHAGNON, N.A. (1979):   *Mate Competition,
     Favoring Close Kin and Village Fissioning Among the Yanomamö In-
     dians,* in: CHAGNON/IRONS (eds.)

[16] CHAGNON, N.A./IRONS, W. (eds.) (1979):   *Evolutionary Biology
     and Human Social Behavior — An Anthropological Perspective,* North
     Scituate, Mass.: Duxbury

[17] CORNING, P.A. (1979):   *The Synergism Hypothesis — A Theorie of
     Progressive Evolution,* New York: McGraw-Hill

[18] DEUTSCH, K.W. (1966):   *The Nerves of Government,* New York:
     The Free Press

[19] DICKEMANN, M. (1979):   *Female Infanticide, Reproductive Strate-
     gies, and Social Stratification,* in: CHAGNON/IRONS (eds.)

[20] DILLMANN, C. (1984):   *Amateure gegen Profis,* in: Die Zeit,
     03.02.1984, p. 13

[21] DYE, R. (1976): *Who's Running America? — Institutional Leadership in the USA,* Englewood Cliffs, N.J.: Pr.-Hall

[22] EIBL-EIBESFELDT, I. (1976): *Menschenforschung auf neuen Wegen — die naturwissenschaftliche Betrachtung kultureller Verhaltensweisen,* München: Molden

[23] EISENBERG, L. (1979): *Die differentielle Verteilung der psychiatrischen Störungen auf die Geschlechter,* in: SULLEROT (ed.)

[24] ELIAS, N. (1969): *Der Zivilisationsprozeß — soziogenetische und psychogenetische Untersuchungen,* 2. Aufl., München: Francke

[25] EWEN, L.A. (1978): *Corporative Power and Urban Crisis in Detroit,* Princton: Princeton Univ. Press

[26] EYSENCK, H.J. (1983): *Partnerbuch,* München: Molden

[27] FISHER, H. (1980): *Woman's Creation — Sexual Evolution and the Shaping of Society,* New York: McGraw-Hill

[28] FISHMAN, A. (1983): *Judaism and Modernization: The case of the Religious Kibbutzim,* in : Social Forces 62, 9 - 31

[29] FLOHR, H./TÖNNESMANN, W. (eds.) (1983): *Politik und Biologie — Beiträge zur Life-Sciences-Orientierung der Sozialwissenschaften,* Hamburg: Parey

[30] FRIEDMAN, J./ROWLANDS, M.J. (eds.) (1978): *The Evolution of Social Systems,* Pittsburgh: Univ. of Pittsburg Press

[31] FROHN, J. et al. (1973): *Der Technische Fortschritt in der Industrie — Messung in 34 Industriebereichen,* Berlin: Duncker & Humblot

[32] GEORGESCU-ROEGEN, N. (1971): *The Entropy Law and the Economic Process,* Cambridge, Mass.: Harvard Univ. Press

[33] GILLIGAN, C. (1982): *In a Different Voice,* Cambridge, Mass.: Harvard Univ. Press

[34] GODELIER, M. (1978): *Territory and Property in Primitive Society,* in: Social Science Info. 17, 399–426

[35] GODFREY, L.R./COLE, J.R. (1979): *Biological Analogy, Diffusionism, and Archeology,* in:Amer. Anthropologist 81, 37–45

[36] GREELEY, A. (1978): *Erotische Kultur — Wert und Würde der Sexualität,* 2. Aufl., Graz: Styria

[37] GROSSMANN, W.D. (1983): *Systems approaches toward complex systems,* in: <u>MAB-Information Nr. 19</u>, Schweizerischer Nationalfonds, Bern

[38] GROSSMANN, W.D. (1987): *Strategic Concepts Made Applicable with Dynamic Geographical Maps,* in: MÜLLER, N. (ed.): Problems of Interdisciplinary Eco- systems Modelling, <u>MAB-Mitteilungen 25</u>, Bonn: Deutsches MAB-Nationalkomitee

[39] GRUCHY, A.G. (1978): *Institutional Economics: Its Influence and Prospects,* in: <u>The Amer. J. of Economics & Sociology</u> 37, 271–281

[40] HABER, W. et al. (Hrsg.) (1983): *Ökosystemforschung Berchtesgaden* 2 Bde, <u>MAB-Mitteilungen 17 und 18</u>, Bonn: Deutsches MAB-Nationalkomitee

[41] HAKEN, H. (1978): *Synergetics, An Introduction,* Berlin: Springer

[42] HARRIS, M. (1975): *Culture, People, Nature — An Introduction to General Anthropology,* 2nd. ed., New York: Harper & Row

[43] HARRIS, M. (1977): *Cannibals and Kings — The Origins of Culture* New York: Random House

[44] HASSAN, F.A. (1980): *The Growth and Regulation of Human Population in Prehistoric Times,* in: Cohen/Klein (eds.): Biosocial Mechanism of Population Regulation, New Haven: Yale Univ. Press

[45] HEINSOHN, G./ KNIEPER, R./STEIGER, O. (1979): *Menschenproproduktion — Allgemeine Bevölkerungstheorie der Neuzeit,* Frankfurt/M.: Suhrkamp

[46] HEINSOHN, G. (1984a): *Privateigentum, Patriarchat, Geldwirtschaft,* Frankfurt/M.: Suhrkamp

[47] HEINSOHN, G. (1984b): *Zins, Hexen, Habermas — Gesellschaftserklärung oder Wirklichkeitsverleugnung,* in: <u>Neue Praxis Heft</u> 2/84, 180–186

[48] HEPPENHEIMER, T.A. (1980): *Eine Arche auf dem Sternenmeer — Besiedlung des Weltraums,* Zürich: Schweizer Verlagshaus

[49] HERODOT (1971): *Historien,* Hrsgg. von Haussig, H.W., Stuttgart: Kröner

[50] HIRSCH, F. (1977): *Social Limits to Growth,* London: Routledge & Kegan Paul

[51] HOBCRAFT, J.N./GOLDMAN, N./CHIDAMBARAM, V.C. (1982): *Advances in the P/F Ratio Method for the Analysis of Birth Histories*, in: Population Studies 36, 291–316

[52] HODGES, R./CHERRY, J.F.(1983): *Cost-Control and Coinage: An Archeological Approach to Economic Change in Anglo-Saxon England*, in: Research in Economic Anthropology 5, 131–183

[53] HOCHHUT, R. (1973): *Frauen und Mütter, Bachofen und Germaine Greer*, in: Hochhut: Lysistrate und die NATO, Hamburg: Rowohlt

[54] HOMANS, G.C. (1983): *Steps to a Theory of Social Behavior — an Anthropological Account*, in: Theory and Society 12, 1–45

[55] HUNKE, S. (1960): *Allah's Sonne über dem Abendland*, Stuttgart: Fischer TB

[56] INOSE, H./PIERCE, J.R. (1984): *Information Technology and Civilization*, Oxford: Freeman

[57] JANSSEN-JURREIT, M. (1980): *Sexismus — Über die Abtreibung der Frauenfrage*, Frankfurt/M.: Fischer Taschenbuch

[58] JANSSON, A.-M./ZUCETTO, J. (1978): *Energy, Economic and Ecological Relationships*, Stockholm: Swedish Natural Science Research Council, MAB

[59] KEPPLINGER, H.M. (1981): *Gesellschaftliche Bedingungen kollektiver Gewalt*, in: Kölner Zeitschr. für Soziologie & Sozialpsychologie 33, 469–503

[60] KERBER, H.R./FAVE, L.R. della (1979): *The Empirical Side of the Power Elite Debate — An Assessment and Critique of Recent Research*, in: Sociological Quart. 20, 5–22

[61] KLIEMANN, W./MÜLLER, N. (1976): *Logik und Mathematik für Sozialwissenschaftler 2*, München: Fink UTB

[62] KOLLONTAI, A. (1982): *Ich habe viele Leben gelebt*, Berlin: Dietz

[63] KRUUK, H. (1972): *The Spotted Hyena — A Study of Predation and Social Behavior*, Chicago: Chicago Univ. Press

[64] LASSWELL, H.D./LERNER, D. (1965): *World Revolutionary Elites*, Cambridge, Mass.: MIT Press

[65] LAUE, T.H. (1987): *Die Ausbreitung der "westlichen" Kultur als Welt-revolution betrachtet*, in: Beiträge zur Konfliktforschung 2, 5–26

[66] LAWICK-GOODALL, J. van (1971):   *Wilde Schimpansen — 10 Jahre Verhaltensforschung am Gombestrom,* Hamburg: Rowohlt

[67] LEM, S. (1982):   *Summa Technologiae,*   2. Aufl., Frankfurt/M.: Suhrkamp

[68] LEMCKE, K. (1981):   *Das Nördlinger Ries: Spur einer kosmischen Katastrophe,* in: Spektrum der Wissenschaft, Jan., 110–121

[69] LENSKI, G. (1970):   *Human Societies — A Macrolevel Introduction to Sociology,* New York: McGraw-Hill

[70] LENSKI, G. (1973):   *Macht und Privileg — Eine Theorie der sozialen Schichtung,* Frankfurt/M.: Surhkamp

[71] LIETH, H. (1976):   *Biophysikalische Fragestellungen in der Ökologie und Unweltforschung, Teil 1: Versuch eines Vergleichs von Biomasse- und Intelligenzentwicklung in der Menschheit,* in: Rad. and Environm. Biophysics 13, 329–335

[72] LIETH, H. et al (eds.) (1981):   *Wechselwirkungen zwischen ökologischen, ökonomischen und sozialen Systemen agrarischer Intensivge- biete,* in: MAB-Mitteilungen 7, Bonn: Deutsches MAB-Nationalkomitee

[73] LOPREATO, J. (1980):   *Pareto's Sociology as a Sociobiological Key,* in: Rev. Européenne des Sciences Sociales XVIII, 133–162

[74] LUHMANN, N. (1974):   *Einführende Bemerkungen zu einer Theorie symbolisch generalisierter Kommunikationsmedien,* in: Zeitschr. für Soziologie 3, 236-255

[75] LUHMANN, N. (1985):   *Soziale Systeme — Grundriß einer allge- meinen Theorie,* 2. Aufl., Frankfurt/M.:

[76] LUHMANN, N. (1986):   *Ökologische Kommunikation,*   Opladen: Westdeutscher Verlag

[77] LYON L. et al. (1980/81):   *Community Power and Population In- crease: An Empirical Test of the Growth Machine Model,* in: AJS 86, 1397–1400

[78] MAHR, B. (1986):   *Poker-Phase oder Die Unberechenbarkeit einer Vision* in: Kursbuch 83, März, 27–46

[79] MARCETTI, C. (1981):   *Society as a Learning System: Discovery, Invention, and Innovation Cycles Revisited,* Paper RR-81-29, IIASA, Laxenburg, Austria

[80] MAYHEW, B.H./LEVINGER, R.L. (1976): *On the Emergence of Oligarchy in Human Interaction*, in: AJS 81, 1017–1049

[81] McGUIRE, M.T. et al. (1983): *Social Dominance in Adult Male Vervet Monkeys: General Considerations*, in: Social Science Info. 22, 89–123

[82] MEADOWS, D.H. et al. (1972): *The Limits to Growth*, New York: Potomac

[83] MENSCH, G. (19752): *Das technologische Patt*, Frankfurt/M.: Umschau

[84] METHE, W. (1981): *Ökologie und Marxismus — ein Neuansatz zur Rekonstruktion der politischen Ökonomie unter ökologischen Krisenbedingungen* Hannover: SOAK

[85] MEYER, J.W./ROWAN, B. (1977/78): *Institutional Organizations: Formal Structure as Myth and Ceremony*, in: AJS 83, 340–362

[86] MUELLER, D.C. (ed.) (1983): *The Political Economy of Growth*, New Haven: Yale Univ. Press

[87] MÜLLER, N. (1973): *Strategiemodelle — Aspekte und Probleme einer sozialwissenschaftlichen Praxeologie*, Köln: Westdeutscher Verlag

[88] MÜLLER, N. (1979): *Empirische Herrschafstheorie — Zur Beziehung zwischen Kontextdifferenzierung, politischer Herrschaft und politischer Sozialisation*, Köln: Westdeutscher Verlag

[89] MÜLLER, N. (1980a): *Functions on Life-trees for Explaining Social Phenomena*, in: Policy Analysis and Info. Systems 4, 317–330

[90] MÜLLER, N. (1980b): *Strategy and Reflexivity*, in: Lewin, F./ Vedung, E. (eds.): Politics as Rational Action, Dordrecht: Reidel

[91] MÜLLER, N. (1981a): *Einstellungswandel versus Hierarchisierungs- oder Kontextwechselartefakte*, in: Ztschr. für Sozialpsychologie 12, 303–324

[92] MÜLLER, N. (1981b): *Einige Funktionsmechanismen sozialer Systeme und ihre Bedeutung für die Beschreibbarkeit sozialer Systeme*, in: ALBERTIN/MÜLLER (eds.)

[93] MÜLLER, N. (1985a): *Real-Structure-Modelling: a methodology for the description of large-scale social units*, in: Social Science Info. 24, 603–624

[94] MÜLLER, N. (1985b): *Modelling Standard Actions of Individuals and Institutions for Controlling NO_3 - concentration in Drinking Water in a Region of Intensive Agriculture (South Oldenburg, FRG) — Evidence from a Pilotmodel,* in: Syst. Anal. Model. Simul. 2, 19–53

[95] MÜLLER, N. (1987): *Taking a Commune as an Example; the analysis of the Relevant Communal Structures,* in: MÜLLER /SCHÖN/THOBER (1987)

[96] MÜLLER, N./SCHÖN, K.P./THOBER, B. (1982): *Projekt HSDMEL — Abschlußbericht,* Osnabrück: Univ. Press

[97] MÜLLER, N./SCHÖN, K.P./THOBER,B. (1987): *Real-Structure Modelling: A Simulation-Based Methodology for the Description of Large Scale Social Units,* Köln: TÜV, ISR series

[98] MÜLLER, N./STACHOWIAK, H. (eds.) (1987): *Problemlösungs-operator Sozialwissenschaft — anwendungsorientierte Modelle der Sozial- und Planungswissenschaften in ihrer Wirksamkeitsproblematik,* 2 Bände, Stuttgart: Enke

[99] O'CONNOR, J. (1974): *Die Finanzkrise des Staates,* Frankfurt/M.: Suhrkamp

[100] ODUM, H.T. (1971): *Environment, Power, and Society,* New York: Wiley

[101] ODUM, H.T. (1983): *Systems Ecology — An Introduction,* New York: Wiley

[102] OEVERMANN. U. (1972): *Sprache und soziale Herkunft — ein Beitrag zur Analyse schichtspezifischer Sozialisationsprozesse und ihre Bedeutung für den Schulerfolg,* Frankfurt/M.: Suhrkamp

[103] OFFE, C. (1975): *Berufsbildungsreform — Eine Fallstudie über Reformpolitik,* Frankfurt/M.: Suhrkamp

[104] OGADIRI, H. (1981): *The Theory of Growth in a Corporate Economy,* Cambridge: Cambridge Univ. Press

[105] OLSON, M. (1982): *The Rise and Decline of Nations,* New Haven: Yale Univ. Oress

[106] O'NEILL, G. (1975): *Testimony,* in: Co-Evolutionary Quarterly 7, Fall, 10–19

[107] OTTEN, D. (1986): *Der Prozeß der Industrialisierung - eine neue Soziologie und Geschichte der gesellschaftlichen Arbeit,* Bd. 1: Aufbruch und Expansion, Hamburg: Reinbeck

[108] PARKER, S./PARKER, H. (1979):   The Myth of Male Superiority: Rise and Demise, in: Amer. Anthropologist 81, 289–309

[109] PASINETTI, L.L. (1981):   Structural Change and Economic Growth — A Theoretical Essay on the Dynamics of the Wealth of Nations, Cambridge: Cambridge Univ. Press

[110] REICH, R.B. (1983):   The Next American Frontier, New York: Times Books

[111] RICHARDSON, J.J./JORDAN, A.G. (1983):   Overcrowded Policy-making: Some British and European Reflections, in: Policy Sciences 15, 247–268

[112] SAMUELSON, P.A. (1981):   Volkwirtschaftslehre Band I, 7. Aufl., Köln: Bund Verlag

[113] SCHMEIKAL, B. (1981): Self-Reference Sociogony, in: Quality and Quantity 15, 603–609

[114] SCHMIDBAUER, W. (1974):   Zur kulturellen Evolution der Agression, in: SCHMIDBAUER (ed.): Evolutionstheorie und Verhaltensforschung, Hamburg: Hoffmann & Campe

[115] SCHNEIDER, S.H./MORTON, L. (1981):   The Primordial Bond — Exploring Connections between Man and Nature through the Humanities and Sciences, New York: Plenum

[116] SHERFEY, M.J. (1974):   Die Potenz der Frau — Wesen und Evolution der weiblichen Sexualität, Köln: Kiepenheuer & Witsch

[117] SERVICE, E.R. (1977):   Ursprünge des Staates und der Zivilisation — der Prozeß der kulturellen Evolution, Frankfurt/M.: Suhrkamp

[118] SIMON, J.L. (1981):   The Ultimate Resource, Princeton, N.J.: Princeton Univ. Press

[119] SIMPSON, M.J.A./SIMPSON, A.E. (1982):   Birth sex ratios and social rank in rhesus monkey mothers, in: Nature 300, 400–441

[120] SOLLA PRICE, D.J. de (1967):   Science Since Babylon, 3rd print, New Haven: Yale Univ. Press

[121] STACEY, J. (1979):   Toward a Theory of Women, the Family and Revolution — A Historical and Theoritical Analysis of the Chinese Case, Brandus Univ., PhD Thesis

[122] STACHOWIAK, H. (1982): *Bedürfnisse, Werte, Normen und Ziele im dynamischen Gesellschaftsmodell: Ein Forschungsprogramm für die °80 er Jahre ?*, in: STACHOWIAK et al. (eds.): Bedürfnisse, Werte und Normen im Wandel, München: Fink & Schöningh

[123] STACHOWIAK, H. (1986): *Gegenwärtige Theorieprobleme der Sozialwissenschaften unter pragmatologischem Aspekt*, in: MÜLLER /STACHOWIAK (eds.)

[124] STEINDL, J. (1976): *Maturity and Stagnation in American Capitalism*, New York: Monthly Rev. Press

[125] SULLEROT, E. (ed.) (1979): *Die Wirklichkeit der Frau*, München: Steinhausen

[126] TALMON, Y. (1972): *Family and Community in the Kibbutz*, Cambridge: Harvard Univ. Press

[127] TANNER, N. (1981): *On Becoming Human: A Model for the Transition from Ape to Human and the Reconstruction of Early Human Life*, Cambridge: Cambridge Univ. Press

[128] TAYLOR, G.R. (1977): *Prediction and Social Change — The need for a basis in theory*, in: FUTURES 9, 404–414

[129] TEFFT, S.K. (ed.) (1980): *Secrecy — A Cross-Cultural Perspective*, New York: Human Sciences Press

[130] TUTTLE, R.H. (ed.) (1975): *Paleoanthropology — Morphology and Paleoecology*, Paris: Mouton

[131] UMBACH, E. (1983): *Entscheidung über Zahl der Kinder in der Familie*, Hannover: ISP

[132] USEEM, M. (1982): *Classwide Rationality in the Politics of Managers and Directors of Large Corporations in the United States and Great Britain*, in: Admin. Sc.Qu. 27, 199–226

[133] VOGT, W. (1974): *Zur langfristigen ökonomischen Entwicklung eines kapitalistischen Systems*, in: Leviathan Heft 2, 295–312

[134] WHITING, B.B. (1963): *Six Cultures — Studies in Child Rearing*, Rearing, New York: Wiley

[135] WEIDLICH, W./ HAAG. G. (1983): *Concepts and Models of a Quantitative Sociology — The Dynamics of Iteracting Populations*, Berlin: Springer

[136] WITTVOGEL, K.A. (1957): *Oriental Despotism — A Comparative Study of Total Power,* New Haven: Yale Univ. Press

[137] WOLLMANN, H. (ed.) (1980): *Politik im Dickicht der Bürokratie — Beiträge zur Implementationsforschung,* Opladen: Westdeutscher Verlag

[138] WUNDERLIN, A./HAKEN, H. (1981): *Über die Anwendung der Synergetik auf soziologische Probleme,* in: HARDER/HUININK/RUMIANEK (eds.): Probleme der Mehrebenenanalyse, Bielefeld, Univ. Bielefeld Press

[139] ZELENY, M. (ed.) (1980): *Autopoiesis, Dissipative Structures and Spontaneous Orders,* Amsterdam: North-Holland

[140] ZELENY, M. (ed.) (1981): *Autopoiesis — A Theory of Living Organization,* Amsterdam: North-Holland

Index